Praise for
FINDING JUNE

"A powerful story of a family's evolving relationships as they struggle to deal with an aging parent in the grips of Alzheimer's. Propelled by strong characters and exceptional writing, Finding June packs a powerful emotional punch."
—MARILYN HUNTER—
Author: *Whispering Hope* and *Death in the Distillery District*

"Finding June is an enjoyable, believable read and offers contemporary perspectives on an illness fast becoming a modern-day scourge as a family learns to navigate the complexities of their mother's distorted state together, yet separately."
—DONNA KIRK—
Author: *Death In The Suburbs*

"Wendy Simpson's warm and gently humorous family drama brims with emotion and honesty. Whimsical yet determined June Walker has always put her family first. Still, decades of misunderstandings, hurt feelings, and even deception have taken a toll. Now, facing a diagnosis of dementia, June knows she has a limited time to reunite her family."
—PAULA SATHER—
Paula's upcoming novel: *Muddy Point*

"...reading this book promotes a greater appreciation of life and love."
—KEN PUDDICOMBE—
Author, *Down Independence Boulevard And Other Stories*, Winner Guyana Prize For Literature (Fiction) 2022

Wendy Simpson's upcoming novel is

Quicksand

FINDING JUNE
A Novel

Wendy Simpson

MiddleRoad | Publishers

www.middleroadpublishers.ca

Making Literature see the light of day

Library and Archives Canada Cataloguing in Publication
Simpson, Wendy author

ISBN 978-1-990765-67-4 (paperback)

Editor
www.kenpud.wordpress.com

Cover
Layout: MiddleRoad Publishers
www.middleroadpublishers.ca

Design: Kathryn Lagerquist
Kathryn.lagerquist@gmail.com

ACKNOWLEDGMENTS

This book would never have come to be without my friends and fellow critics in the *Thursday Afternoon Creative Writing* class.

For ideas and inspiration, I have sometimes relied on the experiences and tales of family and friends, most notably my mother, Mary. I occasionally use Google for the facts.

Thanks to all my children—Amanda and Will, Toby and Jana, Will and Keeley and to their children; Edith, Daphne, Hugo, Connor, Iona, June, Charlotte, Keira, Margaret and Caroline. Without all of you there would be no book.

My big sister Bev has listened and helped and answered all my questions.

Thanks to Heather, Mimi and Sue who accepted the assignment as beta readers and helped in so many ways.

And, when I was close to quitting, thanks to the little one who took my hand and said, "This is my Grandma. She's a writer."

DEDICATION

Inspired by the wondrous love of Marge and Bob.

I saw them in my dreams—come flying east and west,
With wondrous fairy gifts—the newborn babe they
bless'd;
One has brought a jewel—and one a crown of gold,
And one has brought a curse—but she is wrinkled and
old.
From *Fairy Days*

—William Makepeace Thackeray—

(1811-1863)

Table of Contents

CHAPTER ONE

June's time was running out.

The kitchen door slammed behind her as she headed out to the back garden, her favourite place on earth. And yes, while deadheading wilted blooms, strangling weeds, drowning beetles, lopping off branches, and poisoning pests was fun, it was the tranquility of the garden that captivated June. She planned to garden as long as she could. There was never a shortage of tasks—digging, planting, mulching. Tonight, she'd have dirt under her fingernails, scratches on her arms and legs and a few bug bites. But what did June care? She had the flowers, the bushes, the vines and the trees. And today, thanks to Nick, the smell of freshly mowed grass. June inhaled deeply and held her breath, soaking in the sharp, sweet green. *Can you smell green?*

She sniffed again, felt a tickle in her nose and remembered the bunnies. She'd found them a couple of days ago, nesting under the cedar hedge. At first, there'd been six furless kits, but today, as she bent close to the nest, she counted only three, maybe four. Poor mama bunny. She'd brought them a gift—spinach, lettuce, a few stalks of celery, two diced carrots and beetroot tops. Nick had laughed and teased her. *Was she going to bake them a cake too? Champagne, maybe?* She'd reasoned that this rough-and-ready salad just might keep them from feasting on the tender plants in her garden. But if they needed the Impatiens or the new Hosta shoots to survive, well, she'd be all right with that too.

June slipped on her gardening gloves and stopped to collect the last of the dead tulip leaves. They'd bloom again next year, as long as the squirrels weren't too ambitious. Would she remember they were tulips? Who would save the honeysuckles from those…those creepy alien-like ones with the pincers…eye—no…she could picture them—earwigs! She'd never figured out how to defeat those hungry little devils, but at least they'd stayed away from her prize-winning roses! She counted the buds and then did her daily check for Japanese beetles. She used a twig to knock the only two offenders into the bucket of soapy water she kept nearby, and she watched them drown.

June spotted a few straggly weeds in the gravel path but then decided to leave them, mostly because they'd worked so hard to get there. As she stepped behind the garden shed, she caught a whiff of the last of the lilacs and walked smack into a swarm of No-see-ums. June flapped her arms, spat and snorted a few from her nose. She stumbled and almost lost her balance, but luckily Nick wasn't watching. She retreated, sweeping through her hair for any strays.

She'd almost forgotten about the peonies she's left outside the kitchen door. Her mother had taught her to soak them upside down in a pail of water to drown all the pesky ants. She gave each blossom a good shake and was about to arrange them in and old earthenware crock when she noticed the crack. *Darn.* She tossed the flowers back in the bucket.

Nothing lasts forever, right? Nothing and no one. She could cry about it or just give up and take to her bed. Or curse the heavens above. *What the hell, God? Why me? Why now?* But blaspheme wouldn't change things. No. She couldn't control everything or maybe anything but June knew, that unlike those damned Japanese beetles she had a choice. She could dwell on it or not. June was going with *not.*

Nick waved from the middle of the yard as he mowed another neat stripe into the lush spring lawn. June waited until he passed by, then turned and watched the swagger of his buttocks as he bent into the lawn mower. June grinned. He looked good, still fit and handsome though a little red-faced and very sweaty now. He was no spring chicken, but then neither was she. He still looked mighty fine to her.

June filled up the watering can, cooling herself in the fine mist from the hose. Nick turned off the mower, pushed it into the shed and came out with the trimmer.

"You okay?" Nick asked.

"Yes, of course. I'm fine."

"Just don't overdo it. Okay?"

"Overdo what? I'm just watering the flowers."

"Right, I know, but—"

She stuck out her tongue, playful defiance that made him smile. He blew her a kiss. She knew he meant well but really, he worried about her much far too much.

The gas trimmer roared to life, startling June. The watering can wobbled in her hand and soaked her sandals. She checked to see if Nick had noticed, but he was busy trimming around her flowerbeds. She could tell by his face that he was getting tired, not that he'd ever admit it. He'd already mowed the front yard and cleaned the pool today, netting a whole trashcan full of soggy Whirligigs, keys from their Manitoba maple tree. Nick wanted to have it taken down. The branches were weak, the wood soft and infested. He called it a weed and worried that the aggressive root system would crack the house foundation. But she refused to give up on it, so they had it trimmed every year. He was such a worrywart.

Nick shooed her away as he neared the patio, the trimmer *whup, whup, whupping* like an approaching helicopter. She kicked off her wet shoes, walked to the pool deck and gave the large container of red and white geraniums a good drink.

They didn't use the pool much anymore. Nick used to do lengths after work, even in the dark. And Martha and Peter had often dropped by on the weekends for a BBQ and a swim. Sometimes, if they'd had too much wine, they'd stay the night. But that was when they were first married. June used her fingers to do the math—sixteen years ago. Martha had been a beautiful bride.

June knew she was being silly. Martha and Peter had visited plenty of times since then, Christmas, Easter and Thanksgiving, when Peter's parents often joined them. They'd celebrated countless birthdays, anniversaries and promotions in June's dining room. Sure, there'd been many family dinners, lots of visits—just not lately.

When June had complained about Martha, Nick pooh-poohed her concerns. "We see plenty of Martha," he'd said. "It's not personal, June. They're just busy living their own lives." But that was because he saw her at the office. When June invited Martha and Peter over for a meal or movie night or just a quick visit, Martha scarcely bothered to come up with an excuse anymore. *Sorry, no. Maybe next weekend?* was the closest June had come to pinning her down since last Christmas. Something was up. She just knew it. Martha had drifted away and June missed her.

"Oh, Martha," she muttered. "What am I going to do about you?"

Maybe she'd call Peter, twist his arm a little. But no. Martha would hate that and she could get prickly. June didn't want to push too hard. On the other hand, as her mother often said, *must needs.* She couldn't wait much longer.

The pool looked nice today, clean and clear. She crouched down and dipped in her fingers, wiggling them to create ripples across the glassy surface.

"June!" The weed whacker sputtered to silence. "Careful! Maybe just step back a little."

June straightened up and sent Nick a sidelong glance. "Okay, but I'm fine."

Nick waited for her to move before he returned to trimming. She released a long slow sigh as she sat down on the diving board and was again treated to the smell of spring grass. She'd mowed it herself more than a few times, opting for graceful S curves instead of boring straight lines. One time, she'd mistakenly directed scads of grass clippings into the pool. She'd scooped out what she could but, in the end, she'd just left them, counting on the skimmer to take care of the mess before Nick noticed. He was always so fussy about the pool. What he didn't know wouldn't hurt him, right?

June nodded and smiled when Nick looked up. She wanted to shout, *See. I'm fine,* but a sudden a sense of uneasiness made her shiver. She shook it off. Nick knew all her secrets now, both old and new. She'd tried to keep her early memory problems from him—*owls in the loft,* she'd called it, when she first couldn't remember simple things. "Yeah." Nick had agreed, "we're getting old." But he'd soon figured out that her memory slips were different and more frequent than his inability to remember where he'd left his keys or his iPad. He'd held her hand, they'd cried together the day Dr. Motsinger confirmed that, although it was too early to definitively diagnose Alzheimer's or a specific type of dementia, there was little doubt that June was in the early stages of the disease.

"Nick," she called. He'd switched to the leaf blower and couldn't hear her over the high-pitched whine. "Yoo-hoo!" *Honestly, the man and his toys.* She wanted to tell him about the grass in the pool, but that probably didn't matter anymore. Her biggest secret, that whole terrible fiasco, had been unearthed a long time ago. They'd somehow figured it all out and June loved Nick all the more for it—his honesty, his courage and in the end his forgiveness.

She smiled and waved at Nick who had worked his way around to the back fence. June loved this backyard, the flowers, the trees. Even Nick's silly putting green didn't bother her anymore. It had replaced the play structure that had occupied the twins for so many years—at various times a castle, a pirate ship, a clubhouse and on some hot summer nights, a bedroom under the stars. Jonathan and Martha. Her babies, her twins, they'd shared so much when they were little—a bedroom, toys, popsicles and even head lice. He'd needed June more. But he'd left her, fled from home, moved so far away. Too far for her to visit now. She missed her Jonny. He was much more like her than Nick or even Martha. Sure, Jonathan had found some troubles, complicated his life and hers but she'd left him with enough wisdom to figure things out. If only Nick could see it.

Martha was still here, just across town but apparently she was very busy. Busy like her father with work. June knew the firm and the clients always came first.

"Are you done yet?" asked June as Nick swept the sidewalk.

Nick looked up and nodded. "For today, anyway."

"Great, take a seat and I'll be right back," said June. She headed for the house without waiting for a reply.

When June returned, she found Nick settled into the rattan rocker. She'd put together a snack for them; two tall glasses of lemonade, some digestive cookies, the ones with dark chocolate on one side, and a bowl of sweet cherries, all of which she balanced on a silver tray.

"Don't," she cautioned Nick against helping. "I can do this." She set the tray on the table, handed a glass to Nick and took the other for herself. She wiggled into the cushioned armchair and sipped her drink.

"Lovely!" she declared, taking it all in: her handsome husband, their beautiful backyard and her icy cold drink. She'd remember this forever.

"Yes, it is. My putting green looks good and healthy this year." Nick chuckled.

June rolled her eyes at him and smiled. She watched as two squirrels played a rapid game of tag in the willow tree. How often had she spread a blanket under its cool canopy for a picnic with the twins? "There's still a fairy house up there."

"What?"

"In the willow. There's a fairy house."

"June." Nick's wrinkled brow said he didn't believe her.

"No, really. Martha put it there. In the hollow. She'd wanted Jonathan to climb up for her, but he wouldn't, so she did it herself. She even put little fairies in it, Fifi and Elana and…and I think Goldie. Remember? Your mother gave them to her the Christmas before she passed away. When the twins were five."

"What?"

"Martha gave them all names—the fairies, not the houses."

"Hmm."

"I'll bet it's still there."

"Maybe. But it's been a really long time."

"Yeah, but maybe…" Her voice trailed off as the squirrels moved from the tree to the bird feeder, cleaning up all the bits that had fallen to the ground. They scavenged and chattered as if disputing the winner of the last game of tag. June leaned back and sighed. Such a beautiful day.

"This house is too much for us."

It was a statement, a declaration of some sort. June didn't move. She barely breathed. What house? The fairy house? She'd been daydreaming or had she drifted off?

"We should sell."

"Sell what?"

"This house."

"What?" She sat up and swept her arm across the idyllic scene before her. "Sell this? Why?"

"Well, it's a hell of a lot of work." Nick set his empty glass on the tray with a thump. "And it's too big for the two of us."

"But you love this house. Besides where would we go?" June leaned back and feigned indifference.

"One of those retirement places, or a condo. You know, maybe something new and modern? There are some nice ones downtown, by the harbour. We could walk to the shops and restaurants."

So, he really had been thinking about this. June popped a cherry into her mouth. "No," she mumbled.

"No?" Nick's eyebrows shot skyward. "You won't even consider it?"

"No, not yet."

Mercury ambled onto the patio and plopped down next to June. He groaned as he settled his head onto his front paws. Like most Golden Retrievers Mercury liked to be close to his humans. June reached over the arm of her chair and ruffled the soft fur on his back.

"We couldn't leave. Mercury would hate living in a condo."

"Yeah, that's probably true," said Nick. "You know the doctor told us to start thinking about the future. We need to be practical."

"I know. But not the house." *Not the house.* "You can't be serious." Suddenly close to tears, June couldn't hide the quiver in her voice.

"Now, don't get upset. I just thought you might like the idea."

June sat still, rigid and defiant.

Nick shifted towards her. He smiled. "Don't worry. I was just thinking out loud, you know, considering the options. We're okay here, for now anyway."

June relaxed a little. Maybe he had a point—just maybe. The house was a lot of work and Nick looked tired today. They really didn't need this much space anymore. Nick often grumbled about the expense of keeping up such a large house and his endless honey-do list. He'd been complaining and muttering about a lot of things lately. But no. This was home and she wasn't going anywhere.

"Why don't I just hire someone to do some of the work around here? Some handsome young man with a scruffy beard and good knees?"

Nick huffed and looked offended.

June laughed. "Don't look so serious. I was just kidding. I'm not planning on replacing you." June got up quickly, causing Mercury to moan and roll onto his side. "Would you like another lemonade?"

Nick nodded.

"Okay sourpuss! Extra sugar for you."

Nicked smiled, but June could see the sadness, the worry in his eyes. He was right. They had to think ahead. But she didn't want to count the days or even the moments. She wanted to live them.

And she was running out of time.

CHAPTER TWO

June figured Nick had forgotten about selling the house. He hadn't mentioned it again, even when, just after Cananda Day, a *For Sale* sign went up across the street. But she did find a real estate card on his desk. She wasn't snooping—it was just sitting there, in plain sight. She fed it to the shredder. She waited for him to ask about it, but he didn't, so it was probably nothing.

The summer turned hot and dry, but despite the heat, June kept busy. She had a list now—people to see and things that just had to get done. She'd cut down her bridge games to one a week, choosing to play with the less serious group, friends who didn't mind if she forgot about the two-club convention or how many times she asked, "What's trump?" She filled her calendar with lunches and walks with friends. No one seemed to notice that she was calling more often. She'd even hosted a tea party just to show off her garden.

Only Norah commented on the flurry of activity, calling her a busy bee. June just brushed it off at first, but Norah was her closest friend and pretty smart too. One day, just kidding of course, Norah asked June if was working through her bucket list. June told her they'd been to the doctor but she downplayed the diagnosis. She didn't want Norah to worry.

"Only you and Nick know," June told her. "So please keep this to yourself."

Norah nodded and hugged her close. "Do you know…how long?"

June smiled, watching from the park bench as Mercury chased after an energetic Jack Russell Terrier. "No way to tell, I'm afraid."

Norah's eyes brimmed with tears.

"Oh no," said June, dismissing her concerns. "I've still got plenty of time. Fit as a fiddle. So please don't worry."

June took up swimming again. It helped her think and she loved being buoyant, weightless, alive. Her worries floated away in the water, replaced by the rhythm of her breaststroke and the gentle waves as she kicked through the cool water on her back. She wanted to swim all day, but Nick wouldn't let her go in the pool when he wasn't there.

"Everyone needs a lifeguard," he told her, as if it were indisputable.

She tried to push back but then decided he was probably right. So, she swam early in the morning, several times each week. Nick brought his breakfast outside and watched her, always watched her. When the summer mornings turned cool and the maple leaves started to colour, Nick had the pool closed. June missed her morning swims. She put away her bathing suit in the back of her closest with her summer clothes. *Will I have next summer?*

June baked muffins for her friends and delivered flowers from her garden to her favourite neighbours. She gave a tin full of homemade cookies to Mercury's groomer and put a tip in the mailbox for the postman along with some stamps he'd once admired. When her list was nearly complete, she felt no different. She was happier for all her endeavours, but no sicker, in fact most days she was full of vim and vigour, so much so that Nick complained about her never sitting still. It seemed to June that *Relax, June, you'll wear yourself out,* had become his mantra.

But the one task that was still unfinished, the one that would take the longest and likely be the hardest, was Martha. Martha Mary, her brilliant, beautiful, stubborn and June feared, unhappy daughter.

June wanted to see more of her, spend time together, repair a relationship that was distant rather than broken. Strong and independent almost from birth, Martha had never really needed June. She'd always had a way of figuring things out and never truly understood how much June needed her.

Nick had worked some kind of magic and on a perfect Sunday afternoon in early September, Martha and Peter came for a barbecue. Nick cooked the steaks outside on the grill and June made the potato salad she knew Peter liked. Martha pushed aside the potatoes and creamy dressing and ate only the egg bits. She heaped her plate with green salad and added sliced avocado from the appetizer plate. Martha and Peter barely spoke to each other. Oh, Martha talked to Nick and Peter had lots to say about his parents' plan to sell the family cottage. He was most gracious to June. But Martha and Peter sat beside each other, aloof and curt. What was going on with them? She was still reluctant to ask Peter. Sure, he'd probably spill the beans, but she wanted it to come from Martha. No matter how much June longed to sit and talk to her daughter, understand her indifference, help her through her troubles, Martha would never confide in her. She still phoned Martha, mostly on the weekends. They'd talk for a few minutes.

June would have to fill the conversation as Martha had little to say. June would ask about Peter, and her running. Was she still going at night? That was too dangerous. June would invite her to lunch or coffee but Martha would beg off, unmoved by June's efforts.

June wandered into the kitchen one morning with her usual cheery greeting. "Good morning!"

Nick looked over his cheaters and shook his head. "It's raining." He had prepared his regular breakfast, whole wheat toast and two poached eggs.

"It is," agreed June. "My roses will be happy." She poured a bowl of cereal, added milk and sat down at the table.

"The world's going to hell in a handbasket," said Nick, without looking up from his news. "It will take years before we know the effects of that earthquake in Japan. They claim they can clean it up, but I don't know. A lot of contaminated water leaked into the ocean."

"That's scary," said June

"Very. And Steve Jobs died."

"Hmm?" said June through a mouthful of cereal.

"You know, the Apple guy."

"Yes, I know." said June. "Phones and computers, right?"

"Yes. And lots of other things. A real innovator, that guy. Sad he had cancer."

June nodded. She didn't want to talk about the state of the world or people with fatal diseases.

Nick looked up. "What are you eating?"

"Corn Pops!"

"Why?"

"They're really good. You should try some!" She crunched with obvious satisfaction.

"That's not a healthy breakfast."

"And a banana." She waved it in his direction as she pulled back the peel.

Nick grunted. Of course he didn't approve. He didn't approve of anything she did these days. She hated when they fought but he overreacted to everything. She'd called him a bully last week and that had hurt his feelings. Still, it did seem like they weren't on the same page anymore, about the house, about her diet, but mostly about how she spent her days. June tried to think of the last time they'd sat down and managed a nice friendly chat that didn't involve her medications and words of caution and restraint. She couldn't recall. Oh well, she thought. She didn't remember a lot of things these days. Getting old wasn't fun but she'd make the best of it.

Nick closed the iPad, set his glasses on the table and cleared his throat. "I've been thinking about—"

June was focused on her cereal, chasing the bobbing balls around with her spoon, until she realized that Nick had paused mid-sentence. She looked up.

"—retiring," Nick finished.

"What?" *Oh no no no!* June swallowed a huge spoonful of crunchy sugar trying not to gulp and choke. Nick at work time was *her* time.

"Nick, you love your work. Why would you give it up?" She had to think quickly, make him see this was a big mistake.

"Well, I *am* getting old."

"So? You're still a good lawyer, a partner. They need you." She was starting to panic, feeling shaky and confused. Maybe she really was eating too much sugar. Nick retired would mean Nick at home, all day. Grouchy Nick. Bossy Nick. Stubborn Nick. Whiny Nick. He would try and micromanage her time, hover and judge. Home was her space, Monday to Friday, regular business hours, except when he was involved in a big case, and then she had the evenings too. Every moment was precious now, even those without Nick, her time, her days, her clock was ticking.

"You're not so old, Nick. You can't give up your partnership. Wouldn't you miss going to the office and to court? You love a good trial. And Martha needs you there. She counts on you."

Nick scoffed at the idea. "Martha doesn't need me anymore. Besides, I'm the old guy at the office now."

"So, you're older and wiser. You're the voice of experience!"

"True. Though, some days I really feel it. Besides I'd be here for you, for when you need help."

June wrinkled her nose in disapproval.

"And l could get a lot more done around here if I wasn't working all the time."

Nick was sounding surer of this plan. *Stay calm. Don't panic. Think!* She gave herself a little pep talk as she considered her next move.

"Let's take a trip!" she blurted out a little too enthusiastically, spreading bits of Corn Pops, banana and milk across the table. They loved to travel. Well, they used to love to travel.

"Excuse me?"

Oh dear. Now she'd roused sarcastic Nick. "Maybe you're just tired. You need a break—a little holiday. We could take a cruise or go to a tropical island. No, let's go back to Italy! Yes! Italy. Can we?" She waited for him to register delight, but instead he looked angry.

"June, stop it. We can't go away right now."

"Oh! You're just such a—" Jackass seemed too harsh "—an old stick-in-the-mud!"

"Look June, we've talked about this. The doctor says it's not a good idea. June, you know this."

She hated his calm, controlled lawyering voice. Well trained, he kept repeating her name.

"But Nick," she pleaded, wiggling closer to him. "I just thought it would be fun. And I don't care what the doctor says, I'm fine. Everyone forgets things at our age!" She smiled her sweetest smile.

"June, I'm sorry. I can't discuss this now. It's getting late and I've got a client meeting first thing this morning." Nick rose quickly, pushing back the chair with his calves. It wobbled, quivering as it settled into place. The dishwasher door creaked as he pulled it open. The stale smell of last night's dinner filled the kitchen. "Shit," he muttered. "I forgot to start this again." He placed a kaleidoscopic pod in the detergent dispenser and sighed as he set the buttons and pushed start. "It's full now so just leave your bowl in the sink." He turned to June and added, "There's still some soup in the fridge for your lunch. You can just microwave it."

"I know how to make my lunch, Nick."

"Right. Sorry."

"Nick?" June had something more to ask, something she didn't want to forget.

"Yes, June?"

"Do you think you could try? Maybe just an email?"

Nick was gathering his things, briefcase, phone, car keys. The keys clattered to the floor. He bent down to retrieve them, focusing his scowl on June. "Jonathan?"

June nodded.

"Jesus, June, there isn't time for this now."

"Just try. Please?"

Nick jammed his cell phone into the pocket of his jacket. "Let's talk tonight, okay?"

"Okay." June sulked.

"Sorry, I really can't be late for this." He glanced at his watch and kissed the top of her head. "Stay in today. Okay? It's wet and nasty outside."

June's smile collapsed into a pout. "Wait—" But he was gone, off to work. That was always his excuse. But she knew when he was blowing her off. *See, my memory is fine.*

June finished her cereal and, ignoring the sound of swooshing water, she opened the dishwasher door. Hot water splashed on her jeans and slippers. She found a place for her bowl and spoon and then lingered, allowing the warm steam to caress her face. She used a tea towel to mop up the little puddles on the floor tile and then noticed the grocery list on the fridge. Nick had added Raisin Bran. She stroked it out and wrote in Froot Loops, a little shaky but hopefully neat enough.

She opened Nick's iPad, setting it up on the case. She tapped in the code, his birthday, *0138* and opened Scrabble. The small clay dish Jonny had made in high school sat beside a tall glass of water on the counter. Nick had forgotten to make her take her pills. Well, maybe she wouldn't. That would show him.

Mercury nudged at her leg. She added kibble to his bowl and changed his water. "Let's go for a walk."

Mercury's ears popped up; his tail thumped against the floor. Mercury was the most wonderful Golden Retriever. They'd had a few Goldens over the years. They'd surprised the twins with a puppy on their tenth birthday. Martha had wanted to call her Princess, but they'd settled on Piper. Jonathan had taught her to play catch, fetch and beg for treats. Martha had dressed her in doll clothes and later in her ballet tutus. They should have named her Patience. Mercury was all hers, the best walking companion she'd ever had. He was a gentle soul, still energetic enough to love a good run, but always willing to match her pace.

"Do you think Norah would like to join us? It's fun to walk with a friend, isn't it boy?"

She tipped the pills from the bowl into her mouth, washed them down and picked up the phone, a handset that was never in the same place twice. She'd called her good friend so many times, dialing from memory but today she couldn't recall the numbers, three, two, three or two, four, two? She finally gave up and found the card Nick had made for her. She used her index finger to keep her place under each one of Nick's bold numbers and pushed the digits slowly and carefully, shuddering a little as she remembered connecting with the wrong number a while ago, maybe just last week. She'd dialed it twice and the second time the man's gruff voice told her to *fuck off*. She hadn't told Nick.

The phone only rang a couple of times before June heard Norah's cheery voice.

"Hello stranger! Good morning! I sent you a text. How're you doing?" Norah said.

June hesitated. She knew Norah was her best friend, but for a moment, she couldn't picture Norah's face. June closed her eyes and yes, there she was, blue eyes, short hair, beautiful long eyelashes and the warmest of smiles.

"June?"

"Oh, I'm good," said June. "Yes, I'm good. Very good."

Norah was so sweet, but she talked fast. June had met Norah at the off-leash dog park. They probably would have ignored each other, but Norah's tiny but feisty little chihuahua, Taco, had insisted on provoking June's dog Buddy, a much larger but extremely patient Golden. Taco had nipped and growled at Buddy, even stole his tennis ball, yet they'd become friends, the dogs and the women. That was nearly twenty years ago.

"Great," said Norah.

"Mercury and I are going for a walk. Would you like to join us?

"Did you get my text?" asked Norah.

"No, I think I've lost my phone again. It's here somewhere. Maybe I should hang it around my neck," June giggled. "Want to go for a walk?" she repeated.

"No! It's raining. Freezing cold. Not my kind of day. Come here for tea." Norah never drank coffee. "I made butter tarts. And if you don't come, I'll eat them all myself."

Norah's tarts were delicious. Her pies too. "Maybe." June was tempted. "No. I think I'd like to walk. Mercury could use a good run and I need to blow off some steam."

"Why? What's wrong?"

"Oh, nothing new. Nick's being difficult again. He's so stubborn and thinks he's always right. He doesn't listen to me."

"Oh, dear. But that's just Nick, right? He's looking out for you."

"I don't need him to."

"I know. I know," said Norah. "Okay, then let's do lunch. You head out with Mercury and then meet me at the Greeks at noon."

"That sounds nice. See you there," replied June. They both loved the warm pitas and they usually shared a large Greek salad. "Bye."

"Wait," said Norah. "Be careful. Okay? Don't go too far."

"I won't."

"Promise?"

"Yes, I promise. It's just that, I love these days."

"I know. Just take care of yourself."

"Always do!" June laughed. "See you later."

June opened the back door and confirmed the inclement weather. Undeterred, she chose her raincoat with the warm lining, red Wellies and her ridiculous Tilley hat which managed to cover most of her soft grey curls and prevented the rain from dripping inside her coat. She chuckled as she checked herself in the mirror. She suddenly missed the old Nick who would have laughed with her or at her. He really was a grouch these days. Why did he want to retire now, when he wasn't fun to be around?

There was still so much she wanted to do; see the penguins in Antarctica, go on a safari. She'd never seen the Taj Mahal or the pyramids. But, above all, she really wanted to go back to Italy. She loved Venice, the narrow bumpy streets, the tiny pizzerias, the canals, the sexy Italian men. She wanted to go someday. But maybe it *had* to be now.

June felt her legs tremble. Her raincoat was too heavy. She felt hot and clammy, woozy. She plopped down on the shoe bench. Wait, was Nick right? Had she waited too long? They could still travel, couldn't they? Nick was healthy, suffering only from a bad case of *worrywortitis*. And she was fine, just fine, but they'd have to hurry. Chop-chop. No time like the present. She'd shorten her list, strike India and the pyramids, for sure the Antarctic. She'd read that penguins were very smelly and Nick didn't like the cold. But she wasn't giving up on the lions and giraffes or Italy. June took a deep breath and let it out slowly. There. That should do it. "Mercury, let's go."

Mercury responded quickly and sat still while June attached his harness and leash. Outside it was wet and chilly. Mercury made no effort to avoid the puddles. June turned up her collar and tightened her scarf. She inhaled deeply, savouring it all—the cool rain on her cheeks, the musky smell of the soggy ground, the sloppy sound of her boots on the wet driveway. It was a perfect day for walking.

CHAPTER THREE

Nick leaned back in his chair, resisting the urge to put his feet up on his desk. He was pleased with himself. He hadn't been worried about this meeting, but maybe he should have been. Sam, a friend of a friend from tennis, had been an easy sell over drinks at the club. Their first meeting had gone smoothly. Sam owned a microbrewery facing action from the advertising regulators; large fines and threats of a shutdown had brought him to Nick, one of the best commercial litigators around. Sam had seemed pleased with the proposal for their services that he and young Mark DeLuca had put together. He'd come back today, ready to sign, or so Nick thought. Instead, he'd brought his CFO, a youngster with a fancy MBA from London who was ready to challenge his expertise and strategies and then quibbled about hourly rates, retainers and even the disbursements. Mark had come fully prepared today and had an answer for every challenge. He'd become a hell of a lawyer. Nick smiled. The signed contract was on his desk, backed up by a hefty retainer. Walker, Harris and Leblanc had been hired to handle all pending and future litigation. It was a win.

Back in the day he and Mark would have closed the deal and celebrated with a drink, no matter what time of day, but those days were long gone. The thrill of landing such a big account had left him hungry and, he hated to admit, a little tired. He slid open his bottom desk drawer and selected a protein bar, dark chocolate, almonds and cherries. He'd scoffed at them when Martha had left the box on his desk but now he ate one almost every day.

"Mr. Walker?" Sylvie, his assistant, was standing in the doorway. "There's a call for you. Norah? She says she's a friend of your wife, um, Mrs. Walker."

"Norah? For me?"

"Yes. It came through the general number, not yours."

"Thanks." Nick lifted the receiver and pressed the flashing button. "Norah?"

"Yes. Hi Nick. I'm really sorry to bother you but—"

"No bother at all." Norah was June's friend. They did daytime things together. She'd been to the house a few times for coffee or to drop off some baking or a new book for June, but he didn't know her well. She was younger than June, by five, maybe ten years and lived a few streets away. "What can I do for you?"

"Well, maybe I'm overreacting. I don't know. It's just that—"

"Norah, what is it? Are you in need of legal services?" Sometimes friends asked for his advice. "It's okay. Whatever you tell me is strictly confidential."

"Oh. No. Not that. Sorry, sorry. It's June."

Nick stiffened.

"She didn't come to lunch."

"Lunch?"

"Yes. We were supposed to meet at the Greeks at noon, but June didn't come. I called—" She inhaled noisily; her words lost in her breath. "—and waited over an hour. She never showed up."

"Did you call the landline? She seldom answers her cell phone."

"Yes, and I just checked the house. I thought maybe she was sick or hurt. I banged on the door. And I hope you don't mind but I used the key in the garage and let myself in."

"And was she there?" Of course she wasn't. That's why Norah had called him.

"No. Sorry."

She'd seemed fine, happy, when he'd left her this morning, but he'd been distracted and short with her. Shit. Had she taken her pills? He struggled to keep his voice steady. "Did you look everywhere? Downstairs? The bedroom? The backyard?"

"Yes, everywhere. I walked through the whole house."

"What about Mercury?" He was trying to stay calm, holding back the fear. "Was Mercury there?"

"Oh, right!" Norah cried. "Mercury's gone too."

"Well then," Nick exhaled. "They just went for a walk." He closed his eyes, feeling relief soak into his tension. "June likes the rain."

"Yes, I know." Norah paused. "But that was hours ago."

"What?"

"They went out early this morning, right after you left, I think. June called and asked me to go with her, through the ravine. But it was too cold for me. That's when we arranged lunch."

"Well, they can't still be out there. Right?"

"I don't know. I don't know. What if—"

Was Norah crying? "No, no, I'm sure she's fine, Norah. Just fine." *Then where was she?* "Maybe they—" He stopped, unable to make the *maybes* fit the facts. "You know June," he said with little conviction. "She can be scattered sometimes." His mind was racing. Had Norah noticed June's memory slips? Had June told her about them? Dammit. They should have talked to Norah, enlisted her help. And Martha's. But June didn't want anyone to know yet. "So you have no idea where she is?" asked Norah. "Should I call someone? Maybe her bridge friends. Or search the woods?"

Nick pulled his attention back to the conversation. "No. No. I'll track her down. Maybe Martha knows something."

"But—what if—"

"Don't worry." He bit back the hollow *reasonable explanation* platitude. "You're a good friend, Norah."

"Thanks. I only—"

"I will have June call you later. Bye." He hung up.

Nick located his cell phone under the papers on his desk and pressed the speaker button. *Call June Home.* The phone lit up and a second later he heard the ringing, picturing June hurrying to answer the phone in the kitchen or the family room, maybe his office. He pushed his chair back and walked to the window. The rain had almost stopped. It was misty now. He placed his palm against the glass. It was so cold, if June were still outside—Each unanswered ring reverberated around the room, confirming June's absence. Unable to control his frustration, he jammed his finger on the red button and ended the call.

Shit. There really had to be a good explanation. June had gotten along well all summer, almost without incident. And she really was fine this morning, tenacious and stubborn as ever, but that was June. He loved her for her optimism, her hope, even if it sometimes drove him crazy. But where the hell had she gone? He thought back to breakfast. Had she mentioned her plans? No, in fact, he'd specifically told her not to go for a walk today. It was so cold and miserable but when had that stopped June?

Nick slipped on his jacket and headed to Martha's office, hurrying past Sylvie so she couldn't ask questions. He ignored Martha's assistant, a thin, pale young man who looked too timid to offer much assistance and walked into her office without knocking. "Any idea where your mother is today?"

Martha looked at him, tapped her right ear bud, and held up a finger for silence. "Look," she said. "That all sounds good to me, now just get your client to sign off on it and we can take it to the judge." She waited, listened, and added. "Great. Bye." She swiveled toward him. "Hi Dad. What's up?"

It still sometimes surprised him how much Martha had come to look like her mother—the young June; the smile, the eyes, but mostly the hair, thick auburn curls that Martha had coaxed into waves today.

"Dad?"

"Ah, yeah. Do you know where your mother is?"

"Mom? No, why?"

"Why? Because I asked you." Martha stared at him, her face creased with confusion or amusement, Nick couldn't tell. "Sorry, I mean, her friend Norah just called and she didn't show up for a lunch date today."

"So? You know Mom. She probably just forgot. She's—". Martha waved her hand in the air as if trying to catch ideas. "—shopping or in the garden. Gossiping with the neighbours."

He pointed outside. "I doubt she's doing much gardening today. So, you haven't talked to her?"

"Um, Saturday or Sunday maybe—"

"No today. Did you talk to her today?" Nick tapped his fingers on the back of the leather client chair. "She didn't text or anything?"

"No, Dad, sorry, I have no idea of Mom's schedule today or any day. But I wouldn't worry. You know she can spend hours just wandering around the garden centre."

He nodded and swallowed the information about Mercury. "You're probably right."

"For sure. But you seem upset. Are you okay?"

No point in worrying Martha, besides he and June should tell her later—together. "Yeah I'm fine. It was just Norah. She was wound pretty tight so she set me off."

"Okay," said Martha as her phone buzzed. "Sorry, I need to get this."

Nick hurried back to his office, grabbed his fedora and overcoat and headed for his car. Norah had said June was planning to go to the ravine. That made sense. June loved the walk along the river.

CHAPTER FOUR

June pulled on Mercury's leash, steering him away from the squirrel that had just crossed the path, and towards the trash bin with *Animal Waste* stenciled on the side.

"Hang on, there," she chided him. "Your enthusiasm is inspiring, old boy, but you mustn't pull me over." She held her breath and negotiated the spring door with one hand, disposing of the environmentally friendly bag as quickly as she could. "Our Nick won't let me out of the house again if I come back broken."

June walked toward the bench that marked the end of the trail and sat down with a sigh. Mercury shook from nose to tail, spraying her with the water but nicely drying off his coat. June laughed. "Thanks for the shower." She gave him a liver treat from her pocket. He ate it with vigour and eyed her for another.

"Later," she said, scratching his head. "Shall we go home now?" June looked at the sky and detected a sliver of blue in the distance. "Seems a shame to waste this day. Let's just sit here for a bit. A short rest will do us both some good."

Mercury's ears twitched.

"Yes, I know it's raining, but I love these days." June inhaled deeply, sniffing the air. The musky earth smell delighted her. The cool air made her feel alive. She held out her hand to catch the rain drops. Jonny used to catch them on his tongue.

It rained a lot in Vancouver. Jonny's city. She liked it there…

**

But once, it was an emergency—she'd flown there on the red-eye. Nick wouldn't go with her. "Please come with me. He needs us."

"He's a grown-ass man, June. At least he should be."

"Jonathan's had an accident."

"No, June. That's called a DUI. There's nothing accidental about it."

"But he sounded so scared." They'd had the call on speaker. "He's in jail, Nick!"

"Yeah." He sat on the bed as June moved her clothes from the small suitcase into a larger one. "Jesus. How long are you planning on staying?"

"As long as I need to."

Nick sucked in air through his teeth. "June, he's thirty-eight. Same as Martha, right?"

"Yes, I am well aware of this."

"He needs to clean up his own messes."

"Yes, but he also needs to know he's not alone."

She was angry now. "He needs to know we love him! That he has a family who gives a damn!"

Nick stood and pulled her into a hug. "Slow down. Come on." He rubbed her back. "Jonathan is fine. They've got him locked up for the night but he'll probably be out before you get there."

June nodded but she didn't believe him.

"Look, you go, take care of things for him. I need to be at the office tomorrow. But—"

June pulled away to finish packing. "There's always a *but* when it comes to Jon, isn't there?"

Nick sighed. "Look, I was just going to say, figure out how much trouble he's in and call me. If it's just money, bail him out. Pay the fine. If it's more, like charges, well, I know a few good lawyers out there."

'Okay. Thanks."

June was still worried when she landed in Vancouver. She rented a car and drove the treacherous road to Whistler as quickly as she dared. Jon was still in jail when she arrived. She'd never been inside of a police station before. The officers were polite, but not friendly. Jon was charged and released. She'd driven him home, to a small chalet he shared with his business partners. Jon packed up some of his clothes, his laptop, and his skis. June checked them into a suite at the Hilton.

It wasn't until they were back in Vancouver, meeting with a lawyer that June had learned most of the story. Jonatthan had long struggled with alcohol, but she thought he'd figured it out. He'd built a good business with his friends—*Wild Wanderers*—she'd always liked the name, but now he'd started drinking again. He was facing charges for driving drunk and running off the road and into a parked car. The lawyer had worked out a deal—community service, restitution and mandatory AA meetings. But the DUI was on his record.

It saddened June to leave him there, but after several weeks she flew home. They'd found a nice furnished condo for him in the city, close to his AA meetings and with a spare bedroom. He was working off his community service at the YMCA. She'd promised she'd be back soon. She didn't want him to be alone.

He hugged her tight before she got in the cab. "Don't worry, Mom."

But she did.

**

Grrrr. Grrr. Grrr.

Mercury was watching a raccoon approach the trash can.

"Shoo!" June stomped her feet and laughed as the racoon retreated. "You don't wanna mess with us, right Mercury?" They should probably head home. "Come on."

Mercury jumped up.

"I've got an idea!" June headed away from the familiar path, away from home. "Let's go to the Canine Cafe," she said. "We haven't been there in ages." She loved the atmosphere there, welcoming to dogs and their humans, fresh baked goods, light meals and outstanding coffee. And it wasn't far.

They were out of the woods now, on a street that looked familiar. June paused for just a minute, turned left and walked to the end, squinting to read the sign, *Crestview*. Yes, that sounded right. A path between two houses suggested a shortcut, but June stuck to the safety of the sidewalk. They crossed a footbridge that was new or maybe freshly painted, Mercury lagging behind to sniff and leave his mark on each post. It was raining harder now. "Come on, buddy. We're almost there. I'm pretty sure."

The next street sign read *Poplar Drive*. Not what she'd expected. June looked at her watch. She was getting hungry. "Lakeshore," she said. "Come on, Mercury. We can do this." He pulled her forward, wagging his beautiful tail. "Okay, Lassie," she teased. "Lead on!"

It was almost noon when they turned the corner onto Lakeshore Road. Success! The cafe was probably just a couple of blocks away. Mercury walked by her side shielding her from the road spray. They walked several blocks, past impressively large houses. By peeking through the large iron gates, June could see the lake on her left. That was right, wasn't it? Yes, there was a traffic light in the distance, the red light backed up the traffic, but she kept moving forward. Mercury was panting, his tongue hanging low. June spotted a bench ahead. "Let's have a little sit down," she said, tugging gently on the leash. The rain had slowed to a drizzle. Mercury curled up at her feet. A little rest would be lovely—

June opened her eyes, startled by the sharp voice.

"Lady, are you getting on? Lady!"

A city bus, the door wide open, was shouting at her. The driver, red faced and angry.

"You can't bring that dog." He jerked a finger at her. "Unless it's one of them helper dogs. Well, is it?"

June felt a wet nudge against her hand. He was right, she was sitting next to a dog. She pulled her hand into her lap, alarmed to find a leash draped across her legs.

"Lady, are you okay?"

Why was he shouting at her. "Go away," she demanded dismissing the driver and the dog.

"Okay," he hollered. "S'up to you." The door closed with a swoosh.

June's heart was racing, beating in her ears. Where was she? She glanced at the dog. He was watching her. June stood and looked around. This wasn't her street or the trail in the woods. She shivered. Her feet were cold and achy.

"Where am I?" she whispered.

The dog sauntered away from the bus shelter, his soggy leash dragging on the sidewalk. Maybe he knew the way home, like Lassie?

June started walking, keeping her distance. It was raining, a steady downpour. Bang! Thunder crashed through her bones. She froze. She fought back tears, trying not to panic. Anchored by fear, she looked around, searching, hoping for something, anything familiar. Bright lights, foreign cars and strangers. A man rushed past her, a soggy newspaper shielding his face. Nick hated when his paper got wet. Just ahead she spotted a stroller, a baby and a mother. She could ask her. June hurried forward. A loud horn blast scared her back to the curb. She blinked, spilling a flood of tears; mother and baby gone.

The street swelled into a whirl of flashing lights and incongruous sounds. The sidewalk wobbled under her boots. A sudden explosion. Thunder! Too loud! June's heart was racing, hammering, each beat a taunt; I'm lost—ba boom, I'm lost—ba boom—I'm lost. She felt dizzy, assaulted. She stumbled toward a storefront and leaned against the rough brick. An overhead awning stopped the rain. Breathe. Breathe. Cool air filled her lungs. She opened her eyes. The dog sat at her feet, staring, waiting. "Shoo." She waved her command. "Shoo," she repeated. "Go home. Leave me alone."

He nuzzled against her leg.

"No!" She turned away.

 He nudged her hand.

"What?"

He sniffed her coat, prodded her pocket.

"Don't!" He seemed to be smiling at her. Curious. That smile. Oh! Golden. A retriever. June reached into her pocket and found snacks, tiny cookies. She was so hungry. Ew, they smelled like fish or something rotten. She held them out to the dog, stretching out her palm to keep him at bay. His teeth gently grazed her fingers. His thick tongue felt warm and rough, canine. June spun around and bumped into a young woman with a huge purple umbrella.

"Canine Cafe," she blurted out.

"Excuse me?"

"Where is it? The Canine Cafe?"

'Oh, right." She turned and pointed to the rear. "It's just there. On the other side. Cross at the light and you won't miss it."

"Thank you," said June.

"Do you need help? I mean, I'm going that way."

June nodded and took the arm she'd been offered. "Thank you. You're so kind."

She left June at the light, pointing to the shop beside the drug store. "I hope you'll have a cinnamon bun. They're delicious."

"That's the plan." June smiled, waved and added another *Thank you* as she led Mercury across on the green light.

CHAPTER FIVE

Martha watched as her father hurried out the door. The sound of his footsteps faded quickly. What had gotten into him? It was unlike him to be so agitated and so evasive. How would she know where her mother was or what she was doing today? Martha barely found the time or patience to talk to her mother on the weekends, let alone know her day-to-day plans.

"Sebastian?"

Her assistant's head bobbed up above his monitor.

"Could you please get me a coffee?"

He stood and nodded agreeably. "Of course."

"Black," she reminded him, but he was already gone. She pushed some stray curls behind her ear. She stood and slipped off her jacket and her heels and smoothed her pencil skirt with her palms. Martha worked hard to keep her petite frame neat and trim. It was hard enough being a woman lawyer without looking tiny and weak. What was going on with her father? Their paths seldom crossed at work. They attended the same partners' meetings and they went for lunch together every couple of weeks, but that was about it. She couldn't remember the last time her father had stuck his head into her office.

Sebastian hovered at the doorway, gingerly holding a cup and saucer.

"Come in. Come in!" Darn, that had sounded sharper than she'd intended. Sebastian had only been here a couple of days, hired to take over from her last assistant, who'd had a penchant for leaving right at five. He set the coffee on the outside corner of her desk, avoiding eye contact. Hopefully she hadn't scared him off.

"Thanks for the coffee. Next time a mug is fine. Sebastien—" She waited until he looked up. "You may come into my office anytime, with a question or a problem. My door is always open."

He nodded. "Okay."

"Unless," she added with a smile. "It isn't open, the door, I mean. Or I'm on the phone."

Sebastian nodded again. "Got it."

A man of few words. This might work out. "Great. Thanks again."

He turned and pulled the door shut behind him.

The coffee was good, fresh, but did little to clear her head. She couldn't shake the feeling that her father wasn't telling her everything. It just didn't add up. Why was he so worried about Mom? She'd simply forgotten a lunch date with a friend. For some reason Norah's phone call had really upset him. It was no doubt unusual for one of her mom's friends to call him at work, but, like he'd said, Norah was overreacting—being a busybody.

Martha woke up her laptop and signed in again. She checked for new emails, answered the easy ones and made a few notes on the others before finally identifying the tightness in her chest as guilt. Her father had never been a quiet, patient man, but today he was really worked up. She should have asked him more questions, sat him down and talked to him, found out what was really going on. This was more than a forgotten lunch date.

Martha called her mother at home, and let it ring seven or eight times. Why wasn't the machine picking up? She pressed the saved number for her mom's mobile. Voicemail. The mailbox was full. No surprises there. Her mother probably still checked the ornate brass mailbox on the front porch every day, but she found voicemail impossible. Martha had left messages a few times, but her mother never bothered to listen to them. When Martha tried to walk her through the voicemail steps, even printing out the instructions, her mother had just glanced at the paper and said, "Oh, you worry too much. They'll call back if it's important." Honestly, her mother's optimism sometimes drove her crazy.

When she was young Martha had considered her mom the best of all the moms. She'd filled their days with stories and summer picnics, homemade cookies and long trips on the city bus, even though, as Dad pointed out, they had a perfectly good car sitting in the driveway. But as adults, they had little in common and Martha was short on patience when it came to her mother's ramblings. Martha had called her last Saturday or maybe it was Sunday? As usual, her mother had complained that Martha and Peter hadn't visited in a while. Mom had told her again, for the third time, about the mocha cupcakes and lemon squares she'd made for the bake sale at church. And then the question.

"Have you heard from Jonny?"

"No, Mom." Question and answer always the same. But then her mom had broken from the script.

"Have you tried calling him?" she'd asked.

Call Jonathan? She'd called him plenty over the years. Mostly he hadn't answered. Never had he called back. He was her brother, her twin, but also a selfish shit. *No, Mom.* She wanted to say more but bit her tongue and only added. "I haven't called Jonathan in a while." Then she'd gotten off the phone quickly before Mom could get into telling her about all her friends' grandchildren.

Did Dad really think her mother had gone missing? Maybe she should call a few of her mom's friends, the bridge ladies? It might put his mind at ease. But that seemed silly, a gross overreaction. Instead, she dialed her father's office and was surprised when his assistant picked up.

"Sorry, Martha, he just left," said Sylvie.

"He did? He was here, like, ten minutes ago."

"Yes. Mark DeLuca was looking for him too. He seemed to be in a hurry. Said, he's gone for the day. And—" Sylvie lowered her voice to a furtive whisper. "And he didn't take his briefcase."

"Really?" Now that was unusual. When Martha was little she'd almost believed that the black leather bag was an extension of his arm.

"Did he say where he was going? No, never mind. I'll call him and pick up the briefcase if he wants it. Thanks." She hung up. Dad's phone went straight to voicemail. Great. Now both her parents were missing.

"Hi Dad. Just wondering if you've talked to Mom. Sylvie says you left your briefcase here. Do you need it? Um—are you okay? I'm a little worried, so please call me. About Mom. Or if you want to talk about—" The long beep sounded, cutting her off. *Damn.* He'd call her back. Or she'd try again later. A loud rap on her door broke into her thoughts.

"Yes?"

Sebastian leaned in as he opened the door. "Sarah Martinez is here, waiting in the small client room. Mr. Martinez and his lawyer are in reception."

"Perfect. Thanks, Sebastian."

"And." He cleared his throat and glanced at the orange note in his hand. "Oh yes, the meteor is in the boardroom."

"Mediator." Martha grinned. "Thanks."

The Martinez file was the top one on the pile. She gathered her phone, a legal notepad and her lucky pen. This divorce was a nasty one. But that was okay; Martha had no emotional skin in the game. She always urged her clients to settle as quickly and as amicably as possible. Nasty divorces were costly, good for billable hours but too much angst for her liking. She'd mediate the hell out of this one.

CHAPTER SIX

Nick drove along the service road and parked as close to the trail as he could, ignoring the *Service Vehicles Only* sign. The wind had picked up, beating the rain against his windshield. This was crazy. June had to be at home by now. He called again. No answer.

Fuck! He couldn't ignore the facts. She'd taken Mercury, they'd gone out walking, hours ago.

Nick's favourite golf umbrella didn't survive the first five minutes. He converted it to a walking stick and trudged forward, headlong into the rain, focusing on every movement, straining to hear or see or feel June's presence. He veered right, along a river trail, praying he'd chosen the right one. He tried to avoid the puddles and quaggy ruts but soon his leather shoes were covered in mud—soaked through. Rain dripped from the brim of his hat, drained inside his collar and down his back.

"June! June!" He willed her to appear around every turn. "June! Mercury. Here boy!" Had she fallen? Broken a leg? Hit her head?

He walked deeper into the forest. The trail that led to the bridge was flooded. He stayed near the riverbank, scanning the ravine, then slipped, tripped on a tree root. Mud, soupy clay, soaked his pants legs and splashed up the front of his coat. He stumbled but stayed on his feet. He leaned against a tree and caught his breath. It was only midafternoon but the forest seemed especially dark and menacing.

Chilled to the bone, shaking and fearing the worst, he gave in and circled back to his car. His overcoat was covered in mud and soaked. He popped the trunk hoping to find a bag or a blanket to save his leather seats. He'd just had the car detailed so there wasn't even a golf towel. He reached in further to check under a collapsable folding chair he kept for June, when a gust of wind caught the truck lid. The hinges groaned as it flew up to a full vertical position, giving Nick just enough time to back out before it recoiled and smashed down with a violent thud. "Fuck!" *Decapitation by trunk*. He shook off the close call and yanked open the car door. *Fuck the leather seats. Fuck the clean floor mats.* He started the car and turned the heater and the seat warmer to high. The wipers struggled against the downpour while the heat from his anger and his wet clothes steamed up the windows. *Damn it June. This is your fault. If you'd just stayed put, listened to me. How hard is that?*

He turned the air to cool and made a plan while the windows cleared. He'd drive around, check the streets closest to the house, go to the dog park, then circle around to the other side of the ravine. After that, he'd go home, check the whole house, the basement, the garden. Then he'd call the police.

CHAPTER SEVEN

The clock in the dining room chimed but June missed the count. She lifted her arm to check her watch and felt her book slip to the floor, forcing a grumble out of Mercury.

"Sorry old boy."

It was almost five! Really? She must have fallen asleep. She reached down and ran her figures through Mercury's fur. "Mercury?" His fur was matted and damp. "You smell like a wet dog. Whatever have you been up to?" June sat up and wriggled her feet into her slippers. Her hair was damp too. So, they'd been out in the rain but when and...why? "Mercury, did we go for a walk?"

Mercury's ears twitched.

June looked around for her bookmark and spotted an unfamiliar business card on the coffee table, *PremierTaxi*. She turned it over, *Charles*. She pictured an older man, baseball hat, crooked smile.

"Oh! We had a car ride?"

Mercury's tail beat on the floor where he was stretched on his side.

This was worrisome. A whole day had passed and she remembered little of it. She'd eaten cereal and a banana this morning. She could feel the weight of her wellies, taste the cream cheese icing melting on a cinnamon bun. Yes, that was it. She'd taken Mercury to the Canine Cafe. And she'd done it all by herself.

"We did it, didn't we, old boy?"

Mercury sighed.

There were still a lot of missing parts, what did it matter? "We made it home safe and sound, didn't we? Easy peasy."

Another weary thump of the tail.

But it did matter. She could feel the rain on her face, see the unfamiliar street signs, sense the rising panic. She had been scared. And she didn't remember walking home. She laid back against the pillows, listened to the rain pelt the windows and tried to piece the day together.

She and Mercury had walked to the Canine Cafe. That was clear now. She recalled a sweet young lady who was about Martha's age, a waitress who loved dogs. June didn't know her name, but she laughed when Mercury fell asleep under the table and snored. She'd called him Lazybones. June told her they had walked a very long way and she was very tired too. The waitress brought her another coffee and a chocolate chip cookie. *You two need to rest awhile.* When June stood up to leave the woman helped her with her coat and asked too many questions. Yes, June knew her own address. She'd come home in a car, with Mercury. And the driver had said it was *on the house*, which had confused June. But they were here now, safe and sound at home. And they'd had a lovely day.

June heard the key in the front door, the familiar creak as it swung open, then slammed shut with startling thud.

"June! June! Are you here?" Nick burst into the room.

"Of course I'm here."

"Jesus Christ, June! Where have you been?"

"What? Here. What's the matter? Did something happen?"

Nick's face was red. His trench coat was soaked, caked in mud. He looked cold but hot and sweaty too.

"I called, both phones. Why didn't you answer?"

"I can't find my cell." She hated to admit this but Nick wasn't giving her time to think. "The house phone didn't ring. At least—oh I don't know. I think I fell asleep. But why are you so upset?"

"Norah called me."

"My friend Norah?"

"Yes, your friend Norah called me."

"Why?"

"You were supposed to meet her for lunch."

"Oh? No, I don't think so." June sat up, adjusting the pillows to relieve the tight muscles in her back. "I'll have to call and apologize. How was your day?" June grinned at Nick, hoping to elicit a smile in return. But Nick had that grouchy old man look again.

"My day?"

"You're dripping on the floor," said June, pointing to the dirty puddle forming at Nick's feet.

"Dammit June. I don't care about the floor. I thought you were lost or missing."

"But why? You know I go for walks."

"I told you to stay in today."

"I didn't want to."

"But you were gone for hours." Nick's voice dropped low.

"Yes, I went for a very long walk." June pointed to the dog. "Mercury and I."

"Outside? All day?"

"Mostly. We walked to the Canine Cafe. They have the biggest, most delicious cinnamon buns. I wanted to bring one home for you but—"

"The Canine Cafe? On Lakeshore? June, that's miles from here!"

"I know. It was much further than I'd figured. We came home in a taxi."

"Really?"

"Yes. Charles drove us."

"Who?" Nick's face crumpled. "I thought you were lost."

"Well, I was a little confused, but only for a while, but then we found the cafe. Mercury had a cookie shaped like a drumstick."

"What? You got lost! June! That's why you shouldn't—"

June held up her hand. "No, listen. I found my way." She patted the sofa. "See, I'm here, safe and sound."

Nick sighed.

"Are you angry, Nick?"

"No, just worried." He unbuttoned his soggy coat. "You're safe. That's all that matters. I'm going to change into some dry clothes and then I'll start dinner. You can rest."

"Nick?"

He turned towards her; his emotions lined his face.

"Please Nick. I need you to be brave. I did what I wanted and Mercury and I had a great day. I can't be brave for both of us."

- 35 -

"But—" He shivered in his wet clothes.

"But nothing. I had fun," she said. "Next time, though, I'll take along more money so I can buy you something too."

Nick's eyebrows shot up. He exhaled and hurried from the room.

June had set the table by the time Nick came downstairs. "I've poured a red and a white," she said, pointing to two glasses of wine on the counter, the larger glass half full of red wine, the smaller with white. "Which would you prefer?"

He ignored the wine and June and went straight for the fridge, pulling out glass containers and fresh vegetables.

"I emptied two bottles, instead of opening another. I like both kinds so this works out perfectly, doesn't it?"

Nick nodded. "Yup, all good."

"Can I help?" June offered.

"We're just having leftover salmon, green beans and a salad. You can do the beans."

June emptied the bag of beans into the colander, rinsed them and began lopping off the ends with a large chef's knife. They worked in silence. *How long had the salmon been in the fridge?* She was about to ask when she noticed the grill marks and remembered that Nick had grilled it yesterday, maybe the day before. The salmon was fine but Nick wasn't. He was so quiet, maybe angry. Why was he still upset with her?

June pointed her knife at Nick. She waved it back and forth to get his attention.

He gasped. "Jesus!" He jumped back. "What are you doing?"

June grinned. "Settle down. I'm not planning on stabbing you. I was just offering you my knife."

"Why?" asked Nick.

"For the tension—you know, so thick you can cut it with a knife." She giggled but quickly turned serious. "Why are you mad at me?"

Nick's face collapsed. The cranky lines sagged into sadness. "I'm not angry. I'm upset and worried about you."

"But I'm fine. Really. I felt so good today."

He took the knife from her, set it on the cutting board then covered the beans with cling wrap and put them in the microwave.

June watched his slow deliberate movements. He was still upset.

He stared at her and clicked his tongue. "June, my love, I'm glad you had such a nice day." He held both her hands in his. "But I don't think you were careful. You took a lot of chances. And—"

"Oh, don't nag, please."

"Nagging is caring." The microwave beeped, but Nick didn't move. "And should have had your phone with you."

"That's silly."

"No, it's absolutely necessary. So you can call if you need help. We can programme it so you only need to press one button."

June sighed. "Okay. I can do that." She squeezed his hands, pleased he no longer seemed angry.

Nick picked up a tea towel and used it to take the bowl of beans out of the microwave. He flipped the salmon in the frypan.

"It's almost ready," he said. "Just a minute or two more. You must be hungry."

"I am. A cinnamon bun, no matter how large, is not lunch."

Nick chuckled. "That's for sure." He leaned against the counter next to her. "So, you don't remember that you made a lunch date with Norah?"

June shook her head. "I didn't. I called her this morning, to complain about you." He made a sour face and she patted his cheek. "And she invited me for coffee but I wanted to walk."

"Anything else?"

June scrunched up her face, thinking. "Butter tarts. Norah had made some." She reached for her wine but stopped midair. She gasped. "Oh no! The Greeks. I forgot!" Suddenly, in a recap of her panic, all the dark moments flashed before her, still unclear, still scary. Thunder, buses, horns. Lost! June stood in shocked silence for a moment before the tears began to roll down her cheeks. Nick wrapped his arms around her. She pulled him closer, sharing her pain, her fear, needing his strength. She moaned and wept softly into his chest. "I don't…don't want to…to…go… go away. I'm scared."

"I know, my love. So am I."

CHAPTER EIGHT

Martha arrived home to a dark house, with only the motion light on the front porch to welcome her. She wasn't used to getting home before Peter, but today she'd left work early; 5:30 seemed like the middle of the afternoon, but she'd had a shitty day. The Martinez divorce would ultimately be settled by the mediator, but today's session was acrimonious. How had those two ever been married? She'd come home to be with Peter. They'd been running in different directions lately. He seemed so unhappy and Martha wasn't sure why.

Martha's plan was simple: be home early for dinner and suggest they order take-out—something greasy and void of nutrition; any of Peter's preferred poisons. Maybe she could get him talking over beer and pizza.

Martha pushed open the heavy wooden front door with her shoulder, juggling her umbrella and her bag and flipped on the hall light. She turned off the alarm, whispering the numbers to herself before pressing them. Where was Peter? He was always home by now. She hung up her coat and kicked off her shoes. The rain had spotted the fine Italian suede. She'd brush them when they were dry, just like her mother had taught her. Mom! Shit. She'd forgotten all about the lunch drama. Dad hadn't called, so everything must be okay. But she needed to check in with them.

Martha felt cold and grimy, as if the hostility of the warring Martinezes had permeated her skin. She needed to change, maybe even shower, but first a glass of wine. She chose her best red, uncorked it and poured a large glass. It smelled warm and bold. Her stomach rumbled with hunger. Dinner would be a while.

She pulled open the fridge door. The handle jiggled in her hand. Peter had fixed it a few times, but maybe it was time for a new one, maybe a whole new kitchen.

They needed groceries, but thankfully the cheese drawer was well stocked. She chose the aged white cheddar and some brie for Peter. It was better when it sat out for a while. She shaved off a couple of slices of cheddar, then added olives and seedy crackers to the cutting board.

At least a week's worth of mail waited, unopened on the table. She sat and sifted through it, saving only a couple of envelopes from the recycling pile. The cheese and wine were working their magic.

Martha called her father's cell. No answer, she disconnected to avoid leaving a message. She heard the faint beep from Peter's key fob as he locked his car. He always came in through the side door. She listened as Peter opened the closet in the mudroom, hung up his coat, placed his shoes in the rack and changed into his moccasins. He was a man of routines.

"Hello," she called out.

"Hi," said Peter as he entered the kitchen.

He looked drawn and a little tired, his pale skin contrasting with his thick dark hair, all pepper and no salt. So unfair.

"How was your day?" asked Martha, trying to catch his eye. But Peter was headed to the sink to wash his hands.

"Okay. Same old, same old," he said, turning on the water. He dried his hands on the towel meant for the dishes and then added, "You're home early."

"I am," said Martha. "I thought you'd be here."

"Busy day. The market took a hit, so lots of calls."

"Hmm, that's not good."

"I'm tired and hungry. Is there any dinner?" asked Peter

"I'm sorry. No, no dinner but—" Martha nodded towards the cutting board. "Have some cheese and then I thought maybe we could order in."

"What, like salad and steamed veggies?"

"Or burgers, tacos, maybe pizza?" Her voice climbed up a few notes, trying to tempt him.

"Really? That doesn't sound like you."

"Ouch."

The kitchen was silent, save for the whoosh as Peter opened a can of beer. He lopped off a huge chunk of the brie, ignored the olives and ate the last few crackers. He washed it all down with a swallow of beer and cleared his throat.

"Look, I'm hungry now. Ordering takes too long. I think I'll just make an omelette," he said, as he tied his *Mr. Good Lookin' is Cookin'* apron around his waist and pulled out his cast iron pan. "Would you like one?"

"Oh yes, please! Two eggs."

"Yolks and all?"

"Yes Peter." She forced a smile "Yolks and all. I haven't eaten since breakfast."

"Okay then." He dug around in the fridge and pulled out an onion, a red pepper and some wrinkled mushrooms. He put two pieces of white bread into the toaster. "Cheese?"

"Cheddar please, but no toast."

"Yeah, I figured." He diced the onion with short staccato beats. "Just give me a few minutes."

"Sure. I'll go change." She knew when she wasn't wanted.

Martha closed the bedroom door and immediately regretted leaving her wine on the kitchen table. She really thought he'd like the idea of ordering burgers; she'd come home early and everything. He sure hadn't appreciated the effort. Impossible to figure him out these days.

Martha stripped down to her underwear, folded her suit and the silk blouse and added them to the dry-cleaning bag. She'd have to remember to take that with her tomorrow. Dinner wouldn't take long, so she decided to skip the shower. Instead, she washed her face and moisturized against wrinkles. She leaned in closer to the mirror. Her auburn curls were healthy and bouncy thanks to good genes and a great hairdresser. She stepped on the scale, approved of the number and then turned to the full-length mirror on the back of the door. She was little but mighty. That's what Jonathan had always said when she complained about her height. Five feet, four and a bit wasn't tiny but it justified the collection of very high heels in her closet.

Still, she didn't look bad—even without makeup. Her hips had widened a little with age and a small roll peeked over the waistband of her lace undies, but nothing her Spanx couldn't handle. She'd never loved her breasts, too small, but at least they were hers. She still looked strong and muscular, so the running was worth it. Not at all bad for forty-one. Too bad Peter didn't think so.

Martha wiggled into her comfortable yoga pants, the bigger, older, baggy ones. She reached for her favourite sweatshirt, but hesitated, knowing it was Peter's, not sure of the new rules. Peter was sleeping in the spare room these days.

It had started innocently enough and at first only occasionally. Peter had always been a snorer, but it had become worse over the years. She used to poke him and he'd roll over. Then she had to shake him until he opened his eyes. Fully awake and ticked off he'd take his ergonomic neck pillow and retreat to the guest bedroom. But then one night, a few, no, now many weeks ago, he'd started out in the spare room.

**

She'd had a hard day and decided to retire early. When she woke up the next morning, Peter's side of the bed was untouched. She'd teased him at breakfast.

"Where were you last night? Did you get a better offer?"

Peter frowned. "What?"

"Did you sleep in the guest room all night?'

"Yeah, the game went into overtime. I didn't want to wake you."

"Oh, that's nice. But—"

"It's just easier, practical, right? You don't have to listen to my snoring and I don't have to move in the middle of the night. Win. Win."

"Maybe. But—is this what you want Peter? Separate bedrooms?"

"Well, it's not like we're using our bed for anything else these days." He waved an accusatory bagel at her.

"That's not fair." They'd been married a long time, over sixteen years. Sure, they hadn't had sex in quite a while, but maybe they were just aging out—sliding into middle age. Now that was depressing.

"Peter, what's happening here? I'm worried about you. About us."

"Oh, stop it. I'm fine. I'm just tired is all. I'm sleeping in the spare room so I don't disturb you and so we can both get a good night's sleep."

"But—"

"I said I'm fine."

That argument ended. They'd each gone to work, came home and just carried on, silently agreeing to avoid the obvious.

**

So, now what? Did sleeping apart mean she couldn't wear his sweatshirt anymore? *The great sweatshirt dilemma.* To hell with it. It was soft and comfy and she liked the smell.

Martha returned to the kitchen, ready to help, wanting to talk. Her omelette rested in the pan, a plate with carrots and a few cucumber slices waited on the counter. She glanced into the family room. Peter sat in his recliner with his plate on his lap. The noise of a basketball game filled the room. She slid the eggs onto the plate and set it on the table beside her wine.

The first bite was delicious. She'd always loved eggs for dinner. Mom was a meat and potatoes kind of cook but sometimes she'd surprise them with eggs or pancakes. They'd eaten together, most nights without Dad, but almost always the three of them. The routine had changed when she and Jonathan were in high school. They'd microwave their plates after football practice or debate club. Mom must have eaten alone all those nights. Like this, a table for one.

Martha unlocked her phone and dialed her parent's number; the same one they'd had for more than forty years.

"Hi Dad. Did Mom turn up?"

"Yes, yes. She's fine. She took Mercury for a long walk and lost track of time."

"Great. See nothing to worry about," said Martha.

"Nope, nothing at all."

He sounded distant, restrained. "Are you alright? I mean you seemed a little frantic today."

"I wasn't frantic, Martha. I was concerned about your mother. Surely that's not a crime these days."

"No, Dad." She chuckled uneasily. "It's not a crime." She paused, expecting more, but was met by silence. "Oh yeah. Did you know you left your briefcase at the office?"

"I did?" He sighed. "I didn't mean to, but, well, I don't need it. Not tonight. I have a meeting first thing tomorrow, but the paperwork is ready. Are you checking up on me?"

"No, of course not! Sylvie just thought you might need it, that's all."

"I don't, not tonight."

"Okay. Okay." She hesitated. "I...I just wanted to make sure Mom was safe and sound."

"We're fine here, both of us. But thanks for calling."

"I...I...are you okay, Dad?"

"Yes, fine." He ended the call with a quick goodbye.

Peter walked past her and single handed two beers from the fridge. "Trouble at the Walker house?"

"Maybe. No. At least I don't think so."

Peter shrugged. "You haven't seen them in a while, have you?"

"I see my father often enough." She shifted back in her chair, feeling her chest muscles tightening "But no, I haven't been to the house in a while. Or hung out with my mother, if that's what you mean."

"Hey, don't bite my head off. I was just asking."

"Really? Just asking?" Peter's parents were a little younger, devout church goers and he, an only child, seemed to enjoy their company. "And no, I don't have dinner or lunch with my parents every other day." *Am I trying to start a fight?*

"You know I don't see my parents that often, Martha. We get together for a meal a couple of times a month. And, although you know you're welcome to join us, you always find an excuse not to."

"That's called self-preservation. Your parents can be very—judge-y." They'd never gotten over the fact that Martha didn't attend church. And she hadn't given them a grandchild.

Peter sighed and shuffled back to the couch. "My parents love you, Martha."

"Yeah, I know." She'd wanted to tell him about her mom missing lunch, her dad's meltdown, the Martinez shit show, but instead, they were fighting again. No worse. They couldn't even get a good fight going.

Martha started on the kitchen clean up. Her turn since Peter had cooked. He'd used every bowl, knife and spatula they owned. She fought back tears as she loaded the dishwasher. She still loved Peter. But he was so different now.

She poured herself another glass of wine, took it into the family room and sat at the chaise end of the couch. "Who's winning?" she asked.

"Do you even know who's playing?" said Peter without looking at her.

"No."

"Well then, what does it matter?"

"Fuck Peter. Don't be such an ass."

She stood, downed her wine in two gulps and set the glass on the coffee table. "I'm going to bed." She pulled the sweatshirt over her head. Bruised and furious, she gathered the warm fleece into a ball and slam dunked it into his lap.

"Alone."

CHAPTER NINE

Nick was almost asleep when his whole body convulsed with a spasm. His calf muscles tightened in pain. Shit, not again. He took a deep breath and tried to relax, slowly shaking his legs back to life. Hypnagogic jerks, hypnics according to the internet, their severity and frequency were increased by anxiety and stress. Great, so he could expect them on a regular basis from now on. Well at least he no longer thought he was having a stroke.

He rolled over and faced June. She was still so beautiful and so strong. He placed his hand on her arm. Had she been lost today? Maybe. But she'd made it home and was so fuckin' proud of herself. Had he overreacted? He'd been afraid for her, for himself.

Nick flipped his pillow to the cool side, closed his eyes and tried to find sleep. Counting sheep wouldn't work, so he tried the deep breathing he'd learned from his meditation app. Inhale deeply for four counts, hold for seven, exhale for eight. Breathe in, breathe out. He used to be a good solid sleeper, a brandy before bed kinda guy, but somehow over the last year, he'd switched to Scotch and doubled his intake, finding the whiskey more comforting or maybe more potent. But recently, fearing he was becoming a bona fide alcoholic, he'd given it up—most nights

He propped himself up on his elbow and gently pulled the covers up around June's shoulders. She snored softly, so peaceful. Sleep was the only escape from her inevitable, inescapable future. Sometimes it drove him crazy that June slept so soundly, while he worried away his nights.

Even awake, June was just so God damn blasé about the whole thing. *Oh, I'm fine Nick. Everyone forgets things. No, I didn't miss my hair appointment. They changed it without telling me. Have you seen my phone, my keys, my shoes, my book, my glasses?* And what about that exciting day when she'd walked home from the mall and forgotten her car? Luckily, he'd figured it out before they reported it stolen. They'd had quite a fight that day.

**

"Don't patronize me, Nick. I just forgot. I was thinking about walking then changed my mind and drove instead. Then I walked home. There's nothing ominous about it!"

"But surely you realize that you're getting worse, forgetting things, more often now."

"I do. But I don't want to think about being sick. So, I'm going with forgetful. I'm sorry. I'll be more careful."

"But you are sick!" he bellowed. How did this not upset her? It sent him into waves of panic and sometimes outbursts of rage. "You can't ignore this, June. It won't just go away. Have you been taking the pills?" He was yelling, unable to stop himself. He'd wanted to hug her, save her, protect her, but instead he shouted.

"Yes, every day. Just like the doctor told me, and you told me." She was so sure, defiant, beautiful in her strength.

"Okay, I'm sorry." He ended it there. What was the point? They'd fight again another day. "Just don't forget, okay?"

**

But she did forget, so each day he divvied out the pills, put them in a small bowl and reminded her to take them.

Breathe in, breathe out. They were just at the beginning of this dark journey. June had seemed unworried, declaring instead that old age was a bitch and it caught up with everyone eventually. Nick smiled. He loved her sense of humour. He'd read a lot since then, books, internet searches and then realized that there were no timelines, no solutions, no definitive facts, other than he would lose her. He held out hope for a miracle treatment but the appointment with the specialist was still months away.

Maybe he should just give in and count sheep or cows or maybe lost golf balls. That might put him to sleep. He willed himself not to look at the clock, but he did; 2:03. Shit, he had to be up for work tomorrow. He had a meeting with prospective clients. It could mean a lot of business, big revenues for the firm. Could he leave June alone? She'd say yes, but could he trust her? They'd had a good talk tonight. June promised to be more careful now. Even so…Shit. He'd call Mark DeLuca in the morning. Maybe he could take the meeting, or maybe they could reschedule.

He stretched his legs, checking for cramps. They felt fine now. He got up, used the bathroom and wandered down the hall to his study. It was a good place to think; built-in bookcases, an antique desk from his father's law firm and the stylish credenza which housed the bar. June had put it all together for him and he loved it.

He poured himself a Scotch and leaned back in his leather chair. What would he do if he retired? The idea had just popped into his head this morning. He'd never been the kind that counted down the years—Freedom 55. Jesus, he'd outlasted those guys by nearly twenty years. He loved his work. Surely he had a few good trials left in him. But June only had a few more years, maybe not that long. Walker, Harris and Leblanc would survive without him. They'd assembled a solid group of lawyers over the years. Mark DeLuca could take over his clients and Martha had built a hell of a family law practice. The firm would be fine going forward. But would he?

He'd be giving up the law—his entire life's work. He'd founded the firm, he and the others. He was a named partner but more importantly he had built an outstanding practice, legendary. It had taken years—days and days of billable hours, long nights, most weekends. But he'd done it. It wasn't easy and it had cost him a lot, vacations, his son, almost his marriage.

The old clock in the dining room struck three. Nick had hated that clock when, many years ago, June had found it in an antique shop in Florence. She'd loved the ornate brass design and he'd loved her so they'd bought it. It had taken months to arrive and then cost a fortune to restore. It had annoyed him on the hour, slightly less on the half hour. But he'd grown used to it, almost depended on it now.

June would certainly benefit if he were at home. Realistically, how long could she manage all day on her own? He could hire someone to stay with her. She'd never agree to that. Maybe Norah? He could pay her on the side, but June would figure that out too. There were programs for dementia patients, but absolutely not—he wasn't sending her to daycare.

What would he do all day at home? Sure, June would be better off but he'd be bored. He could golf some days and they could do things together. June wanted to go back to Italy. They'd been young there, carefree and happy. But now, it was risky. He could surprise her, but it would have to be soon.

Nick drained his glass and poured another shot, a practiced two fingers. June needed more help, mostly supervision at this point. He'd have to be around more. That's what he'd suggested this morning. But June hadn't liked the idea. She'd been defensive, argumentative or too proud to accept help.

Well, she might not like it, but it was the best, the only, solution he could come up with. He was going to retire. Retire! Yes, Nick Walker would be stepping away. The legal community would be abuzz. Despite, or maybe because of the alcohol he knew it was the right decision. He finished his drink and returned the crystal stopper to the decanter. It made a satisfying clink as it settled into place. He'd made his decision. Feeling relieved and pleased with himself, he was finally sleepy.

Tomorrow he'd tell June.

CHAPTER TEN

June tiptoed into the living room hoping to find her cell phone. She hated the thing. She didn't trust it at all, but it seemed important to Nick that she keep it close at hand. Besides, she couldn't go for a walk again unless she found it. Nick always had his in his pocket, but she believed hers was enchanted, maybe haunted. It teased her, ringing loudly enough to surprise her but never long enough to find it. She preferred the house phones. They were dependable, uncomplicated and best of all, permanently anchored to the wall, except they weren't anymore.

Nick had been in a foul mood all week, ever since the rainy day when she'd gone for the long walk. Sure, she'd been tired and made a couple of wrong turns. She'd decided to focus on the positive; she'd made it home and had even had a good cup of coffee and a cinnamon bun. But now Nick was talking about retirement—to look after her! She'd tried to talk him out of it, but he wasn't buying her arguments.

"Hi."

June jumped, startled to find him there. He was sitting so still, hiding in plain sight.

"Looking for something?"

Was he testing her? Watching her? "Uh, no. Just getting my readers." It was a lie, but she was pleased she'd found it so quickly. "Weren't you going to vacuum the car?"

"I changed my mind."

"Okay." June turned to leave.

"Here." Nick held out a pair of candy red reading glasses.

"Thanks."

"Don't forget the cleaners are coming today."

"What? Is it Tuesday?"

"No, Saturday."

"Oh. I thought today was—" Nope, she had no idea.

She heard Nick sigh as she walked out of the living room. Damn, she wished she could stop thinking out loud. June headed to the bedroom to check under the bed for dirty socks and errant underwear. She knew it drove Nick crazy but she hated for the cleaners to see their messy lives. In the kitchen she folded the newspaper, replacing each section in the proper order, wiped some splatters off the stove and removed the nearly empty bag from the trash can.

"June!"

June jumped. "Wh—what! Stop sneaking up on me!"

"Please stop." Nick smiled. "The cleaning ladies will be here soon."

"I know, but—" She remembered now, the cleaners used to come on Tuesdays, but that was when the kids were little.

"We pay them to do these things." Nick took the bag from her and put it back in the can.

"I know." She'd always tidied up for the cleaners. It just made sense. Then they could really clean, but no point explaining this to Nick. It was easier when he went to work. "And I'm not cleaning. I'm looking for my phone."

Nick chuckled and reached into his sweater pocket. "I almost forgot. I found it in the drawer, with the tea towels."

"Oh." Heat brushed her cheeks.

"It's okay. It happens to everyone." Nick rubbed her shoulder. "It's okay, really. Why don't you find something to keep you busy? Work in the garden? Take Mercury for a walk?"

"Oh, am I allowed?"

"For Pete's sake." Nick reached for a coffee mug. "Yes, you're allowed. Just take your phone. Also, don't forget Martha is stopping by this afternoon." The espresso machine hummed to life.

"Is she? Why?"

"I asked her to. I did tell you."

"But the cleaners will be here," she replied logically.

"They'll be gone by noon. Stop fretting. I've got this, June."

"Yes, I know." But she used to have it. She stuffed the phone into the back pocket of her jeans and stepped outside through the kitchen door. Mercury was close at her heels.

"Martha's coming today," she whispered to herself, then added, "I hope she doesn't bring any of those cookies from the vegan bakery." Oatmeal raisin sounded yummy, but they reminded June of lumpy hockey pucks, hard and heavy. Maybe she'd suggest a deal—she'd eat a vegan cookie if Martha tried a bowl of Sugar Crisp.

**

June awoke, dazed and flustered. The morning sun had warmed her, but a stiff neck and a dry mouth confirmed she'd must have dozed off, outside, in a chair.

"June, wake up. It's lunch time." Nick gently jiggled her knee. "Did you have a good sleep? The lounger would have been a lot more comfortable."

"Huh?" Fuzzy confusion. Her bum was vibrating.

"Your phone's ringing."

"What?"

"It's stopped now. Don't worry about it, probably just a sales pitch."

What was he talking about? Her thoughts were jumbled, murky but she forced herself to respond.

"I guess I fell asleep."

"Are you hungry? I made egg salad sandwiches. Come inside and eat. Martha will be here soon."

"Martha?" She paused. "Right! You told me that this morning." Triumph over the tangles in her mind.

Nick helped her up, held her arm until they were inside.

"The house looks nice." June wondered how long she'd been sleeping. "You've been hard at work." Nick liked compliments. "And you made lunch. Thank you," she said, feeling pleased that she'd put this all together.

"You're welcome, but I can't take credit for the housekeeping. The cleaning ladies were here, remember?"

No, I don't remember. "Oh right." Convincing? Probably not. She'd never been good at fooling Nick.

They had a quiet lunch and just as June finished clearing the dishes, Martha arrived, carrying an ominously large bakery box. Martha looked tired. June went in for a hug, but too late, as Martha had turned her attention to Nick—something about work. June decided they all needed coffee, more to help tenderize the cookies than for the caffeine. Martha, a bit of a health nut, asked for green tea. She seemed unusually tense. Was Martha okay? Where was Peter?

Nick suggested they move into the family room. Martha carried the tray of hot drinks and a plate of three cookies. Martha was careful about calories. June nudged Mercury away from the sofa and sat down. The room was quiet except for the snoring dog. Nick spoke first, breaking the swelling silence.

"Martha." He paused. "I've decided—and your mother is on board with this—"

June watched his face, not sure where this was going. She sipped the warm, rich coffee, sifting through the day to recall if he'd told her why Martha was here.

"What's going on, Dad?"

"Nothing too serious. I just wanted to tell you that I have decided to retire."

Martha gasped. "Really? That's great! I'm surprised, but this is good news. You've worked hard and deserve to relax a bit." She stood up and gave her dad an enthusiastic hug. "Wow I can't imagine you not going to the office every day. This is such great news, isn't it Mom? Should we celebrate? Have a toast?"

June stared at them, watching them huddled together, hugging, laughing. This wasn't a celebration! She hated that Nick was retiring. It wasn't a decision! It was a sacrifice, because she was a burden. He wanted her to face the dementia, accept it. Okay! Yes, she was sick, disappearing by the week, the day, the minute. Was this all her fault? Had she eaten the wrong food? Drank too much wine? Used aluminum pans? Only questions, no answers, no cures, no hope. And that made her very angry.

June laughed—purposefully sarcastic. "*A toast?!*"

"Mom?"

June 's face flushed with anger. "Don't uncork that bubbly just yet."

"June, please." Nick's scowl said it all.

"What?"

"Why don't we all take a seat and calm—"

"Just tell her, Nick. Tell her why!" June's words leapt out with a fierceness that astounded her. "Tell Martha the real reason you're quitting. Tell her! It's my fault. I've ruined everything!"

"June!"

June closed her eyes. "Just—just go away. Both of you!"

"Dad?"

"June, look at me."

"No." June covered her face with a pillow.

"Ok, then at least listen."

June nodded, feeling the pillow graze her face.

"Look June, whether you choose to believe me or not—I want to retire. I'm done. I'm old. And yes, I can be here for you and with you. That was always the plan. We always wanted to be together, grow old together. Remember?"

"Of course I remember," June mumbled into the pillow.

"Great. Then you know that I'm here for you—always—just like I promised."

They'd talked about this, yesterday or last week. "Yes, I know." June abandoned the pillow. *"For better or worse,* right?"

"For better or worse."

June reached for her coffee. They were watching her, waiting. She could feel Nick's concern, Martha's confusion. She took a long sip, then another, drawing strength from the sweet creamy brew. "Okay, let's tell Martha the truth."

"The whole truth?"

'Yup. Tell her you're retiring to be my nanny."

Nick exhaled his frustration. "June, don't—"

"Can someone please let me in on what's going on?" Martha picked up a cookie and took bite. It sounded like Mercury chewing on a stick.

"Yes, sorry. That's been my intentions all along." He turned to June. "You're right. It is time for the truth. No more secrets."

"What secrets?" demanded Martha.

Nick leaned back in his chair and closed his eyes. His face was pale and strained. June so wanted him not to tell, not to make it true. "It's okay," she whispered, confirming her decision with a nod.

"What the hell is happening?" Martha dropped her cookie on the plate. *Thunk.* Mercury wiggled his ears and went back to his nap.

Nick swiveled in his chair to face Martha.

"We probably should have told you sooner, right at the start, but—"

"It's my fault. I didn't want to tell you—or anyone." June sat forward, straightened her spine and squared her shoulders. She twisted her fingers in Mercury's fur. "I forget things, lots of things. I don't feel sick, but the doctor says I am. I'm losing my mind. It's happening slowly and I don't like it. I've been trying to ignore it, pretend everything is fine."

"Mom?" The colour had drained from Martha's face. "What are you talking about?"

"Well," said June, "I've been experiencing some co...cog..." She reached for the term the doctor had used.

Nick filled in the blanks. "Cognitive decline?"

June nodded.

"But that's normal at your age, isn't it?" Martha swept her hand to include them both.

"Yes, it is," agreed Nick. "But this is something more. It's actually the onset of—" He swallowed.

"Dementia," said June.

"Dementia?" gasped Martha. "No way. Surely one forgotten lunch date and a misplaced phone don't add up to—" She lowered her voice to a whisper. "Dementia?"

"Sadly, they do," said June.

"Yes," said Nick. "At the beginning, in the early stages, there's no real difference. You know, everybody wonders, *where are my car keys* or *what did I come in here for* or *did I turn off the stove?*"

"Yeah, I get that," said Martha with a wry smile.

"But it's more," said June.

"More, like how, Mom?"

"Sometimes I just don't know where I am, what day it is or I don't recognize normal things." June was trembling, but she took a breath and steeled herself to finish. "Or I forget the way home."

"Oh Mom." Martha's face was pinched and drawn. "But why did you wait so long to tell me?"

"I'd hoped it wasn't true." June grinned to hide her embarrassment.

"Me too," said Nick. "And, I think everyone has a deep and instinctive fear of admitting weakness or disability. It's hard to accept."

"Okay, I get that, but I'm your daughter. You should have trusted me."

"You're right," said June. "I'm sorry."

"And stubborn," said Martha. "I'm sorry, Mom. I can't imagine how hard this is for you and Dad." She looked sad and tired, as if she'd aged in the last few minutes. "You know, I thought something was up the other day when Dad was looking for you." She gasped. "Were you lost in the rain, Mom?"

June smiled. "Only a little, And Mercury was with me."

"But—"

"Nope. No buts." June waved her finger, negating all further objections.

"Dad?"

Nick shrugged. "Yes, they were fine."

Martha sighed, obviously unconvinced.

"Look," said June. "Both of you need to understand some things." June waited to make sure they were listening. "I'm okay. Today and tomorrow, I will be fine. Probably next week too. I can still look after myself and make my own decisions. I want to be me for as long as I can. I want to garden and bake, visit my friends and…" She raised a defiant hand in the air. "I am not going to give up until I absolutely must!" She choked back a sob and collapsed into the sofa. Mercury shifted and nuzzled her leg. June sighed. Her secret was out. She felt lighter, less angry.

Nick sat down next to her and swooped her into his arms. He was a good hugger. He held her close, whispered in her ear. "It's okay. You're good—all good."

She believed him. Trusting this man was second nature. She leaned into him, breathing in his energy.

June felt Nick's tears on her neck. She was crying too.

"Oh, Mom," sobbed Martha.

Tears all around. This was not at all like the Walkers.

"What can I do?" asked Martha, dabbing her cheeks with a paper napkin.

"Plenty," replied Nick, pulling away from June. "I'm only going to work for another three or four weeks. I can hand off most of my files and then consult on an ad hoc basis. Once I'm home every day I'll be able to handle things here, but in the meantime, we'll need a little help."

Martha nodded. "Sure, anything. I can come by more often, arrange for meal delivery or temporary help, even work from here sometimes."

Oh no! Now there are two of them. June dried her tears with the back of her hand. "I'm sure I'll manage just fine." She stood, picked up her coffee cup and headed toward the kitchen. "You don't need to treat me like a child."

She looked back to see Mercury heave himself up, sniff at the remaining oatmeal cookies, and follow her without stealing one.

CHAPTER ELEVEN

"*J*une, are you ok?" Nick's booming voice carried easily from his study. Such a wretched question. It jarred her nerves every time he asked.

She leaned toward the bedroom door and hollered, "I'm fine! Please stop asking me that." Yes, she was fine, just a little stuck, strangely tangled in her underwear.

"Sorry. Do you need anything? I'm going downstairs to start breakfast."

"I'm getting dressed. I'll join you in a few minutes." Good grief. He barely gave her a moment's peace. Retirement. There was no game plan for this. They'd been working on it for over a year now, Nick here at home, all day, every day. He sometimes had calls from the office or watched a ballgame, but more often he followed her around like a lost puppy, offering help, watching her. She was fine getting dressed on her own.

Yet today she was having trouble, wrestling with a bra that refused to co-operate. She had taken it off last night without undoing the hooks and was now trying to slip back into it like a T-shirt. But the straps were twisted and tangled, pinning her arms, the cups weirdly unavailable to support her breasts. She struggled and eventually managed to extricate herself from its lacy grip. She eyed it with mistrust. Yes, it was just a bra. With renewed energy she unfastened it, circled it around her waist, clipped the hooks, slid them around to the back and inserted her arms one at a time. *See, no trouble at all*, she thought, sweating as she pulled a brightly patterned shirt from the hanger and slipped it over her head. She paused, knowing the next step was pants but there were none on the hangers. She wanted her black leggings. *Where are they?* She circled the large walk-in closet, eyes darting from hers to Nick's clothes. She caught sight of herself in the mirror. Skinny bare legs protruding from her saggy granny panties. She shuddered, alarm creeping into her gut. She really needed her pants.

"Nick! Do you know where my leggings are? I can't find them." June ran her fingers along the edges of the hanging clothes, sweaters, Nick's trousers and polo shirts. Someone had stolen all her pants.

"Nice undies."

"Sweet Jesus!" June spun around, unbalanced and found Nick's outstretched hand. "You scared me!"

"Sorry, I came to help."

"I don't need—" June glanced down at her bare legs. "Yes. Nick—" She leaned in, dropped her voice to a whisper. "Someone has stolen my pants."

Nick chuckled. "I see that."

"No. All my pants are gone!"

Nick gently settled her into the chair he'd moved into the closet several weeks ago. It belonged in Martha's room. She didn't want to admit it, but it sure made getting dressed a lot easier. If only she had pants.

"Hmm, let's see if maybe they're in here, somewhere."

"No, I checked. They're all gone. Stolen! Even my leggings!"

"What the hell are leggings?"

"Pants, black, stretchy, comfy."

"These?" Nick held up a pair of jeans, picked from the laundry basket.

"No. Those are black jeans. I need the leggings that go with this shirt."

"Got it." He opened a drawer with a yellow label: *June Bottoms* and pulled out the missing pants.

June hadn't noticed before, but all the drawers had bright yellow or orange stickers.

Nick smiled and flipped the leggings over his shoulder. "Your shirt's inside out. Here, let me help."

She raised her arms as he lifted the shirt, deftly reversing it and slipping it back onto her body. Oh, he was such a smooth operator. She remembered the first time he'd undressed her, impressive moves even back then. She'd been scared, but he was so confident, so gentle as his hands slowly explored her body. She'd never forget how he'd whispered her name as he drew her close, his kisses so soft she barely felt them, seductive, exciting. That was the moment she knew. Nick Walker. She'd love him first but he'd loved her more.

"June? Are you with me here?"

"Yes, of course I am." She was feeling a little smug having retrieved that memory. "Just thinking. About us."

"Nice," said Nick. "Good things, I hope."

"Always." June smiled.

Nick handed her the leggings, label to the back and left her on her own as she slowly wriggled into them. June glanced in the mirror again, this time with some approval. Good work old girl. Looking pretty good. She could see Nick in the bedroom making the bed, fluffing the comforter and arranging the pillows.

"I can do that," said June.

"It's okay. I don't mind."

"I know, but just leave it, please." *Why did he have to try to do everything?* "Just stop. You don't even know where that pillow goes!" It was the silk one with tiny pearls.

"I'm sorry. I was just trying to help."

"I don't need help. What I really need is for you to…to… to butt out. I'm not an invalid, you know." She punctuated her anger with a stomp of her bare foot.

Nick dropped the pillow on the bed and stepped back, his hands raised apologetically.

She'd expected a snarl, an angry rebuff, but he just stood there. "I'm sorry. But that pillow is mine. It goes on my side."

Nick didn't move. He didn't look angry, just sad. She stepped close and hugged him, snuggling into his chest and savouring his touch, his strength and especially the Nick smell. University. That was when she'd first inhaled it.

"Law school was fun, wasn't it?" She could feel his heart, the warm, familiar beats.

"Well, that's going back awhile and as I recall, more work than fun."

"For you. I know but we had some good times, right?" Before he could answer she added, "Could we go to Rosa's for dinner tonight?" June looked up into Nick's soft blue eyes.

"Oh dear, that was a long time ago."

June didn't hear him. Her mind had twisted, she'd drifted away, back to…

She breezed into Rosa's, smiling at the maître d, asking for a table for two. Damn, they looked good tonight, young and oh so sophisticated. She loved this place.

"Let's order that Caesar salad they make at the table and some Mateus—a whole bottle," said June.

"Sure" agreed Nick. "We could, if this was nineteen sixty-one."

"What?"

"Never mind, my love." He reached for her hand and said with a chuckle, "Yes, Caesar salad and wine. Throw in a pizza and we have tonight's dinner."

June didn't get the joke, but she smiled at her beautiful man. Rosa's was so much better than the cafeteria at the law school, in fact, it was perfect. The bow-tied waiters, white linen tablecloths, candlelight and her Nick—so dapper in his three-piece suit.

"Oh Nick," she said. "This is our place."

"It is?"

"Yes! Rosa's Place!" She started to hum.

"Ah," said Nick. "Elvis." He gently swayed her side to side and sang, *"But I can't help falling in love with you."*

The song, the words, the voice—gifts from heaven. Nick and June, lovers dancing. June holds him, tastes his lips, his low sultry whispers fill her heart.

"June?" murmured Nick. "Are you ready for breakfast?"

Slowly, without even trying, she came back to herself, back to now, still feeling Nick's strong embrace. She held onto him, unsettled but still feeling the glow of that date at Rosa's. She knew she was no longer back at Rosa's, lost in her past. That's what they called it, now, *getting lost*. It held the hope of being found. She had so many memories. No, not memories. Realities. Today and yesterday were much more baffling, recent memories wiped out by the same quirk that made long ago so real. It would be lying to say it didn't scare her. But sometimes it just didn't matter. Like now. "I'm so hungry. Can we have waffles?"

"What? Not pizza?" His grin was infectious and then, there it was. One of those strange moments in which she remembered both what had truly happened this morning and just as clearly, going to Rosa's. She could still smell the garlic. She loved that he teased her this way, acknowledging and somehow cheating the disease, stealing time.

"Do we have any strawberries?" June peered into the fridge.

Nick was filling the waffle maker with thick goopy batter. "Only frozen. But there might be blueberries in there somewhere. I think Martha brought some on the weekend."

June snorted, a disapproving chortle for Martha—not the blueberries.

Martha came by more often these days. It was clear she'd taken June's illness to heart and was trying to help. But poor Martha, she didn't seem able to do anything but take her on as a special project. Martha never stopped in for just a visit. She sometimes stayed for dinner but she always came prepared, with advice, brochures, products for the memory impaired and armloads of healthy food. One Saturday she'd gone through their kitchen and declared most of the food unacceptable. Nick had stopped her from purging everything by promising to make sure fruits and veggies were at the top of their grocery list.

She shopped with Nick these days, like when they were newlyweds. At first it felt strange having him there, but now she liked it. She pushed the cart and Nick oversaw the list which always included her favourites, sweet cereal, ice cream and soft gooey cheese. Once in a while Nick added a couple of strip loin steaks and a nice bottle of red wine.

But Martha had done the research on memory loss and aging so her bags from Whole Foods were full of yams, salmon, blueberries, nuts, cabbage, and even collard greens. Sometimes she brought them bags of flax, chia or pumpkin seeds, and small tins of disgusting, slimy sardines. She insisted these were all essential and medicinal. Nick, now their chief cook, incorporated the Martha ingredients into their meals as best he could. Salmon was easy and delicious. Neither of them liked collard greens. The cabbage and the Brussel sprouts produced flatulence and bouts of giggles. The birds appreciated Martha's gourmet seeds. June hid the sardines in the back corner of the pantry. Martha meant well but—June wished she could just get Martha to sit, have a cup of tea and talk.

"I found the blueberries," June announced as she pulled them out of the fridge. "And some zucchini."

"Oh, those might be pretty old." Nick flipped the waffles onto the plates with a flourish, eliciting a smile from June.

"That's ok. I'll use them today. I'll make zucchini bread."

Nick grimaced, pretending to gag.

"Don't worry. I'll give it to Martha. Peter will like it and she doesn't have time to bake."

Nick nodded. "I like that plan."

After breakfast June set about finding her zucchini bread recipe, locating it at last in her old *Kate Aikens* cookbook, still held together by a thick red elastic. She'd always found it relaxing to bake cookies and cupcakes for the kids, but now it was exciting. Not everything turned out, of course, the measurements, ingredients and baking times had to be exact, but like many things these days, the results weren't all that important to June. She mostly loved the smells, cinnamon scones, apple pie and ginger cookies. Nick ate what he could although lately he'd joked about his pants shrinking.

June knew that Martha didn't approve of her baking. Just a few weeks ago she'd tried to convince June that it was dangerous and unhealthy.

**

"It's fun," argued June. "I feed my disasters to the squirrels." She laughed.

"Well, that's just strange," said Martha. "And I'm not sure baked goods should be part of a squirrel's diet."

June sighed. "It's fun, Martha. And your father's here to make sure I don't burn down the house."

"I know, Mom, but what about a puzzle? Or some word games? There's lots of good ones online now."

"A waste of time. I'm not interested."

"Well then, what about some exercise?"

"What?"

"Have you been getting any exercise? It's good for your brain, you know."

"Of course. Your father and I walk Mercury most days."

"I know. But I was thinking about other things. Weights are good for elderly bones."

"Weights? Really? You want me to become a bodybuilder?" June pictured herself as one of those muscle-bound women she'd once seen on TV, bulging muscles, huge breasts and oily skin. "Don't be silly."

"No, Mom." Martha's sigh was so loud even Mercury eyed her

suspiciously. "Small weights just to add some resistance. Here—" Martha reached into her bag and pulled out two pink dumbbells, setting them on the table in front of June. "Just try them, like when you're watching TV. It's good for you."

"They're very small. Thanks," said June, far from grateful. "Does Peter lift weights?" She was hoping to change the subject, get Martha to talk about her husband so she could ask about her marriage.

"He used to," said Martha.

"How *is* Peter these days? We haven't seen him in ages," said June.

"He's fine, Mom. Busy." Martha held up a flat plastic case. "And look, I also brought you a yoga DVD."

Martha was too smart for her. "I don't even know what that is," said June, trying to sound as petulant as she felt.

"Stretching."

"I know what yoga is."

"Dad said he'd set it up for you."

"What?"

"On the TV. You just follow along, like an exercise class."

"Oh." She smiled, nodded, hoping Martha would stop.

Nick put the weights beside her favourite chair and she used them while watching the news, curling them towards her and lifting them high over her head. She liked the budding feeling of power in her arms, and giggled every time Nick called her Arnold, even though she had no idea why. He set up the yoga so it played on the TV in the bedroom. If he was too slow or forgot, June would remind him. "Martha says I have to do this."

June hated that Martha was right, but she loved the yoga. She would bend and stretch along with Veejay, a thin sinewy man dressed only in very short shorts. Veejay was so handsome and lithe and he taught her to breathe slowly while making her believe she was folding herself in impossible ways.

"Veejay," tittered June, realizing too late that she'd said it out loud.

"Pardon?"

"Oh, I just meant—I really should do some yoga today."

"Sure. Just let me know when you're ready and I'll set it up."

"Okay," said June, pleased with her quick thinking and her date with Veejay. She wasn't sure if yoga was helping her memory but Veejay sure made her feel better, stronger and so much happier. Baking made June happy too, so first she was going to make zucchini bread.

Nick finished eating and cleaned up the breakfast mess, a new routine June still found unsettling.

"There you go, all ready for my sweet baker. Do you need any help?"

"No, I'm fine," June replied with only a hint of impatience.

"Just be careful with the oven. I'll take your cakes out when they're done, okay?"

"You're starting to sound like Martha. I'll be careful." She smiled sweetly. *Now just go away and stop spoiling my fun.* Nick set his coffee and iPad on the counter and settled onto a stool. He returned her smile, that sweet boyish grin she found hard to resist, but oh no, this was her baking space and he was sitting there just to keep an eye on her. She'd scare him away soon enough.

June began by setting out the ingredients and equipment, bowls, measuring cups, flour, sugar, thumping each one down on the granite counter. She needed the food processor to shred the zucchini, but she couldn't quite remember where it was stored. She opened and closed each door and drawer with untamed enthusiasm, finally locating it in one of the large pot drawers. She knew in an instant it wasn't worth the effort, too heavy and lots of finicky parts. She slammed the drawer. She could feel Nick's irritation. Good.

"Need help?"

"Uh-uh."

"Okay then. I'll be in the family room.," he said. "Just holler if you need me." His disgruntled look wasn't as satisfying as she'd hoped, but she was happy to be alone.

June set the oven to 350 and read through the recipe. She used to know this one by heart. She hummed as she measured the dry ingredients and opted for the box grater to prepare the zucchini. She shredded them, squeezed out the liquid and measured, surprised that she had slightly less than two cups, not the required three. Not to be deterred, June searched the fridge. Carrots would work but the colour might be weird, not beets for sure, maybe apples. Then she spied the perfect replacement and added several handfuls of fresh green spinach along with the zucchini to the bowl of her KitchenAid mixer.

Next, she measured the spices into the flour then poured it all into the powerful mixer, remembering too late to lower the speed. She giggled as a cloud of flour dust puffed from the mixer. She pushed the lever forward, faster now, the shifting cloud filled the air, billowing into the light. June stuck her finger in the batter for a quick taste. It was greener than usual and needed something. More sugar? No, chocolate chips would do the trick. She dumped a bag of peanut butter chips into the bowl before realizing her mistake. Oh well, they were all natural so they'd be fine. She scraped the dough into the pans, slid them into the oven. She was pleased with her efforts, two yummy zucchini breads.

"How'd it go?" asked Nick when she joined him.

"Great!"

"Smells good."

"It's the cinnamon and cloves."

"Did you set the timer?"

"Oh no. I forgot. I'll do it now." The warm spicy smell welcomed her back to the kitchen, but the mess—oh my god. What happened in here? She felt Nick behind her as she pondered the white floury footprints on the floor. "Did—did I do this?"

"Oh, don't worry," said Nick. "I'm on cleanup duty. How about a nice cup of tea?"

June sat at the table with the local newspaper spread out in front of her. She'd only been allowed back in the kitchen after Nick had declared it shipshape. Was that before lunch or after? They'd had grilled cheese for lunch and tomato soup. Yes, that was right, but she'd lost the rest of the day. The whole afternoon was gone. Her stomach growled. It was past their regular suppertime, but Nick said they had to wait for Martha because she was bringing dinner. June hoped it was takeout, maybe a pizza or Swiss Chalet? She loved the sauce.

June adjusted her readers and tried to focus on an article about this year's Fall Fair. She wanted to go on opening day to see all the flowers while they were fresh. She'd once won first prize for her roses. The words were playing tricks on her today, bobbing and blurry. It happened sometimes. She gave up and pushed the paper aside.

The back door swung open without warning. June almost jumped out of her chair. She'd been worried about burglars lately and home invasions. So, Nick had decided they couldn't watch any more crimes shows. She missed *Law and Order*.

"Hi, Mom."

"Oh, thank goodness it's you."

"Who were you expecting?"

"Oh—" Someone, she was sure of that.

"I'm here and I come with food."

"Right," said June. "Of course. I knew that."

Martha set two paper shopping bags on the counter.

June couldn't smell chicken. No pizza box.

"Oranges were on sale so I bought you a dozen. And some kale chips."

June wrinkled her nose and wondered if her Blue Jays liked kale chips. "Have you had your hair done?"

Martha chuckled softly. "I have—cut and colored. Thanks for noticing."

"Well, you do look better. No, I mean, you look good—younger."

"Oh. Thanks, I think. What's this?"

June had wrapped the zucchini loaves in plastic and covered them with a single sheet of paper. She'd written *Martha* in big bold letters that barely fit on the page.

"Zucchini bread. Freshly baked this morning."

"Why the sign?"

"You told me to label things."

Martha nodded. "Right." She picked up a loaf and turned it over several times.

"It looks—different. What's in it?"

"Zucchini, of course. But I didn't have quite enough so I added some spinach, and peanut butter chips, I meant to add chocolate but—"

"Oh dear."

"I made it for Peter."

"Oh. He'll like that. But, Mom, I really don't think you should be baking. It's too complicated for you now. And dangerous. It's just not safe. Besides, all that sugar isn't good for you and Dad."

June laughed. "We're fine."

"I know, but I worry." She reached into the largest of the bags. "I also stopped in at the new vegan deli near the office and picked up this eggplant lasagna. It's fresh so it just needs a couple of minutes in the microwave."

"No meat?"

"Well, plant-based meat. You really can't tell the difference."

"If you say so." June took the casserole from Martha and put it in the fridge. It looked healthy and sad. A generous layer of old cheddar might help. And maybe some sour cream?

"It's for tonight," said Martha, taking the aluminum pan out of the fridge. She unwrapped it and cut it into quarters, scooped one generous serving onto a dinner plate and popped it in the microwave.

So, we are going to have to eat this?

"Should I make a salad too?"

"No, I think we'll have more than enough vegetables." Maybe Martha wouldn't notice if she served the cheese and sour cream on the side?

"Fair enough. Um—Mom. I brought some brochures for you and Dad. They're from retirement homes."

June grunted.

"Now don't get mad." Martha set them on the counter. "Just look at them. No pressure. Some of the places are really nice."

"Not interested."

"I know." Martha sighed. "Where's Dad?"

"In the other room." June glanced at the white-haired grinning couple on the top brochure. She turned on the water, full blast, ending all conversation. Martha rolled her eyes and left.

June turned off the tap, squeezed out the soapy sponge and began wiping some crumbs off the counter. The sponge picked up speed as it approached the glossy pamphlets, colliding and sending them skittering across the floor. Nicely done. She could hear Martha calling to Nick. He must have fallen asleep.

"Mom! Mom! Something's wrong with Dad! Call an ambulance! Call 911!"

Ambulance! No! No! Oh God. June reached for the phone. It wasn't on the wall. Shit, shit, shit! Where is it? Her eyes darted frantically around the kitchen at last spotting the handset on the table. Relieved, frantic and terrified, June grabbed it. And paused. She held the phone, uncertain, perplexed. She had no idea how to use it.

CHAPTER TWELVE

June knelt beside Nick. He was slumped in the chair, pale and motionless. His glasses were on the floor. June picked them up, careful not to smudge the lenses. "Nick. Nick, wake up."

His eyes opened slowly. "I'm sorry," he whispered. "Not feeling so good."

She could barely hear him. She touched his cheek "What…what's wrong?"

His mouth twitched, but no words, just a hint of his smile.

"What's wrong with him? Martha! What's wrong!?"

Martha was on the on the phone. "We need an ambulance! Ten Acorn Terrace! Hurray! He can't breathe. Nick Walker. Seventy-five."

"Seventy-four," said June. But Martha ignored her.

"His daughter, Martha Walker. Okay." Martha placed two fingers on Nick's neck. "Yes, I can feel it. It seems slow."

He looked so frail, broken. June was afraid to touch him. *Tell them to hurry!*

"Yes," said Martha. "A CPR course for work. Okay. It's on speaker now." She set her phone on the table next to Nick.

The operator said, "The ambulance is on the way. Three to four minutes out. Just stay calm, Martha. Unlock the door. Outside lights on."

"Okay!" Martha ran out of the room.

June gently placed blanket over Nick's knees. "It won't be long, Nick. They're coming to help you." June leaned closer to Nick and rested her forehead on his arm. He was sleeping now, just sleeping, right? June closed her eyes. Helping him rest. But suddenly lights and sirens, voices—strangers in the house—uniforms, heavy boots, big men.

"Let's move back a little, Mom." Martha pulled her away.

The man cut through Nick's shirt. "No! Stop!"

Martha held her, too tight. June struggled to be free.

- 69 -

"They're here to help Dad."

June felt dizzy, confused and angry. She twisted her arm out of Martha's grip and spun to face her. "What did you do to him? He was just fine before—before you got here."

"Mom! I didn't do...do...anything to Dad. How could you ever think—"

They were wheeling Nick across the room, out the door. June wanted to follow them but was too scared. She reached for Martha's hand. "Is he dead?"

"Oh no. You know Dad. He's too stubborn for that."

She smiled but June wasn't sure.

Martha pulled her into a hug. "It's going to be okay, Mom."

She pushed back. "It's not okay! They took him away."

"To the hospital. Dad's had some sort of attack."

"Attack! Someone hurt him?"

"Oh, no! Nothing like that. He just can't catch his breath or maybe his blood pressure is off. I'm not sure, but that's why he's going to the hospital. We can meet him there."

"Is Jonny home yet? I want him to come too."

Martha sighed. "Jonathan's not here, Mom. But I'll call him later."

Jonny was late from football again. No, he'd given that up.

"Mom! Are you okay?"

June starred at her daughter. She'd lost her name. Jonathan and—? "No. No. I'm not okay."

"I know. This is really hard. But if we get moving, you can see Dad at the hospital very soon." She held up June's mucking-about sweater. "Come on. Put this on. It's a bit chilly outside."

"No." June shook her head. "Really, Martha! I can't go anywhere in that old thing." She opened the closet and took out her tweed jacket, centered herself in the mirror and expertly tied her scarf. "Let's go," she said. "Jonathan lives in Vancouver. He won't be meeting us there."

June ignored the nurse who was pumping up the cuff on Nick's arm and scooted the stiff plastic chair closer to the bed. She threaded her fingers through the safety rail and clutched his hand. It was warm. He winked and smiled. He didn't look sick. There were lots of wires, beeping machines, oxygen in his nose: but he looked just fine. She wiped her tears on her sleeve.

"Don't cry." Nick sounded scratchy.

"I thought you were dead."

"Mom! I told you—" Martha stood near the open door, the only space left in the small room.

Nick chuckled. The wires bounced on his bare chest. "Oh, I hope not."

He squeezed her hand, more like a little squish but she felt it.

"This nice nurse here says I'm doing just fine."

She didn't look like a nurse. She was wearing purple sneakers and ridiculous pajamas, a riotous print of flowers and toothy beavers. Whatever happened to proper nursing uniforms—clean and starched, crisp and white?

"Yes, Mr. Walker. Your vitals are looking good," said the nurse. "Dr. Revello will be in shortly. He's the cardiologist on call tonight."

"Thanks," said Martha.

June could tell Martha wanted to ask more questions but the nurse hurried away. They waited and waited. Nick fell asleep. June made sure his chest went up and down with each breath. Martha left for coffee and a bottle of water for June. She returned quickly, empty-handed but accompanied by a nice-looking doctor, properly dressed in a white coat.

"Hi folks. I'm Dr. Revello. I guess you've had a bit of a scare tonight. So sorry about that."

He looked at June and smiled—dimples, soft blue eyes and a sexy five-o-clock shadow. He placed his stethoscope on Nick's chest, listened and then hooked it around his muscular neck. He talked quickly, too quickly for June. He was talking about Nick's heart. Something about angina. It was best to just watch him, not listen at all. He had such a nice smile. He wouldn't smile if Nick was really sick, right? Martha kept asking him questions, lots of questions. Good work. Keep him talking. She wondered if Nick would agree to grow a bit of stubble, not too much but a little was very enticing. Surgery? What? The doctor was still smiling but now he was talking about an operation.

"Nick needs an operation?"

"It's minor," Nick said. "Not really an operation at all. It's more of a procedure."

"I don't like it." June pouted.

"I know but it needs to be done. My heart isn't working properly. Things are a bit clogged up and this will fix it. It's called an angioplasty and Dr Revello is an expert. Right Doc?"

Martha jumped in. "I knew it. It's your diet. Too much red meat, right?"

"And genetics," said the doctor." He turned to June. "Your husband is correct, Mrs. Walker. I've done a lot of these opera... um, procedures and I haven't lost a patient yet." He grinned.

"Will he live?" She noticed the doctor's shoes—fancy joggers.

"Yes, I'll make sure he does."

"Okay," said June. But she wasn't sure. It didn't add up. The doctor—Nick, hurting, damaged. Her memories, emotions—unsettled, shifting from fear to trouble and worry. Thoughts—clearer now—finally making sense. "I'm not so worried about the cuts on his face and arms, I know they'll heal but you said his lung collapsed. That's serious, isn't it?"

"Mrs. Walker?"

Martha touched her arm. "Sorry," she said to the doctor. "My mother gets confused sometimes."

"June," whispered Nick.

"What?" It was a simple enough question.

"Stay with us, June," said Nick. "Today we're here about my heart. Not the car accident."

**

The beating heart monitor pulsed in time with the windshield wipers.

June was driving. It was dark, snowing and she was exhausted. They should have waited until morning but both sets of parents were expecting them, a casual Christmas Eve with her mom and dad and a traditional dinner with Nick's parents tomorrow.

The signal light, blinking, flashing orange, and then the oversized tires as the black pickup swerved into her lane. She pulled the wheel to the right, hoping to connect with the shoulder but the impact sent them airborne, missing the gravel and the ditch, landing them in a snowy field. June was saved from all but a broken nose and the accompanying black eyes. Nick, slouched in his seat, had been punched in the ribs about the same time the side door came crashing into his right shoulder, smashing his arm.

**

June touched her face. Her nose no longer hurt. Nick was worse off. Still in the hospital. But he looked so old. She was confused, worried. Wading through fog. Exhausting, scary, like trying to navigate a maze blindfolded. "When can we go home?"

"Sweetheart. The accident was a long, long time ago. I know this place is making you remember. But we're fine now."

Nick held up his arm. The cast was gone. She looked at him, trying, struggling to untangle the pieces, the injuries; nose, arm, cast, lung—a broken heart.

"Are you having an operation?"

"Yes, but it's not serious. Honestly June, I'll be out of here in no time."

"I don't like it here."

"Me either. You go with Martha tonight and I'll be home soon."

June nodded. This made sense. And Nick looked much better now.

"Let's get going then," said Martha. "We'll have a sleepover."

"A sleepover? Really Martha. I'm not a child. But I am hungry. Did we have dinner?"

"Not yet," said Martha. "We'll find something at home."

"No eggplant."

"No eggplant," agreed Martha.

"Let's call it a night, then," suggested Nick.

June rose quickly and blew him a kiss. And then, without hesitation, she blew one to Dr. Blue Eyes too.

CHAPTER THIRTEEN

June was cold, shivering, awake and not at all sleepy. She sat on the side of the bed and wriggled her freezing toes as they came back to life. Martha called them icicle toes. Were the twins cold too? No, they'd be snuggly warm in their flannelette pajamas. She reached for her robe, always on the end of the bed. It was gone. She'd get her blanket, the woolen one in the family room. She didn't want to wake Nick so she would manage without the light.

Star light, star bright.

She made her way into the hallway and down the stairs, slowly running her hand along the wall to steady herself. She shivered in her thin nightgown. The house was darker than she'd expected. Her fingers searched for the light switch.

Night stars, Bright stars. Fairy lights. So pretty. Sparkly.

She lowered her foot carefully for the next step but found the cold floor. She'd forgotten her slippers. Everything was in the wrong place, but light from the moon helped her find the family room. It was cold in here too. Maybe the furnace was broken. Where was Nick? Was he still sleeping? She closed her eyes, squeezed them tight, to help her think. Oh yes! Her blanket.

June had found her special blanket in a small wool shop in Edinburg. The tiny Scottish lady had made it herself, in fact she'd been working at her loom when they wandered in. The blanket was the colour of fresh sage and had a wonderful, tasseled fringe. She'd loved it immediately, but Nick had said it was too bulky to carry home and much too expensive. She'd been upset, sad to leave it in the shop. But then, it found her on Christmas Day.

"Why did Santa bring you a blanket?" Jonathan had asked. "Don't cry Mommy. You can play with my new truck."

"Oh, don't worry, sweetie. This is the very best present ever," she'd reassured Jonathan as she hugged Nick. The perfect day.

And now, the blanket was not on her chair and her chair was…where? June shuffled her feet, moving in a circle, once, twice. Had someone stolen it? Was she dreaming again? Her dreams had seemed so real lately. Nick always helped her figure them out. She'd dreamt Nick was in the hospital. She'd tell him in the morning. He'd have a good laugh. She swiveled again, slowly so her head didn't spin.

"Nick! I need my blanket," she shouted as loud as she could. No answer. Where was he? "Nick!" Was he hiding? Jonny loved to play hide and seek. "Come out, come out wherever you are."

Maybe he was in the closet. She crept across the room on tippy toes, took a deep breath and yanked open the door. "Gotcha." Nothing but coats. Coats! Warm coats! She ran her fingers over them and chose a long suede one with a thick fur collar. Perfect! An orange fleece hat with earflaps begged to be included. She pulled it on and fastened it under her chin. A plaid scarf and red fuzzy mittens completed her ensemble. She buried her face in the fur and struck a pose in the hall mirror. *You look marvelous darling.* She strutted back into the family room, her best runway walk, waved and blew kisses to her fans.

Martha burst into the room. "Mom? Where are you? Did you call me?"

"Goodness Martha, quiet down. Must you always holler?"

Martha turned on the light. "Mom! What on earth are you wearing?"

"I'm cold and I can't find my blanket. Did you take it? Have you seen your father? I've lost him too." Maybe Nick had her blanket.

"Sorry, it's not here. I didn't think to bring it with us. I'll get you a different one, or I can turn up the heat. Would that help?" Martha looked at her and laughed. "You look like an explorer ready to tackle the Antarctic."

"Don't make fun of me." She flopped onto the sofa. "I'm...I'm..." She wanted to say glamorous but Martha might laugh again. "I'm cold. It's freezing in here."

"I'm sorry. You're right. It is cold. Come on now, I'll help you get back to bed and I'll get you an extra blanket."

"My green one? It's lost, possibly stolen." She looked around and suddenly realized why everything was off. "Martha, is this your house?"

"It is."

"No, it isn't. Peter's not here."

Martha chuckled. "Oh, he's here. In bed. Snoring like an old warthog."

"Really, Martha," scolded June.

"Well, it's true. But still, I'm surprised all your squawking didn't wake him up."

"I don't squawk," said June with all the indignation she could muster. "So exactly what I am doing in here, in *your* house?"

"Staying safe," chuckled Martha. "But apparently not. Mom, you're here with us while Dad's in the hospital. Remember?"

June scowled.

"Dad's had some trouble with his heart. We saw him earlier today, remember?"

"Stop asking if I remember," June snapped. "Of course I remember. He's at...at the...doctor place. The one downtown, on the street with the boulevard and the cherry blossom trees, right?"

Martha chuckled. "In the spring, yes, beautiful cherry blossoms. Memorial Hospital."

"Yes. Of course. Why is he still there?"

"Mom," said Martha. "He's going to be fine, but he has to stay a few days longer than we first thought. That's why you're here. Now, let's get you out of these things." She pulled the red fuzzy mittens from June's hands and tugged at the hat that was still tied under her chin.

"Don't! Stop it!"

"Mom, you're squawking again." Martha smiled and winked. "Come on. Let's get you back to bed."

"No. The doctor said Nick would be home by Thursday. Tomorrow is Thursday. I know it is. And then a follow up appointment in a week, no two weeks."

"How in the world did you remember that? You really amaze me sometimes."

June smiled. It was nice to be amazing. She rose slowly, regally, slipped out of Martha's coat and laid it on the couch, then added her hat and scarf. "Can I see him tomorrow?"

"Dad? Yes, of course. We can go first thing in the morning."

June nodded. "I miss him."

"Me too, Mom."

"It's very late, Martha. You should be in bed."

"So should you."

Martha held out her arm. "Ready M'Lady?"

They climbed the stairs side by side.

"Do you think Dr. Blue Eyes will be there?"

Martha laughed. "More than likely, Mom."

CHAPTER FOURTEEN

*M*artha finished her wine, gulping the last swallow. The dishwasher was in the middle of the rinse cycle. She sighed and washed her glass by hand. The soapy water felt warm and comforting. The last few days had been hard. Back and forth to the hospital, a plethora of scans and tests and not a lot of answers. Then today, the news that her dad needed bypass surgery, a much more serious diagnosis than they'd initially thought. The operation was scheduled for tomorrow afternoon.

Using the railing to help her tired body up the stairs, Martha started compiling a to-do list. Just in time she remembered the squeaky stair, second from the top, and stepped over it. Mom's door was ajar, just a little, as she'd requested. Martha had meant to buy another nightlight for the hallway but she'd forgotten. She moved quietly into the guest room. Mom was sleeping—so calm and peaceful. It was easy to imagine her as sound and healthy. If only she had a magic wand. The only nightlight they owned glowed in the bathroom. Hopefully that would help if Mom woke up in the middle of the night again.

The first night had been the worst. Martha had heard her just after midnight and rushed in to find her crying, frightened and confused. She wanted Dad: *Nick, Nick, Nick*. Mom didn't know her—her own daughter. They'd both been scared. When Mom finally agreed, Martha hugged her tight, laid with her in bed and told her stories, childhood memories, until Mom understood enough to relax and fall asleep. The next night she'd wandered downstairs, apparently looking for a blanket. Instead, she'd found Martha's winter coat, a hat and mitts, and seemed to think she was dressed to see the queen. What if she'd fallen down the stairs? Peter had suggested a gate or a lock on her door, but they both seemed so wrong.

"Good night, Mom," she whispered. "Please sleep tight." It was a hope and a bit of a prayer.

Martha yawned, tired, maybe too exhausted to sleep, but she'd give it a try. She still hadn't decided what to do with Mom tomorrow. She'd freak out if she knew Dad was having this surgery. What if he didn't make it? No, don't go there. They could visit him in the morning, then wait it out here. She might be okay with that. But Jonathan. Mom wanted

Jonathan. Mom always wanted Jonathan. Martha wanted Jonathan too—so she could give him shit, maybe strangle him. She'd left him so many messages, texts, even called his business. Apparently, he'd left the company. Thanks for letting us know.

Peter was sprawled across the bed, snoring. This might be the only good thing that had happened this week. She and Peter were sleeping together again. Only in the literal sense and it had taken a heart attack and a house guest to get them back together, but Martha would take it. She barely had enough energy to brush her teeth and contemplated skipping her nightly face ritual but no—the war on wrinkles was an important one.

She climbed into bed, hoping her fatigue would lead quickly to sleep, but then tuned into her *sleep sounds* app just to make sure. Seconds, minutes, maybe hours later Martha awoke, confused, jarred by a noise that filled the room. An alarm? The phone? Instinctively, she lunged across the bed for the phone on Peter's nightstand, the landline that he'd insisted they still needed. She grabbed the receiver before she realized she was splayed across Peter's bare chest.

"Hello?" She was greeted by the dial tone.

"It's your cell phone," Peter mumbled, barely conscious, groaning under the weight of her body. Oh, right! She ransacked the sheets. Her heart pounded. Had Dad taken a turn? Praying the caller wouldn't hang up, she finally found the phone under her pillow. "Hello?" A quick glance at the time confirmed that this was not an hour to expect good news.

"Hey. Took you long enough to pick up."

"Jonathan! It's about time." She pulled herself upright. "I thought maybe you were dead, devoured by a grizzly bear or something." Jonathon had somehow converted his love of the outdoors into a fulltime career of skiing and mountaineering. He'd started a wilderness excursion business with some friends and it had done quite well.

"No. No bears. Would you miss me?"

"Probably not." Martha used to like to banter with her brother but tonight she was angry.

"Is it Jon?" Peter whispered. "Try to be nice."

Martha chose to ignore him. She'd heard his *you attract more bees with honey* speech too many times.

"Where the hell have you been? I've been trying to reach you for days!"

"Oh, Boo-Boo Bear, settle down. You're going to blow a gasket."

She put the phone on speaker so Peter could see what she was dealing with. "Seriously! What are you, ten?" She'd always hated the nickname. Her parents had thought it was cute, not understanding that Jon used it to mock her whenever she followed the rules or threatened to tell on him when he didn't. He liked to think of himself as Yogi, loveable, mischievous but no stranger to trouble. "You woke us up, you know. It's the middle of the night here."

"Yeah, sorry, I don't pay much attention to the clock. But I got your messages. What's up?"

"What's up? Are you kidding me?"

Peter shook his head, put his hand on her shoulder. It was both infuriating and comforting. She didn't need him to keep her calm but liked that he was trying.

"Did you listen to any of my messages? Maybe read the texts?"

"Yup, Dad's having ticker troubles. I got that. Sorry, I've been busy. Working, living, that sort of thing."

"Don't be a shit, Jon. Dad's sick. It's more serious—"

"Come on. We all know that he's indestructible."

"What the hell, Jonathan," Peter barked. "That's not even a little funny."

Martha started in surprise. She shifted closer to Peter.

"Do you have any idea what we've been going through, what Martha is doing for your parents? Grow up man!"

So much for the staying calm approach. Martha hadn't seen this much passion from Peter in years. She liked it.

"Whoa! Stand down. Hello Peter. I didn't know you were there." Jonathan exhaled. "I was just kidding."

Martha resisted the impulse to fill the dead air.

Jonathan gave in first. "Okay, so lay it on me. What's going on?"

Martha could hear it in his voice, the smile, the boyish grin that almost always got him out of trouble. He was a charmer. But tonight she wasn't buying it.

"So, you want to know what's going on? Dad had a heart attack. He's having by-pass surgery tomorrow. Oh yeah. And I can't tell Mom. She's having trouble grasping things and she'll flip out if she knows."

"Shhhhit! But your message said it was angina and it wasn't that serious."

"Oh, so you were paying attention." Martha couldn't resist the gibe, spurred on by Peter's nod of approval. "It's a lot worse than they thought. Dad almost died!" She knew it was a little dramatic but so what? "The doctors did a lot of testing and figured out his arteries are blocked. And he needs a new valve. It's a real operation now. Open. Heart. Surgery."

"That doesn't sound good."

"It isn't. It's major. But really, I don't think I asked enough questions. I was distracted by Mom and missed my chance. She keeps flirting with his doctors."

"Oh God. That's awful. So, Mom's getting worse?"

"Yeah, it's pretty bad. Not always. But she's definitely in her own little world sometimes."

"And she's staying with us," said Peter.

Jonathan chuckled. "I'll bet that's fun."

"Delightful. Nothing quite like living with your mother-in-law." But Peter quickly added. "It's fine really. She gets confused, thinks I'm Nick or the gardener. Or you. She talks a lot about you."

"Really?"

"Oh yeah," Martha said. "She thinks you're here, but in high school, playing football, or rehearsing, out with friends. She's convinced you'll be home any minute."

"So, there's no point in me coming, is there?"

"Smart-ass. Strangely, she never thinks you're in class or at the library studying."

"Oh Martha, will you ever change?"

"Not likely. So, are you coming home? I sure could use your help. Mom would love to see you, in person." Guilt was such a handy little tool.

"Oh, I don't know if I can. I'm pretty busy these days."

"As am I."

"I mean, it's complicated."

"It always is. It's just that, well, I'm not sure how I'm going to work all of this out." She reached for a tissue and noticed Peter had buried his head in the duvet and was trying to go back to sleep. Seriously! He had the attention span of a gnat.

"Martha?" Jon's voice had lowered, softened. "Um, I think I can come home. I mean, I do have some spare time. But truthfully things are pretty shitty here."

"What? Sorry, I can hardly hear you." She took the phone off speaker and held it to her ear.

"I want to come home, really, but—"

"Jonathan! I'm a little short on patience these days."

"Hey, you sound just like Mom, like, same voice and everything!"

Martha waited.

"Look, I'm broke. There's no way I can come up with the money for a plane ticket. Jesus, this is humiliating."

"Oh. What about your business? I called there."

"Of course you did. Well, it's a really long story that ends in me being unemployed and basically penniless."

"Oh geez, I'm sorry. I thought you'd straightened all that out."

"You knew?"

Martha sighed. "About the drinking? Yeah, Jon. Of course I knew."

"And what else?"

"What do you mean?" Martha waited. "Jon. What else is there?"

"Jesus. Mom never told you?"

Martha could hear him breathing

"Look, I really screwed up but I'm on my way to making it right. I'll tell you, sometime. I promise. Just please don't make me get into it now."

"Jon, you're scaring me. Are you all right?"

"I am. Most days. And I'm working on it."

"Come home. Mom really needs you. I'll send you the money. Okay?"

"That's not at all embarrassing."

"Jon, we're family. No judgement, I promise."

Jonathan laughed out loud making her realize that it was the first time she'd heard his laugh in such a long time.

"Right," Jonathan chuckled, "No judgement, in this family?"

"Come on, we're not all that bad, are we?"

"No comment." He paused and then added. "Thank you."

"I'm doing it for me more than you. I miss you. Don't worry, I'll put you to work when you get here." Martha glanced over at Peter. He'd always been so good with her family, maybe better than her.

"It's a deal. I just hope I can handle it. You know, Mom's problems and all of Dad's shit."

"Come on. You're a middle-aged man. Don't you think it's time to stop being pissed off with your father?"

"Yeah, probably but it's not as easy as all that."

"I know. But…" Martha was exhausted. "Just get here and we'll work it out."

"Sounds like a plan, Boo-Boo."

She grimaced, ready to censure him again, but she let it go.

"Just come—as soon as you can. Check out the flights and let me know what the tickets cost. I'll send you an email transfer. Okay?"

"Well—"

She heard him swallow, exhale and felt his bravado dissolving into the phone.

"To be honest, I think you should buy the ticket and let me know the details. My sponsor would say that I'm not ready to handle that kind of money."

"Oh Jon."

She agreed, asking no more questions. They said the good-byes quickly, leaving Martha to wonder and worry about how to fill in the blanks.

CHAPTER FIFTEEN

June cleared her throat as she entered the kitchen. "Good morning, Martha." She said it more loudly now, as apparently Martha hadn't heard her the first time. She was hungry. She'd missed breakfast and was hoping for muffins or, even better, croissants. Martha disapproved of croissants, but Peter liked them as much as she did, with butter and lots of jam. Peach jam was the best.

"Oh Mom. Yes, good morning—again. Are you okay?" Martha was smiling but she didn't look happy.

"Of course I'm okay. I had a very good sleep for a change."

"Oh. Then I guess you don't remember—" She stopped and took a deep breath. "So, what's up?"

"I'm hungry."

"But you just finished breakfast, like twenty minutes ago."

"No."

"Yes. Scrambled eggs and toast. I haven't even washed the pan yet. See?" She held up one of those fancy non-stick skillets. It looked quite clean to June.

"I need a croissant. Peter bought them and he said I could share." June moved slowly toward the table and sat in her usual chair.

"Do you think you can wait just a little while? Maybe have some water or a cup of tea? I can add some honey to sweeten it up."

June shook her head. "No. I'm hungry." She shook her head again. "Very hungry."

Martha removed a croissant from the paper bag from the bakery and sliced it in half lengthwise. She worked slowly, gathering a plate, the butter and jam. Her shoulders and back were stiff, a sure sign that she was annoyed. But June wasn't going to change her mind.

"Should I warm it up?" Martha spoke without turning around.

"Yes. Please."

Within minutes June was eating the soft, buttery treat. Too bad

Martha couldn't soften up a bit. June had told Nick that Martha was grumpy sometimes. But he always took her side. He'd said that Martha was helping them, doing her best. The peach jam tasted so good. Nice and sweet. Nick had told her to try and remember to be nice. "More jam."

"Pardon?"

June pointed to a naked spot on her croissant, missing butter and jam.

"No Mom. There's plenty already."

June tapped her plate and stared at Martha until she gave in and scooped a scant spoonful from the mason jar, handed it to her and without a word turned back to the dishes in the sink. June spread a little on her croissant and then popped the spoon into her mouth. She licked off all the yumminess and was careful not to smack her lips. Martha was happier at the office, so why wasn't she at work? She and Nick had talked about this too. June tried to work it out in between bites. Maybe it was—

"Peter slept on the sofa." *Oops. She wasn't going to ask about that.*

"Mom?"

"I saw the blanket and pillow."

Martha's cheeks turned pink. "He…we…it's…He snores—a lot."

June laughed. "Yes, I've heard him." The croissant or maybe the extra jam, was clearing a path through her mind, as if each sweet flaky bite was adding layers to her thoughts. "Are you getting a divorce?"

"Mom!" Martha pulled out a chair and collapsed into it. "Why would you say that?"

June took Martha's hand. It was damp, warm and a little soapy. Martha's eyes had filled with tears.

"Martha?"

"Oh Mom, I don't know what's going on. Peter and I, well we just don't see eye to eye on anything. We have nothing in common anymore—nothing at all."

That didn't sound so serious. A tear rolled down Martha's chin and landed on the table. June watched as a second tear dropped, then a third. June was astonished. This wasn't like Martha and she knew Peter and Martha loved each other. What was going on?

"It's me," said June. "You're not at work because of me."

Martha looked up. "What?"

Suddenly June could see all the reasons for Martha's pain. "First me, then your dad, you're having trouble at work and now Peter."

Martha nodded. "Everything in my life has changed." She crossed her arms on the table and buried her face.

June rubbed her back while she cried, adding a few shushes and then hummed a familiar lullaby.

Martha lifted her head and smiled. "I'm not very good with change, Mom. I don't know how to pivot."

"What does that mean?"

Martha chuckled. "You know, accept change, go with the flow kind of thing."

"Hmm. I think you've pivoted very nicely." June ate the last bite of her croissant. "You've...let's see...you've changed a lot. You cook now, like whole meals and the other night you ate an ice cream sandwich. I saw you. Honestly Martha, that's quite a pivot!"

Martha laughed. "Oh Mom."

"But, have you quit your job? I can't believe they'd fire you. You must tell your father about this."

"No, no. It's fine, Mom. I've just taken some time off. It's temporary, so I can look after you and Dad. The people at the office have been kind and generous. No worries there."

"Well, that's good. You know, your father put a lot of time and effort into that law firm and—"

"Mom. It's Peter. Me and Peter. I think my marriage is in big trouble, maybe over."

"No." June licked her finger and used it to gather the tiny flakes from her plate. "I like Peter."

"Me too, some days. But now, most of the time, he's an ass."

"No he's not! I really like him. Now. I didn't quite get what you saw in him at first but he's grown on me. And lately he's been a real sweetheart. Martha, he even likes *Wheel of Fortune*!"

"Oh Mom, you just don't see the other things."

"Like the snoring?"

"I can live with the snoring." Martha ran a finger around the edge of her cup. "It's the other things. He's obsessed with sports on TV. He never wants to go out for a nice meal or take a vacation or even go for a walk with me, let alone a run. He's, he's…I was going to say boring but I think he is just not interested in me anymore."

"Marriage is hard."

"Yeah, tell me about it."

"Is Peter cheating?"

"Mom!"

"What? It's just that, when your father and I hit rough spots—"

"Are you saying that Dad cheated?"

June held up her plate and smiled. "Another croissant. Please?"

Martha shook her head. "You'll have to wait for lunch. But how about a cup of tea?"

June set the plate on the table. It landed unevenly and rocked for a few seconds before coming to a full stop. "A latte."

"Really? You never drink coffee anymore."

"I'm pivoting"

Martha didn't move.

"With lots of milk *and* sugar."

"Okay then." Martha turned on the coffee maker. "But I am going to need more information about these rough spots. Like how you got through them and…and…did Dad have…an affair?"

"Oh dear! That's between us, your father and me. But no, at least I don't think so. Just bumps in the road, you know, we argued a lot, made each other hopping mad. The point is—" What was the point? What did she want to tell Martha? Surely not the whole truth, not now, not yet or not ever. "The point is, is that we worked through our problems, learned to forget, get past—" She recalled it all. Forgiveness had saved them. "Look Martha, people change. You and Peter have been together a long time."

"We have," agreed Martha. "I think that's part of the problem. We might be bored with each other." Martha set a large cup of coffee in front of her and sat down.

"You should have had children." June felt Martha stiffen, stare over her head as if June wasn't even there.

"Mom," she said after a few moments. "Please don't—don't go there. You...you...know that sad story."

"I do?"

"You do."

"Well, it is awfully hard to be a lawyer and a parent. We all make choices, right?"

"I can't have children."

June grinned. "Not with Peter sleeping on the couch."

"Mom, I want babies. Wanted them. I—"

"I want more croissant." But what was wrong? Martha was crying. And she just been crying? Martha was a tough cookie—she never cried.

"Oh Martha, Mommy's here." Had Jonathan been teasing her again? He was such a little devil. "Where's Jonathan?" she said aloud. "Jonathon! Come here. Now!" Martha would be alright if he said sorry.

"Mom! Jonathan is not here!" Martha jumped up. Her chair screeched along the floor before tipping over. "I talked to Jonathan last night. He's flying home soon."

"Don't be silly Martha. Jonathan can't fly."

Martha picked up the chair and roughly slid it back to the table.

"Careful, dear. You'll scratch the floor."

Martha held her breath, her cheeks puffed with air. She exhaled impolitely and started counting, out loud. "Eight, nine, ten..." She stopped at thirty. "Drink up, Mom. We need to be at the hospital in an hour or so to meet with Dad and his doctor."

"The hospital? Why?"

Martha turned away. "And just like that she's gone."

"Who's gone?" asked June, but she really didn't care. The cup in front of her was filled with foamy milk. She stirred it slowly and watched as the tiny bubbles deflated into the rich, dark liquid. The acrid smell of coffee assaulted her. "I don't like this. I want tea."

CHAPTER SIXTEEN

Martha could feel her mother's impatience. She was straining forward against the seatbelt as if trying to outrun the car.

"Mom. Please sit back. You'll go straight through the windshield if I have to brake suddenly."

Mom scowled and pushed forward even harder. "I want to go home."

"Really, Mom, it hasn't been that long."

But it had been. Two months—eight long weeks. After today, no more yoga pants and runners. Martha would be back in her tailored suits and heels. She couldn't wait. Couldn't wait to be back in the office, in charge and in control.

Today, finally, after a couple of setbacks and a slow recovery, her father was leaving the hospital. It was homecoming day for both of her parents. Martha prayed it went well, that all the stars would align and she could get Mom home and settled without too much drama. The day had started out well and they were out of the house before noon. A bit of a minor miracle since some days just getting Mom dressed was a challenge.

Dementia was such a mystery and after reading a mountain of books Martha was still pretty much in the dark. She tried to be patient and kind but just keeping her mother safe was exhausting. She could have used some help. Peter tried, but Jonathan had bailed completely. The plane ticket she'd bought him hadn't been used—cancelled the night before the flight. She'd sent him dozens of texts. They were read but not answered. She'd tried calling him but it went to voicemail and just yesterday when she'd planned to give him a giant piece of her mind—voicemail or not— she heard, *the number you have dialed is no longer in service.* What kind of person does that? What kind of brother does that! She was tired of his excuses and way too exhausted to care.

Martha looked over at her mom, still sitting bolt upright.

"Eyes on the road, Martha."

"Yes ma'am." Martha smiled. "Don't worry, Mom, the house hasn't gone anywhere."

"I am not worried. I want to see the magnolia tree. It will be covered in flowers."

"Oh yes. They were so pretty. But they'll be done by now."

"No! I see those flowers every year."

"I'm sorry, Mom. I really am. I wish you could remember, back in the spring the tree was beautiful."

"It always is—the best in my garden club. I won a ribbon once."

"Yes, for your roses. You've always had a green thumb."

"So why did I miss the magnolias?"

Her mother's eyes were wide, her expression earnest.

"You didn't. The tree was magnificent this year, but it only lasts a week or so. You loved it."

"I don't think so." Her mother collapsed back into the seat. She tilted her chin upwards, closed her eyes and exhaled a dramatic sigh.

Martha stifled a laugh and stole a quick glance at her mother. When had she gotten so small? Her head barely reached the head rest. She definitely needed to eat more. She loved ice cream. Maybe she'd drink milk shakes with lots of chocolate ice cream, enough to disguise one of those protein drinks Mom refused to try.

"What's wrong with Nick?" Mom demanded, her eyes now aimed at Martha.

"Oh geez! Mom… um…don't worry. He's fine."

"Will he be home soon? He works too much. I told him we should travel, see the world!"

"Mom?" Martha tightened her grip on the steering wheel. These moments, the switches and flips—it was hard to keep up.

"Don't you just love Italy? The wine? The food? The men?"

Martha smiled. "I do. In fact, Italy is one of my favourite places."

"Mine too."

Her mom's head bobbed enthusiastically, accentuating her need for a haircut. Maybe she could find someone to come to the house? Martha reminded herself to add it to her list. She turned into her parents' driveway and was relieved to see that the flowerbed, thanks to the gardeners, was in full bloom.

"Okay, Mom, we're home. Your flowerbeds look great."

Her mom sat still, silent. Martha nudged her shoulder.

"Mom?"

"That tree…"

Martha followed her mother's gaze. "The magnolia? Yes, it's lovely isn't it, even without the flowers.

"No, it's big." Her mother's face twisted with doubt. "That's not my tree."

"It is your tree, your magnolia. Look at the flowerbeds, Mom. They're beautiful."

"Is this…my house?" Her mom was breathing heavily. Her head moved slowly, back and forth, from tree to house to tree. "It looks…everything is different."

"No, it's not. Maybe it looks different because you've been away." She lightly touched her mother's hand. "Come on. Let's go inside and you'll see."

Martha helped her mother out of the car and guided her along the walkway. Mom stopped at the steps.

"What's wrong?"

Mom shook her head. Martha could feel her tremble and shrink back. "Mom? It's okay. There are only four little steps and then you'll be in the house. Go on. I'll be right here, behind you."

Martha nudged her forward. "Hold the railing and lift one foot then the other onto the step. Come on."

Her mother slowly climbed.

"Good work, now the next step." Good lord. How were her parents going to manage here? Her mom hadn't had trouble with the stairs at her house, but now, she seemed unwilling, unsteady. When she reached the top step her mom straightened up and stepped confidently onto the front porch.

Martha exhaled. "Well, that was fun, wasn't it? Are you okay?" She asked this question a hundred times a day.

Her mother was smiling, grinning. The morning sun bounced off the large brass mailbox and illuminated her face. "Of course I am. I'm just checking for mail. It's important to keep up with your correspondence, Martha. Did I tell you we have a new mailman? I should bake him some cookies. Can we have lunch soon? I'm really hungry."

Martha unlocked the front door as her mum opened the mailbox and pulled out several flyers and a few envelopes.

"Probably nothing but bills," June declared as she stepped through the front door, dropping the mail on the hall table without looking at it.

"Mercury! Here, boy. Mama's home." June waited then called again. "Where's Mercury?"

Martha grimaced. "Oh, don't worry. He's fine." She reminded herself to breathe and just try to go along with her mom's logic-defying mind. "He's not here right now." Mom knew that Norah had been caring for Mercury, in fact, they'd come for a few visits at her house. She tried to summon her patience; one, two, three... She used to count her daily steps, now she just counted.

"Is he outside?" Mom started toward the door.

"Wait. Mom. Can you just sit and relax for a few minutes? In here, where I can see you. Please?" She needed to unpack the car, bring in the groceries.

Her mom paused as if considering her request. "No. I want to see the garden. Maybe the lilacs are blooming."

"In a few minutes, okay? I need you to stay inside, where you're safe."

Mom laughed. "Safe? Martha, I'm just going out to the backyard. Let me know if you need any help with lunch."

"Mom, it's November, the lilacs are—" She stopped. Mom looked happy. "Sounds good. Stay away from the pool."

Martha worked quickly, bringing in the food she'd bought yesterday, the oversized suitcase and her mom's blanket. She'd almost forgotten it, had only remembered when they were already driving away and she'd had to go around the block to return home to pick it up. Her mom had even teased her about how absentminded she was getting. That'd sent shivers down Martha's spine. All her reading had almost convinced her that dementia wasn't hereditary, but, it couldn't be completely ruled out.

Martha folded the blanket and laid it on the sofa. Mom's attachment to this ragged piece of wool drove her crazy. It smelled old, even after she washed it. Mom wanted to take it everywhere. Against Martha's wishes, Peter let her bring it to the hospital when they went to visit Dad.

"It keeps her calm," Peter had reasoned. "Like a security blanket. And where's the harm, Martha?"

He was right, of course. She hated when that happened. It was strange how she and Peter had found a bit of peace with her mother in the house, at first, anyway. But they'd soon learned to be pleasant in front of Mom and save the fights for the bedroom. Their king-sized bed had become the sparring zone until they were both exhausted enough to sleep. Sometimes they actually talked and listened, working their way through the pains and frustrations of their years together. The darkness allowed them to be honest and it hid the hurt.

**

One night they each admitted they weren't happy. That's when divorce came up. Martha had cried at the suggestion, but Peter said maybe it just made sense. He was stoic, infuriatingly logical.

"Look, Martha, the way I see it…" Peter had hoisted himself up on his elbow. She'd felt uncomfortable with him lurking above her and had pulled the duvet up around her shoulders. "Jesus," he'd said. "Are you afraid of me now?"

"No, of course not. I'm chilly."

Peter snorted. "Okay then, the thing is, we can keep doing this forever or we can go our separate ways. Those are the only choices."

"So, working on our marriage isn't one of the choices?"

He grinned, that smug, superior toothy smile that Martha hated.

"It is an option or would be if you had any time for me—for us."

"That's so unfair coming from you. All you have to do is go to work, watch sports on TV, drink beer and work in the occasional game of golf."

"What? I help out Martha! I spend hours with your mother."

"Don't yell at me."

"I'm not—" He exhaled loudly and dropped back onto his side of the bed, his head sinking deep into the pillow.

Martha stared at the ceiling. "I'm sorry…" But it wasn't an apology. "I'm sorry that we've come to this."

"Me too." Peter rolled over, facing away from her. "I feel like I don't belong here anymore. We just have nothing left."

"I know." Martha's eyes stung, but there were no tears. Peter was right. They had nothing in common. She hated the platitudes, but for once he was right. They'd agreed to sleep on it, think it over for a few days. She had imagined herself alone, not lonely but independent and free. She could picture herself working late without feeling guilty, spending time on a beach with a book and a piña colada, Peter's least favourite kind of holiday. She'd watch rom-coms and documentaries, take her laptop to bed and be able to enjoy March without the madness of basketball. Maybe she could finally commit to a vegetarian lifestyle, or in this world of new possibilities, she could become a vegan! She'd meet a new man or date lots of them who'd wine and dine her and they'd have new and exciting— not-Peter—sex!

They would have the perfect divorce. She'd prepare the documents and they could meet over coffee, share a couple of laughs and sign without tension or drama. She'd presented the idea to Peter while he cleaned up after dinner. Mom was resting, watching *Wheel of Fortune*, so they had a few minutes.

"I've been thinking about what you said the other night." She doodled on the legal pad she'd taken from her briefcase.

"I say a lot of things. Could you be more specific?"

"You know, about us separating, moving on, being free."

"Oh, I don't think I said that, but okay."

"You said we had nothing left and I am agreeing with you."

"Oh."

"Does that surprise you?"

"It does. It's not like you to give up so easily."

"I'm…not giving up. I'm facing reality. There's a difference."

He nodded and opened the dishwasher.

"Peter."

He loaded the dishes carefully, precisely arranging them in the racks. Martha resisted throwing her pen at him.

"Peter! Do you think we should separate?"

He finally looked at her. His face was tense, his eyes sad. "I do." It echoed for only a moment, then stillness chilled the room.

"Well," said Martha, finally breaking the silence. "I guess that's it then." She forced herself to smile at Peter. "Lucky for us, divorce is my specialty."

"Yes, lucky for us." Peter swung a tea towel over his shoulder and leaned against the counter. He studied her as a slow sardonic grin crept across his face. "You're awfully agreeable this evening. What's with that?"

"I'm just hoping to keep this friendly, easy—non-confrontational. I've yet to see two people agreeing and separating amicably, but I have to believe it's possible."

"But then they wouldn't need your services."

"True."

Peter's brow wrinkled; a sure sign he was thinking things over. "Okay, then you write it up, fair and square and I'll sign. But…just tell me this, have you already found my replacement?"

"What?"

"Are you sleeping with someone else?"

"Of course not!" Martha laughed. "As if I'd have time for that."

"I've always wondered about some of your friends at work, especially a couple of the guy friends—" He added air quotes which Martha hated. "They always seem happy to be *working late with you*." He laughed but Martha knew he wasn't joking.

"Don't be such an ass, Peter."

"I'm just saying."

So much for a perfect divorce. Well, fuck it. If Peter wanted war, she could do that too. She sighed. They hadn't talked since that night. Probably a good thing.

When he'd offered to pick up her father and bring him home today, they'd spoken through her mother, with Peter asking June if she'd like him to bring Nick home and June agreeing, after a nod of approval from Martha.

**

Martha stood at the kitchen window and watched as Mom walked through her garden. Was she talking to the rose bushes? How would Martha tell her about the divorce? She wouldn't understand. Mom loved Peter. They'd become so close over the last few months. And Mom was good at marriage. How had she done it all these years? Despite their differences her parents were still in love. She wished she could pour a couple of glasses of wine, sit on the patio with her mother and tell her that Peter had found a new place to live, closer to his work and that their marriage was over. She craved sympathy, support and a really big hug. How paradoxical life was—now that she really needed her mother, she was gone. Not dead, not yet, but still unable to talk to Martha when she needed her most. Not her mother's fault, but the irony wasn't lost on Martha. She regretted all the times her mother had wanted to be involved in her life and she'd just blown her off. No wonder Jonathan was her favourite. Flighty, utterly irresponsible, needy, chatty Jonathan. Karma really was a bitch.

Lunch was all but ready when Mom wandered in from the back yard. She seemed relaxed, happy to be home.

"The garden looks good, doesn't it?" Martha pointed to the table. "I hope you're still hungry."

"Yes, I am. Things are looking pretty good outside. Not many blooms this time of year. I think we need to hire someone to do the weeding again. Your father will be pleased that the pool is covered." Mom sat down in her usual chair and inspected the food. "This looks yummy. I like soup and sandwiches. Simple but good."

Martha nodded. "Eat up. You need the calories. I'll make a pot of tea too."

"Thank you, Martha. Thank you so much—for everything."

"No problem, Mom."

Martha watched as her mother filled her spoon with chicken broth, waited as her hand steadied and navigated to her mouth. It was a slow, painstaking journey.

"I thought your father would be here by now. I guess it takes a while to get discharged. It was so nice of Peter to pick him up."

Martha nodded, awed by her mother's sudden clarity and soup skills.

"He'll be tired when he gets home, don't you think?"

"What? Oh yes. I think so." Martha swallowed a bite of her sandwich and wiped a few crumbs from her lap. "Mom? You seem...is this a good time to talk? There are a few new things…some changes."

"Of course. What's up?"

"So, you know Dad had an operation, right?"

"Yes. I know that."

"Well, I've hired a nurse to look after Dad and help around the house."

Martha waited for her mother's objections. She knew the idea of a stranger in the house would upset her. And although her father needed rest more than a nurse, this was the best way to convince her mom that the nurse was non-negotiable.

"A nurse? Is that really necessary?"

"Yes. Absolutely necessary." Martha had found a lovely woman, a nurse who was willing to cook and take on some of the housekeeping.

"Are you going back to the office then?"

"Yes, it's time."

Her mother smiled. "You miss it, don't you?"

"I do. I have a meeting tomorrow. That's why we need someone here. Gloria, her name is Gloria. She's from the Philippines. She's been here for several years and she'll be more of a helper. She'll make sure Dad has everything he needs, monitor his pills and do things around the house. Meals, laundry. That sort of thing."

"Okay, that makes a lot of sense. You know Martha, sometimes I need a little help too."

There was no missing the twinkle in her mom's eye. What a rascal.

Her mom patted her hand and added, "I'm so sorry. I know this is hard on you. I never wanted to be a burden."

"Oh Mom." Martha rose to pour the boiling water into the teapot, but instead bent low to hug her mom, holding her tight, trying to keep this moment from shifting away. Willing her to stay.

Mom pulled out of the hug. "So, where *is* Mercury?"

"Oh," muttered Martha as she wiped away tears. "He's with Norah. I talked to her this morning. He's having a great time terrifying the squirrels at her place."

"Good, I hope he hasn't been digging." Mom set her spoon on the table. "Martha?"

"Yes?"

"Will you take him when I'm gone? He's such a good dog."

More tears, a waterfall of wonder and sadness. "Of course, Mom. Don't worry. He's part of the family."

"And Jonathan?"

Martha chuckled. "Well, I'm not sure I want to take in that stray!"

"No, I wouldn't expect so, but could you, maybe, find a way to forgive him, maybe help him? He's not strong—not like you. He's different, but you need each other, or you will, at some point." Mom clutched Martha's wrist, squeezing hard. "Don't forget—"

Martha heard the front door open. "Oh! They're here."

Her mother's face erupted with pleasure. "Nick!" She clapped her hands, giddy with childlike excitement. "Oh goody! Maybe he brought ice cream. I hope it's cookies and cream!"

CHAPTER SEVENTEEN

June had heard the question. She even knew the answer. Monday. Today was Monday. Monday. But she wasn't about to tell her, this stranger. She played this game with Nick; if yesterday was Sunday, then today is…" If she needed help, they'd say the rhyme. Monday's child is fair of face. Tuesday's child is full of grace. She could tell by Nick's smile which day was right.

June pressed her lips together and wiggled her feet further under Mercury's soft fluffy belly. His ears twitched away a bug or maybe he was dreaming. He seemed unconcerned about the strange woman who sat across the table. June wasn't so sure. She allowed herself a quick glimpse, pretending to look past her, over her head, at the hollyhocks climbing up the side of the pool shed. Not too scary; short spiky grey hair, lots of wrinkles, a big smile. Everyone always smiled at her now. Their cheeriness was annoying. She, this woman, seemed ordinary, acceptable but unknown. Nick put neon sticky notes on everything these days, drawers, shoes, even the toilet had a sticky that said *Flush*. This woman needed a label.

The woman picked up a pitcher, hand painted with hummingbirds and flowery vines. "Would you like some water?" She didn't wait for an answer. The ice cubes plopped into the glasses. Tiny drops of water sprayed onto the patio table.

That was her pitcher. She used it for flowers, not water. Tulips, not ice cubes. June sighed, exhaled a noisy sputter. Wrong, wrong, wrong.

"Are you okay?" asked the woman.

No, I am not okay. June squirmed, her legs restless, unsettled. Mercury groaned. Her sweater felt heavy and rough. She pulled at the collar, yanked at the sleeves. She just wanted it off. "Argh!" She had the words, *itchy, scratchy, irritating*, but they were stuck, caught somewhere between her brain and her lips.

"June, stop. You're stretching it." The stranger pulled the sweater back onto June's shoulders, then straightened the sleeves. "It looks so pretty on you. Lavender is your colour."

June could yell and scream and still not get rid of the sweater or this woman. She had no choices anymore. This stranger telling her what to do. She'd had enough. "Leave me alone!" *Be nice, June.* Nick's words, not hers. *Be Nice.* What did that mean now? Give in? Give up? She knew what she wanted, what she needed, and right now she needed to get rid of this damn sweater. June clawed at the wool, making the itch worse instead of better.

The woman sat down across from June, her smile less happy now. "Don't scratch, June. You'll hurt yourself."

June turned away and leaned back in the chair. She closed her eyes and wished the woman away. A quick peek confirmed her wish had failed. *Okay then, I'll just pretend you're not here.* June leaned back in her chair and looked up, up, up into the trees, her trees. The canopy of lush green leaves danced in the wind. She searched the branches for squirrels, blue jays, her fairies. They mostly came to her at night, but sometimes— magical fairies, bright like tiny perfect diamonds. She could feel the soft breeze of their silky wings, see the spontaneous spectacle. She clapped with joy. "Bravo! Bravo!"

"June?"

"No!" Gone, frightened away by this—

"Oh, I'm sorry." The woman lowered her voice to a whisper, then pulled her chair closer to June. The metal scraped the patio stones. June covered her ears.

"Sorry. Sorry. I don't mean to frighten you. Are you okay?" The woman leaned forward, catching the sun in her hair. It was pink! Not all pink but sprinkled with bits of cotton candy. But that couldn't be right. Her hair would be sticky, but it would explain the spikes. Maybe her comb was stuck in there. June giggled.

"June?" She touched her hair, adjusting the peaks as if reading June's thoughts.

"Yes, yes. I'm fine." Fine. Fine. Fine. Fine, even if she wasn't.

"Good. Good."

They sat, quiet, still until the woman, who was not wearing a sweater, spoke again.

"I wanted to tell you that Mercury made a new friend this morning. A Labradoodle named Gordon. They've been sniffing around each other for the last few weeks but today they played together. We were at the off-leash park, you know, the one over by the school, and Mercury was like a puppy again."

She was talking but June only heard nonsense, no words, gobbledygook. Mercury was here, snoring at her feet. Her tongue felt dry, her lips too. The water looked good. She leaned forward, reached slowly. Her hand trembled then bumped. The glass tipped, bounced and rattled across the patio. The cold icy water felt good on her restless legs.

"Oops," said the woman. She used a towel, red with white stripes, to soak up the water. "Here. Let's move you over here, to a dry chair, okay?" She reached across June's back and helped her stand. She smelled like gardenias, Chanel gardenias.

"Norah."

"Yes!" She nodded and shifted June into a dry chair, Nick's chair, the one that rocked. "Yes June. I'm here. Are you okay? Would you like some dry clothes?"

June shook her head. "No."

"Okay, it'll dry fast. But here, let's make sure you don't get cold." Norah placed a dry towel over June's legs, picked up the glass and refilled it. "Good thing we're using plastic these days, isn't it?" She smiled and sat next to June.

"Norah." June placed her hand on Norah's and saw tears in her eyes. "Don't cry. It was just water."

"Oh June." Norah squeezed her hand but June pulled away, twisting her fingers, hiding them in her lap. Mercury stood, yawned, then stretched and moved closer to June before collapsing into a sleepy heap. "Where's Lady?"

Norah chuckled. "You remember Lady Godiva? My goodness. Sometimes you amaze me. Well, unfortunately, Lady isn't with us anymore. She's in doggy heaven. I miss her but I think Mercury misses her more. He looks for her every time he's at my house. It's been, wow, almost a year now. She had cancer and I just couldn't let her suffer. I named her after the chocolates, you know, not the naked woman."

June watched her lips, tried to listen. Lady was old—dead. Mercury was old. He would die too. Sometimes she wanted to die—

"Well, hello, ladies."

June looked up to see Nick walking towards them. She smiled, lifted her arms to greet him. He bent and hugged her, then kissed her forehead. His lips felt soft and warm. Nick.

"So how are we all doing?" Nick sat down, avoiding the chair with the damp towel.

"Good, good," replied Norah.

June nodded.

"How was your walk, Norah? I hope Mercury behaved." Mercury lifted his head and Nick rewarded him with rubs and pats.

"Oh, he was great. I was just telling June that he has a new friend."

June could hear the vacuum in the house and the hum of a jet. She looked up and saw soft trails across the blue sky. The airplane was just a speck now, far far away.

Nick touched her shoulder, moved his face close. He spoke slowly to her.

"Well, my dear, do you have anything to tell us today? Any stories or tall tales?" He winked. June giggled. "No. No."

"Oh, come on. Surely you can find something to tell me."

"I spilled my water."

"I noticed that. But that's okay. I spilled my coffee yesterday."

"Oh dear," said Norah. "Not your excellent coffee!"

"In the kitchen," said June. "Nick tripped over Mercury. He smells like coffee."

"The dog," said Nick, "Not me. Yes, it was quite a mess."

June giggled. "A big mess."

Nick turned to June and held her hand. "I'm going to go to the store and pick up some groceries. Are you okay here with Norah?"

'No." She shifted in her chair, watched as a bird pecked at the feeder. Bits of seed scattered through the air.

"June, I won't be long. I promise." She ignored him. "How about some nice juicy peaches or strawberries?"

"The local ones are ready now," said Norah. "They're so yummy."

"Fine."

"Gloria is here if you need anything, like a snack or the bathroom."

Norah nodded. "Thanks."

Nick kissed June again, first on one cheek, then the other. "You're my special girl."

June grabbed the sleeve of his jacket.

"I won't be long my love, really. Just a quick trip." He patted her hand and released her grip. "Bye, love you."

He jingled his keys and walked away, blurred by her tears. She stood up, ready to follow, but the woman blocked her way.

"No, we'll wait here. He'll be back soon." She coaxed June back into her chair. "Would you like me to read to you? We could do a puzzle. Or take a little walk around the yard."

The gate slammed shut.

"What do you think, June?"

What? No, she was busy. She was waiting for Nick. All day, all night, tomorrow too. Waiting.

CHAPTER EIGHTEEN

Nick set his plate on the table—eggs and two slices of rye toast. He'd tried the sprouted bread Martha had bought at the farmer's market but it tasted like cardboard. He placed a small bowl of yogurt with fresh raspberries in front of June. She pushed the bowl away. It skidded across the table and stopped when it met the butter dish.

"Don't do that. You'll make a mess."

June bit into her bagel, and without pausing to chew, added another mouthful.

"Slow down, June. Swallow. And take smaller bites, please. You're going to choke."

She spoke through the food. "I want Cocoa Puffs."

"Yes dear, I know but we don't have any. Have some yogurt. It's good for you." He started to move the bowl toward her but she turned up her nose. God, she'd changed so much in the last few months. She hadn't lost any weight, she ate enough for both, but somehow, she was smaller, weak, and droopy, as if her bones and muscles had forgotten how to support her. Only her obstinance had only grown stronger.

June stuck her finger into the cream cheese container, licked it and smiled. "Strawberry."

Nick chuckled. "Yes. But maybe use a spoon next time." Her smile was still so beautiful, ingenuous, almost youthful. He moved his hand across the table and covered hers, feeling the warmth of her fingers, the slight quiver radiate into his. "I love you."

She took another, slightly smaller, bite of bagel, chewing and swallowing any chance of the words Nick longed to hear.

They ate together, in silence except for the clinking sounds of dishes and cutlery as Gloria unloaded the dishwasher. Nick pushed back his chair and carried his plate to the counter.

"Well, I'm heading up to my office. Either of you ladies need anything? Coffee?"

"No thank you," said Gloria. June stared out the window.

"What?" Nick laughed, exaggerating his dismay. "You're turning down the best coffee in town?" He tapped his espresso machine. "Don't worry. I still appreciate you." He placed a cup under the spout and set the dial to extra strong. He'd ordered these beans online, skeptical at first, but his choice had been a good one. Kona coffee lived up to the hype. He waited as the machine whirled into action, first grinding and then through a series of grunts and steamy hisses, squeezed out his much-needed cup of ambition, the first of the day.

On his way out of the kitchen, Nick stopped in front of June, momentarily blocking her view to the outside. "I'm heading up to my office, sweetheart." June remained still. "I'll check on you in a little while." He kissed her cheek, but still no response. Just as well. He had no desire to fill her in on today's task.

Nick had known for a while that they couldn't stay in the house. The front door ramp had helped some and he'd considered a chair lift for the inside stairs, but mobility wasn't June's biggest problem. She was wandering now and Gloria spent most of her day keeping June close.

The ice cream incident had scared both. They hadn't noticed when June left the house one afternoon. She'd been napping in her chair while Gloria worked on dinner. Nick was in the garage when Gloria sounded the alarm. June was missing.

Nick had hurried out to the street and quickly spotted her, heading towards him, all smiles, triumphantly eating a large vanilla soft-serve. Nick had paid little attention to the melodic tune as the truck passed the house, but June had heard it, remembered the appeal of a simple ice cream cone. He was upset, with himself, with Gloria but not with June. The joy on her face was so familiar, so missed. She looked like June again—a strong, carefree, unbroken June. He'd waved down the driver as he drove away and tried to pay for the cone. "It's on me," he'd said. As Nick led her home, holding hands like lovers, June offered him a lick and she'd laughed when he'd lopped off the curly top with his tongue. They were happy. June was safe but for how long?

Nighttime wandering was worse. Sometimes he barely slept. He'd locked the bedroom door to keep June in but one night she panicked when she couldn't open it and it had taken him hours to console her, to get her back to bed. So, he'd tied some jingle bells on a string and hung them against the closed door. He'd installed a baby gate at the top of the stairs and left the hall light on all night. But none of this could change June's moods—the outbursts, hysterics and stubbornness. She'd refuse a bath or reject the shower, suddenly afraid of the water, the shampoo or even the towel.

Nick was tired. The last few nights had been rough. They probably needed a night nurse, maybe daytime help for Gloria too. He'd tried to ignore it, but what they really needed was a safer place to live.

As he climbed the stairs Nick pictured Jonathan, a skinny reckless boy, careening down the polished railing, jumping off just in time to avoid smashing the family jewels into the newel post. He thought of Jonathan more often lately and almost always as a young boy, a happy boy, June's boy. Nick knew he'd made some mistakes, but had he pushed the boy away? He didn't think so, but now he was gone. Nick didn't even know how to reach him—his own son. He should be here. Nick tapped the railing. Home, here with his family.

Nick loved this house. He felt grounded here. Like some corny country song, this house was their foundation, their shelter and safety. Even through their troubles he and June had never considered leaving this house, leaving each other. It was filled with memories and a hell of a lot of stuff. Moving wouldn't be easy.

He'd spent so many years here, almost his whole adult life. They'd bought it for a song, well, it had been bit of a stretch back then. But now they were sure to make a shit load of money on the sale. First, he needed to find them somewhere to go.

Did he know anyone who'd moved recently? Friends or colleagues who'd downsized? One of his golf buddies had moved up north to his cottage but he couldn't think of anyone who'd moved to a retirement home. How hard could this be? He did a quick online search and watched a couple of videos, which didn't help at all.

He decided to call Dr. Stemmler's office. After all this doctor had been the first one to suggest that June shouldn't be living in the house anymore. He dialed, set the phone to speaker and started jotting down the things they'd need, care and activities for June, and a garden. She'd benefit from a spa, massages. He'd like to have a golf course nearby, nine holes would be alright, a pool and privacy. Independence for sure and lots of space; two bedrooms, and he'd like a study. And a gym.

The doctor's office wasn't any help, other than giving him an email address and a number for the Region's senior services. He decided a call would be more efficient. He was making short work of this.

His call was added to the queue with a current wait time of approximately twenty-four minutes. He picked up yesterday's crossword, still pondering a nine-letter word for *whirlybird*. Helicopter had ten. He'd counted twice. When someone finally answered he asked for some guidance about senior housing. The line seemed to go dead.

"Hello, are you there?"

The woman's voice was gruff and impatient. "Yes. Yes. That information is available online. "Our website is—"

"Wait! No, I want to talk to someone about this. Could you please answer some questions for me?"

The woman, who hadn't identified herself, said, "Yes sir, but calm down. This call is being recorded."

"Look, sorry, could you just answer some of my questions? I'd really like to know if you have someone who can help me find the appropriate home for my wife and myself. Is there a specialist? Maybe someone I can hire? Like a real estate agent?"

"You're kidding, right? You're looking for a personal assistant?" She cackled. "No, sir, we are fresh out of those."

Her condescension angered him. "Excuse me?"

She sighed. "Look, are you both, like healthy?"

"Healthy?"

"Yes, like able to take care of yourselves."

"Why would I be asking for help—" Nick was up for the fight but bit his tongue. "Well, I'm fine but my wife has dementia. So, we need a place that will accommodate her decline and be a good place to live too. Is there something like that?"

"Well, have you considered the aging-at-home option? This seems to work for many seniors these days. There are a lot of in-home service providers—"

Was she even listening? "No. I'm asking about residential accommodations because we are currently aging at home and it's not working anymore." Nick doodled on his list, a figure that seemed to be morphing into a witch, with horns.

"Well, sir, homes are very specific and different ones appeal to different folks." She paused. "Since I don't know you or your wife, how about I email you our list.? You can check them out and find a suitable one. Do you think you can do that?"

Nick bristled at her tone, now patronizing, sickly sweet. He recited his email address, the sound of the clicking keys was the only sign she was still on the line.

"Thank you for calling us today. It was a pleasure serving you. Is there anything else we can help you with?" She sped through the script.

He shot back, not even bothering to hide the sarcasm. "On no, you have been ever so helpful. I hope you have a—" The line went dead.

What had he expected? Well, more than this. He should report her, but what good would that do? He didn't even have her name. Shit, he'd finally decided they needed to do this, make this unthinkable move, and now, well he sure hadn't gotten very far. Maybe he'd dragged his feet too long, trying to believe they were doing okay. He'd probably procrastinated less for June than for himself. He liked it here.

Nick tore the page from his yellow legal pad and wrote *MOVING* in large block letters at the top of the next one. Number one: find homes to prospect. His computer dinged with the expected email, no message, just a seven page attachment. Jesus, it seemed to be every place on the planet. They weren't arranged in any logical order, not even alphabetically. The name of the residence was followed by a terse description; retirement home, independent living, long term, continual care, assisted living, nursing home. Who knew? They just needed a place to live.

His coffee cup was empty but he wouldn't let himself go get another. If he still had a secretary, um, an assistant, he could assign this task to her. But he didn't, so he'd figure it out on his own. He didn't even consider calling Martha. She had enough on her plate these days. He hated that she was alone now. He'd thought Martha and Peter were happy enough. What the hell had happened? June had suspected something, but he hadn't. He hadn't picked up on the problem—just like Jonathan.

Nick forced his mind back to the ominous list, choosing almost at random. He could do this. He'd sorted out far more complicated documents at the office. After the first few calls, he was able to dodge the plethora of questions and protect the personal details he was reluctant to disclose. No, he'd explain, he wanted a basic tour, something quick and informative. A few had the gall to ask for financial information. Jesus! He'd schooled them on current privacy laws. Finally, inanely proud of himself, he'd locked down a few appointments. He picked up his pen and wrote *eggbeater* in empty squares of his puzzle.

**

June seldom wanted to leave the house these days, reluctant to go to any kind of appointment, especially the medical kind, so Nick decided to keep the details of today's trip to himself. They were going to a retirement home, the first choice on his list. He wanted her to come with him, to get her reaction, but maybe he was hoping for too much. He stepped into his loafers and took his overcoat out of the closet.

"Where are you going?" June looked at him with determined suspicion.

"Out. For a drive. Would you like to come with me?" He was prepared for reluctance or an outright refusal.

"Road trip!" June declared. "Are we going to the cottage?"

"No, no." Damn. They'd sold the cottage years ago.

"We need to pack! I'll tell the kids to get their things ready."

"June—" She'd always made the drive to the cottage fun, even though traffic problems could turn the two-hour trip into four long hours. How had she even remembered this? Some days she couldn't find the kitchen.

"Come on, Nick. We need snacks and the travel games and my suitcase!"

"Sorry love, not that kind of trip. No need for luggage."

Not in the least discouraged, June flung up her arms and laughed "Where are we going?"

He went for the uncomplicated truth now. "Sunnyview Retirement Home. We've been invited to come for a visit."

June stared at him, confusion flooding her face.

"We're just going for a quick look-see, okay?" Maybe bringing her was a mistake. "If you don't want to come—"

"Can we get chocolate milk? And, and…donuts?"

Nick chuckled. "Yes, but maybe on the way back, okay?" She was still lost in the road trip, as excited now as the kids have been with each rest-stop adventure.

June nodded, seemingly satisfied and now eagerly stuffing her arms into the coat Gloria held up. She sat on the bench as Nick crouched low to slip on her sneakers, tying the laces in double knots just to be safe.

"Okay. Let's go!" shouted June. She jumped up without warning, almost knocking Nick off balance. He steadied himself with an outstretched hand, his fingers bending under the weight.

"Jesus, June." Nick used the bench to hoist himself up, as his knees popped and complained. "You need—" He was about to scold her but stopped. June was beaming, her happiness tangible, untouched by age or disease, as if some enigmatic spark had restored her. Nick took one quick step forward and folded June into his arms. She hugged him back, a long, warm embrace that lasted longer than most.

"Ready?" asked Nick, making no effort to fight back the tears.

June nodded. "Can I have two donuts? Or a box of those little ones?"

Nick took her arm and led her out the door.

"Jonathan likes the little chocolate ones."

"Sure, we can do that."

They walked slowly, navigating their way down the wooden ramp, supporting each other, slow and steady on the gradual decline.

**

Nick checked his watch. They were right on time, but still they waited on this uncomfortable metal bench. The girl behind the desk assured them that someone would be with them soon, so they waited. June fiddled with the buttons on her cardigan, buttoning and unbuttoning. Nick scrutinized the staff, silently berating each one who failed to approach. He'd trained his secretaries, the articling students, hell even his kids to be on time. Nine minutes passed, ten. He felt June leaning against him, deflating.

"Excuse me." He tried to not bark. "We have an appointment."

The girl looked up from her computer. "Yes, so sorry. Um, mister, let me see—"

"Walker. Nick and June Walker. We have an appointment."

"Yes of course. We have it right here, on the schedule."

"Look." Nick fabricated a smile as he approached the desk. "I arranged this a few days ago. I spoke to someone who told me we were confirmed for this morning at ten."

"Oh, here it is. You're Mr. and Mrs. Walker."

"Yes, I know."

"Stan will be here in a minute. He's with a family right now." She leaned forward and whispered, "Mrs. Kumar passed away this morning."

"Oh." Nick shrunk back. "I'm...yes, well...well that is a shame." He looked at June. She'd slumped forward. How much longer would she last? "Well, maybe we should rebook, for another day, next week? My wife is getting—"

"Hello. You must be the Walkers."

Nick turned around quickly, surprised to find someone behind him.

"Hi, I'm Stan, Stan Schneider."

He was a tall man, skinny, purposely unshaven, young, but then everyone seemed like a kid these days, with a complexion that seldom saw the sun. Stan extended a hand toward Nick, the other planted firmly in the pocket of his faded jeans. An ill-fitting sports jacket and a tie with a limp knot did little to elevate the outfit but his rubber soled sneakers accounted for his covert arrival.

"Nice to meet you, Stan. Nick Walker and this is my wife, June." Nick shook his hand firmly, and dammit, the guy practically winced. June sat still on the bench and made no effort to acknowledge Stan.

Nick sat down beside her and put his arm around her shoulder. "I was thinking we'd reschedule. My wife is getting tired and it might be best if we headed home."

"Nonsense," said Stan. "Let's just get her a wheelchair." He motioned to the desk and turned to June. "How about you ride in style today? You sit and I'll do the work."

"No, that won't be necessary," said Nick, but to his surprise June stood and sat in the wheelchair an attendant had parked next to Stan.

"Excellent," said Stan. "Let's start off in the lounge, meet some of the resident campers, okay?" Stan didn't wait for an answer as he propelled June towards a large open room, crowded with mismatched sofas, chairs and tables. Stan chirped good morning to a few people. He stopped in front of a bulky woman wearing a red beret with a feather.

"This is Mable. She's been with us a long time now, haven't you, dear?"

Nick nodded at Mable, mumbled a polite *good morning* and stepped back.

"Oh wait," said Stan. "You need to meet Clyde too. He's our in-house entertainer." A stately white-haired gentleman with an oversized moustache saluted and bellowed from across the room, "Hi y'all."

June smiled and returned his wave as Nick took command of the wheelchair and pushed her back toward the hallway. He smiled as best he could as he steered her around walkers and canes, careful not to run over any slipper-clad feet. An old man in an older velvet wing-back chair reached up and grabbed the arm of June's wheelchair. He leaned towards her and whispered, "Hello cutie," followed by an attempt at a wink.

Nick cringed, but June seemed unconcerned. Had she even noticed?

Stan hooted. "Now Sammy, you know better than to flirt with our new girl. All your other ladies will be jealous." He turned to Nick, "Okay now, let's have a peek at the dining room. I've arranged lunch for you later."

Lunch? Nick's gut tightened into a knot. "Uh, maybe. Can we see some of the amenities first, perhaps a suite?"

Stan laughed again, "A suite? Oh no, we have shared, standard or king size rooms. They are extremely comfortable, cleaned once a week and you're allowed to have a kettle, auto shutoff only, and even a microwave."

Oh god, what had he gotten them into? Stan prattled on about movie nights, the in-house hairdresser, chair exercise classes and weekly excursions to the mall.

"The shuttle always stops at Walmart—one stop shopping, right? A quick lunch at McDonalds and then back home for a little R and R."

Nick wanted to flee. Instead, they walked on, following Stan past heavy metal doors labelled with large numbers and residents' names written on jagged pieces of masking tape. Some doors were propped wide open, exposing women or men still in bed or parked in loungers or wheelchairs. June was quiet, her head bowed, which, Nick felt, was probably for the best.

"The carpet is dirty," said June. "I don't like it."

"June." Nick tried to shush her.

"Oh, you're right little lady," said Stan. "That's on the improvement list but right now it's not in the budget. We hope to get something a little fancier, maybe that new luxury vinyl stuff that looks exactly like hardwood."

Nick noticed an exit sign. How close were they to the parking lot? He could move pretty fast pushing this thing.

"Here we are," said Stan, indicating a door which was slightly ajar. He knocked twice. "Helllooo, Barbara? Babs, my dear. I've brought you some visitors." He pulled back the door to allow Nick and June to enter.

Nick hesitated. He heard laughter, cheers, a game show played on the TV. A tiny woman sat in her bed, a wheeled tray table across her lap. She gazed at Nick, not even startled, just blank. She was eating, a late breakfast or maybe an early lunch?

"Oh no. We don't want to bother anyone." Nick felt his heart sink. This could be June—would be soon enough. "I've—we've seen enough." He nodded to the woman, tried to smile. "Thanks," he said. He noticed framed photos, children's artwork tacked to the wall. She was a mother, someone's granny.

"Okay then," said Stan. "It's a little early but how about lunch?"

"What? Sorry, but no. I think we'd best be on our way. This has been a lot for my wife."

"I want to go home," said June.

Nick smiled. "Yes, let's go."

Stan seemed to understand. "It's a lot to take in, isn't it?" He patted June's shoulder and reached for the handles on the wheelchair. "I'll show you out."

"We're good," said Nick as he propelled June forward and hurried for the front door. "Thank you for your time." He collected their coats from the rack and threw them over his arm.

"See you soon, then?" It sounded more like a plea than a question. "Look Nick, just gimme a call if you'd like more info. Or better still, come back for lunch."

"Will do," said Nick, without looking back.

CHAPTER NINETEEN

M artha entered the house through the kitchen, the unmistakable aroma of her mother's beef stew greeted her like a warm hug. "Hi, Gloria. Wow, it smells wonderful in here." Martha inhaled deeply.

Gloria closed the oven door. "It's beef stew and butter rolls. I used your mother's recipes."

"I can tell. It smells like I'm back in high school."

Gloria smiled. "Thank you. Your mother seems to like this food the best. It's her food, I suppose."

"Yes, you're probably right."

"I like to cook."

"Well, you are amazing, and not just in the kitchen." Not for the first time, Martha marveled at her luck in finding this wonderful woman to help her parents. "I hope you know how grateful we are to have your help."

Gloria acknowledged the compliment with only a quick uncomfortable nod, the colour rising in her cheeks.

Not wanting to embarrass her further, Martha changed the subject. "Where are my parents?"

"Mom's in the family room and your father is upstairs, in his office."

Martha found her mother napping in front of the TV, a wildlife documentary barely audible. She lingered for a couple of minutes, removed the spill-proof tumbler from her mother's hand and gently tucked her blanket around her legs. Mom looked calm, peaceful, undamaged. Normal, not that napping in the afternoon had ever been normal for her mother.

Martha climbed the stairs slowly, realizing for the first time that the old family photos, her and Jon as babies and in their school uniforms, had never been updated. Unlike her friends, her mother had no grandchildren, no new photos. She and Jonathan remained frozen in time on the stair wall. If she and Peter had been able to—nope. She wasn't going there today.

Dad was in his office, *The Imaginary Office*. It had been named by default. As far as the twins were concerned, Dad did his lawyer work in his downtown office, which one day, Mom, likely peppered with questions from two unrelenting four-year-olds, had called his real office. So, Jonathan had, logically, christened this one *The Imaginary Office* and it had stuck, so much so that for one birthday they'd given Dad a name plate. He'd loved it and mounted it beside the door that very day. Jon had helped with the drilling. Martha ran her finger along the cool brass. The years had aged the finish, but the words were still clear.

"Hi, Dad."

He looked up from his computer. "Oh, hi. I didn't know you were coming today."

"I had some time, a client cancelled." She dropped into one of the soft leather chairs. At some point, probably in high school, she'd used this office as her quiet space, to read and do homework, away from Jon and his noisy friends. She hadn't spent much time in here since then, but it hadn't changed. The timeless elegance was a little retro now but it still emanated comfort. She loved all the old books, fiction, politics, the classics, a couple of shelves of case books and, of course, several editions of Black's Law Dictionary.

Her father sighed deeply, not a sound she was used to.

"That sounds serious. What's up?"

"Not much. But do you happen to know of any good homes for the old and ailing? Somewhere other than a pine box?"

"Dad! That's not funny."

"I know."

He ran his fingers through his hair. He looked old, a little haggard and he needed a haircut, something else she wasn't used to. Dad had always been fastidious about his grooming, scheduling regular trims for his hair and unruly brows. Both were shaggy now. The foul taste of guilt rose in her throat. She'd been neglecting her parents. She'd been placated by her dad's determined independence, fooling herself that his repeated assurances that they were just fine meant she only needed to spend a few hours a week visiting.

"I'm trying to find a suitable place to move—for your mother and I."

"Seriously?" She knew it would come to this. But she'd thought they were fine for now.

"Yes, Martha. Seriously." He spoke quietly, but louder and harsher than a whisper.

"I'm a little surprised. You love this house. And Mom's comfortable here."

"You're right. I do love this place, but things have changed. Your mother really isn't safe here anymore." His face was steeped in sadness.

"We could hire more help or install a stairlift?" She was grasping at straws, a quick fix to mitigate her guilt.

"No, it's more than that. Your mother's confused, some days completely lost and she can't be trusted to stay in one place. It's a lot for me now, too much. And I can't...I'm tired Martha, and I've got to believe this will be best for both of us."

Martha was overcome with guilt. "Oh, I'm sorry, so sorry. Why didn't you tell me? I should have been paying more attention." She moved to hug her father but he leaned away.

"No. No. No need for sympathy. Your mom and I have been fine. It's just...she's declining and every morning my knees remind me that I'm not getting any younger." He chuckled. "But I've figured out what we need to do, our next stop in this unpredictable journey we all so optimistically call life."

"Oh, Dad." Martha gave him no choice. She rose and wrapped her arms around his shoulders.

"Martha."

She squeezed again, this time hoping she could soak up a little of his strength and wisdom.

"All right. Enough already." Dad laughed. "I'm okay. And I have been handling things very well for the last few years."

"I know, but—" This was probably true. She'd been so caught up in work and her Peter problems that she really couldn't be sure. "Are you sure you're alright? You seem a little down."

"I'm fine—just frustrated."

"Why?"

"Well, I've done a lot of research and visited a couple of the homes, but they're all shit, sorry, let's say, less than desirable."

Martha chuckled. But Dad wasn't joking. Despite his genial grin, he looked exhausted. His face was drawn and tense. He was way past frustrated. He'd always been so good at hiding his feelings, an unreadable poker face, but now he wasn't even trying.

"I don't know, maybe I've lost perspective."

Martha smiled. "Who you? Nick Walker—the master of detail and precision?"

"I know I'm nitpicking. Am I being too analytical? Too critical?" He handed her a grey file folder labelled *MOVING*.

"This looks ominous." Martha sifted through the papers. "You made a spreadsheet. Now that's impressive."

"Don't make fun of me. It's the only way I can keep things straight."

"I'm not, Dad, really. I am impressed." She picked up a stack of brochures. "Have you been to all these places? And you made notes and—oh God, this one sounds horrible." She began to read aloud. "Place smells like onions fried in pine disinfectant." Martha pretended to gag. "Windows need cleaning. No suites. No gym. Liver every Friday." Martha grinned. "Okay then, we are not moving you in there, are we?"

"No. No we are not and actually none of these places are any good." He pulled the file toward him, gathered the sheets of paper into a neat pile and tossed everything into the trash can.

"That's pretty dramatic."

He ignored her, closed his eyes and sank into his chair. He looked defeated.

"Dad? Are you okay?"

He nodded. "Yeah."

Martha stood up and retrieved the file from the trash. "So, why did you pick these places?"

"The woman from social services emailed me the list. I trusted her judgement."

"Clearly that didn't work out." Martha frowned. "Let's try again. Trade places with me."

"Okay, even though you're kinda bossy, I could use your help."

She moved over to replace him at the computer, kissed him on the cheek and started typing. "There, these look better, less insane *asylum-ish.*"

Her father leaned over her shoulder and squinted at the screen. "That one looks nice, from the outside at least. I haven't seen anything like that before. How did you find it?"

"I just Googled *luxury upscale retirement and care communities*."

"No shit. I suddenly feel very old." He laughed. "Thanks. Seems like you're good at this."

"Well, it's a start, I guess. But what happens next?" Would they have to go and check out each one? Dad had been going alone. Little wonder he looked depressed. She should go with him, but she had two active arbitrations and a full calendar this week and next. And one last appointment with Peter and the mediator.

"We choose a couple places and book appointments for the tour," replied Dad, confirming her fear of the time commitment. "We'll get the sales pitch, and if we're not careful, lunch, I'm guessing egg salad, maybe tuna and rice pudding."

"What?"

"Yeah. But don't worry. I've learned a few things, the tricks of the trade so to speak. Look, I know you're busy. So don't worry about it. I'll go, take notes and add them to the spreadsheet. Then we can meet and discuss."

Martha picked up her phone and opened it to her calendar. "No, this is just too much for one person. I can't do tomorrow, but Thursday might work. Or I could move things around on Friday, if I have to. But Thursday is better. See if you can get two appointments for the same day."

"But—"

"No buts. I'm going with you." She clicked through one of the websites. "This one really does look promising."

"Humph," Dad grunted. "Does it have a golf course?" He moved toward the bar tray on the credenza.

"Yes, eighteen holes, manicured greens and a two Michelin star clubhouse." She grinned. "Let's try to be realistic."

"I am. Believe me. This is becoming all too real. My new reality is smacking me right between the eyes! What the hell am I supposed to do in these places all day?"

"Dad, you're an active, intelligent man. I'm sure you can figure out how to fill your days." She clicked onto the other website. "Look, this one has a library and a gym. The gardens are nice too. And the apartment is quite big." She looked at her father, expecting him to agree, but he looked irritated.

"Big? Look around you, Martha. We have so much space and even here I sometimes feel like a hostage." He extended a tumbler of Scotch towards her. "Would you like one?"

Martha nodded. "Yes please. With ice." Dad always had the best whiskey.

"So you've changed your mind? Now you don't want to move?" She was trying to sound positive, patient, but even she could hear the frustration in her voice.

"Of course I haven't changed my mind. This isn't a choice, you know. And maybe, just maybe, I haven't quite got my head around that yet."

"Oh. I am so sorry. I forget how hard this must be for you." She knew the fear, the pain when she thought she would lose her house in the divorce. Peter had proposed a sale to split the proceeds. Dad's situation was worse.

"Thanks. I'm okay. I just feel like…some days—like I'm losing so much, so much is already gone." He tipped back his Scotch, clicked his tongue and winked at her. "You know, maybe I should just stay here."

"Alone?"

"Well, you're single now. Maybe we could live here together."

"You're joking, right?" She'd never lived alone, not even at university, but now, with Peter gone, she was finally embracing her independence.

"I think so. Yes, no, maybe." He sighed. It sounded so pitiful.

"Well, Dad, as much as I love you—"

"Don't go there. I was just joking." He smiled as if she needed proof. "But Gloria says that's what they do in her country. All the generations live together."

"We'd drive each other batshit crazy."

"Or worse."

"Or worse," agreed Martha. "We'll figure this out. We'll find a place that works for both you and Mom and hopefully near a golf course."

"Cheers to that." They clinked glasses. "Would you like another?"

Her dad reached for the crystal decanter.

"No thanks, I'm heading home soon." Martha bit her tongue as he poured another generous shot for himself.

"Look," he said. "There are only two things I need, besides your mother, of course. Scotch and good coffee. The liquor is easy. But I'm not leaving here without my espresso machine."

Martha forced a smile, nodded and clicked past the page she'd been reading, *Rules for Residents. 6. Personal small kitchen appliances are prohibited.* Poor Dad.

"Okay, so we have the rules of our mission. You make the appointments and send me the details. But I'm driving."

"Why? What's wrong with my driving?"

Martha laughed. "Nothing a little pressure on the gas wouldn't fix."

"Okay Speedy Gonzales, you can drive."

"I gotta go, Dad." She moved toward the door.

"You can stay for dinner."

"Thanks, but I have to work. I'm in court tomorrow."

"I know. It's a curse." He pulled her into an awkward hug. "Thank you."

He felt soft and fragile, like a teddy bear missing some of its stuffing. Only the smell of his aftershave remained the same.

CHAPTER TWENTY

Nick zipped up his windbreaker and checked his watch at the sound of Martha's car pulling in the driveway. Right on time, just like he'd taught her. He grabbed his flat cap and quietly slipped out the door before June could notice he was leaving. It wasn't an exciting outing but they were finally going to visit the two retirement homes Martha had found online.

Their initial plans had been waylaid, first by Martha's work commitments and then by June. She'd picked up a nasty virus that had required an arduous trip to the hospital and a long wait in Emergency, only to be sent home with a perfunctory diagnosis of, *it's going around. Just make sure she stays hydrated.* Martha had been furious on the drive home, vowing to make heads roll. But the virus had run its course, the worst part being the fever that fueled June's growing paranoia and delusions. So, this morning, as Nick climbed into Martha's car, he realized he wasn't looking forward to visiting a couple of euphemistically named *rest homes* but he was very glad to be getting out of the house.

As they made the rounds in the first place, Nick tried to keep an open mind. The facility was an adequate fit for June but, not so much for him. Was it so selfish to want something decent for himself too? The home wasn't terrible but it felt cold and institutional. As the tour progressed, Martha pressed him to see things a little differently. He'd always zeroed in on the problems and deficiencies but today he tried to be a little more objective, especially when Martha pointed out things he hadn't considered.

Their second stop, EZY Retirement, was the most promising. He hated the name, but it was clean and modern. Martha liked the fireplace in the lounge, and the greenhouse solarium that he thought too crowded and noisy. The hair salon looked small, dark and dreary. Martha laughed when he held his nose and grumbled about the chemical smell.

"That's the scent of beauty! This will be great for Mom and you. It's so convenient."

Nick nodded, acknowledging she was probably right. It wasn't easy taking June for a haircut these days, so he'd let it go far too long. Norah had helped him last time, but that was months ago.

In the games room, a couple of tables of bridge players made Nick wonder if anyone would be interested in a good game of poker.

"And look, Dad, there's a theatre room." Martha pointed to the handwritten sign on the door. *The Magnificent Seven. 11:00 am, today. Don't be late!!*

"A little early for a movie," said Nick as Martha nudged him through the door. The movie hadn't started yet. Several of the recliners were occupied, walkers parked nearby. A few wheelchairs filled in the empty spaces. Nick backed up towards the door.

"Look, there's even a popcorn machine," said Martha.

"Wonderful."

"You're such a curmudgeon sometimes. This place isn't so bad, you know."

Thankfully it was the last stop on their tour. "Yes, Martha, it's fine... just fine."

"Just fine? You said you liked the suite."

"I did."

"So?"

"So nothing. You're right. It's good. Better than any of the others I've seen."

"Well, that's something." She smiled that *I'm-happy-when-I'm-right smile*. But then she didn't have to spend the rest of her life here.

The drive home was a quiet one. Martha opted for the long route through the light industrial district. Nick was lost in thought, trying to imagine himself living at EZY Retirement and was more than a little surprised when they pulled into a parking lot with one of those inflatable wacky waving tube guys. This one had a sombrero.

"Are you hungry?" asked Martha.

They pulled up near a food truck, a dented, well-used vehicle painted with green, white and red stripes.

"I could eat." They'd managed to avoid lunch at both the homes. "What's this place?" The large *TACO* sign was making him nervous. Workers in hard hats and orange safety vests sat eating at picnic tables.

"A surprise—my treat."

"I don't know…" He was worried about his acid reflux.

"Just trust me." She parked and ordered from her phone. They settled on a table that wasn't too sunny and out of the wind. In less than five minutes a young kid came out with a small paper shopping bag.

"Martha?" he called.

"Here," said Martha. She handed him a generous tip.

"So, what have we got?" Nick had never considered himself a taco kind of guy.

"Fish tacos!"

"Really? That's new to me, but they smell delicious."

"They are. They were, well probably still are, Peter's favourite."

Nick bit into the warm crunchy, creamy taco. "Well, let's not hold that against them."

Martha laughed. They ate, trying to contain the messy goodness of the taco. In between bites they laughed and talked about everything, except retirement homes, June, and Peter. Nick noticed guacamole on Martha's chin and wiped it away with the last napkin.

**

Nick collapsed into his favourite chair and let out a sigh of relief. June had gone to bed without much of a fight tonight. After dinner they'd sat together on the sofa and paged through one of June's gardening books, a beautiful coffee table edition of English country gardens. June, fixated, spellbound by the exquisite photos, became petulant when Nick finally closed the book, but thankfully her mood changed when Gloria lightened the bedtime routine with some cheerful songs from her own childhood.

Nick checked his iPad. June was sleeping now. The nanny cam Martha had set up in the bedroom allowed him to relax without worrying so much. He inhaled the aromatic steam from his coffee, a mug of decaf instead of the Scotch he really wanted. He had planned to read, but his book, *Master and Commander,* sat unopened on the footstool. He'd decided to read the series again, but he wasn't inclined to begin the journey tonight. He had other things on his mind.

Nick studied the glossy brochures he'd brought back from the homes and tried to picture himself as a resident, walking the halls, eating in the dining room, watching a morning movie. *Inspired senior living in a community that cares. A vibrant retirement lifestyle designed for you.*

*S*ounded good, but in the end, they were just old folks' homes. The nicest looking place was, with several hundred units, too large for his liking, but it did have a small gym, with weights and ellipticals—all he really needed, according to Martha. He liked the living space at Horizon Sky, despite the echoes of the pearly gates. June would enjoy the solarium. The gym was bigger and had better equipment. They would have a real two-bedroom apartment. It was close enough to the downtown, but there was no parking for residents so where would he keep his car? The phone interrupted his thoughts.

"Dad!" Martha sounded excited.

"Hi, what's up? It's late, you know. Everything alright?" He stretched, yawned and considered pouring a Scotch.

"Oh sorry, yes fine. But I have some news. I was talking to my friend Angela, remember her? From college? Well, her mom runs a company that specializes in home care for seniors."

"What? Oh no, we're past that now."

"Yea, I know, but I just talked to her, the mom, not Angela and—"

"What? Martha please. I'm tired."

"Sorry. Yes. I told her that we were having a really hard time finding a place for you guys and she suggested Whispering Pines. She said it's where she plans to end up. I'm looking at it online. It might just be perfect."

"That's quite a tease, Martha. Wait, I'll look it up." Nick closed the camera app on his iPad and typed *Whispering Pines* into Google. "Yes, that does look nice." He read further. "But Martha it's in the country, in the middle of nowhere."

"No not nowhere. Only about half an hour, maybe forty minutes from here. There's a tennis court," she paused. "And shuffleboard." Martha chuckled.

"Not exactly a selling point." But Nick liked what he saw. "I wonder why this place never showed up in any of our searches."

"I'm not sure," said Martha. "But I'm guessing they don't do a lot of advertising. It's small and they might just rely on referrals."

"Small and expensive I'm guessing."

Martha laughed. "No doubt. But it's time to loosen the purse strings. That's why you've been saving all those millions."

"Yeah, but I was hoping to spend it all on a far more exciting retirement."

"Oh Dad."

"Don't worry. I'm fine. Let's see if I can book us a tour later on this week, okay?"

"Saturday or even Sunday would be better for me."

"Yes, of course. I'll let you know."

**

Nick didn't like leaving June at home alone on the weekends. The young woman he'd hired to help them out on Gloria's days off was personable, but not ambitious, content to leave June in bed too long or to just sit and watch TV with her for hours. Nick had probably fussed too much. June's lunch was in the fridge and a list of instructions and a loose schedule were on the kitchen table. And now they were headed to Whispering Pines, Martha driving a little too fast and Nick drinking his first ever oat milk matcha latte.

"It tastes like grass."

Martha glanced at him and raised an eyebrow.

"Not that kind of grass. The green stuff that goats eat. I could brew this from the clippings from the backyard."

"Seriously!" Martha laughed. She looked relaxed today and he was grateful for her company.

"It's a little too, um, earthy for me. I'd happily trade it for a double espresso."

"It's good for you." She shifted gears and steered off the highway. "And that much caffeine isn't."

"Yeah, yeah."

"We're almost there. See, that didn't take long."

Nick felt some of his drink dribble down his chin as Martha, without bothering to signal, swung the car into a driveway marked only by a small sign that read *Whispering Pines*.

"Slow down, girl, or I'll be wearing this dreadful thing."

Martha laughed. "Cheer up, old man. I got us here in less than thirty minutes."

"And luckily we made it in one piece." They'd been bumping heads about her driving since the first day she'd sat behind the wheel. He'd tried to teach her but couldn't stand the tears. June had taken over, and still Martha had needed a couple of tries to get her licence, probably the only test she'd ever failed.

"Oh, Dad, this looks promising."

They'd driven up the winding drive and were parking in front of a stately building that resembled an English manor, only smaller and newer.

"It's nice," said Nick, noting the well-manicured lawn.

"Look," said Martha. She was pointing toward a field.

"What? Cows?"

"No Dad, a putting green."

Nick squinted. "I see one flag, maybe two."

"It's something. Come on. Let's see if the inside meets your unrealistic list of requirements." Martha smiled and took his arm. He knew she was teasing him with the truth.

Enid, the director, must have seen them drive in. She was waiting at the door and led them to her office. Enid was tall, even in flat shoes she was taller than him. There were no strange smells, the carpets were clean. And as they passed the dining room, Martha pointed out the fresh flowers on every table.

"Roses. Mom would love that."

He noted the small sittings, only two, sometimes four to a table and nodded his approval.

In Enid's office, she directed them toward the window where a small glass table was set with beverages and a plate of cookies.

"Tea? Coffee?" asked Enid. Her smile was warm and seemed genuine.

"Just water please." The grass tea had left him thirsty.

"Nothing for me," said Martha.

"Help yourself to a cookie. Our chef makes them fresh every day." Enid filled a glass and set it in front of Nick. "I'm sorry you didn't bring June. I was looking forward to meeting her."

"It's not always easy to take her out," explained Martha.

"She gets confused," Nick added. "And sometimes a little frightened by unfamiliar places."

"Oh, I understand," said Enid. "May I ask about her diagnosis?"

"Of course," said Nick. "So far, we're working with mixed dementia which really means none of the specialists have been able to narrow it down. The label doesn't really matter much to me. It's just becoming more difficult—"

"But she's not violent or anything like that." Martha spoke directly to Enid.

"Well, that's good to know." Enid seemed unfazed. "But don't worry, we can handle most challenges."

Nick caught a whiff of ginger and cinnamon from the cookies. He sipped his water. This place felt okay. That's all he'd give it for now.

Enid handed Martha a large manila envelope. Ah yes, thought Nick, the package, next comes the hard sell.

Enid smiled at him as if she knew what he was thinking.

"Nick," she said. "This is a big decision you're trying to make. It will change June's life and yours as well. In my experience, you might find this move more difficult than your wife."

Nick shot her a glance, sat up straighter. "Why would you say that?"

"Well, I haven't met June, but I'm guessing that after her initial period of adjustment she will be happy just being here—or anywhere with you. You've been together a long time?"

"Over fifty years."

"Amazing," said Enid.

"Especially these days," said Martha.

"Look," said Enid as she took the chair next to Nick. "I'm not going to try and sell you on Whispering Pines. I'll show you around and let you decide for yourself, okay?"

Nick nodded.

"I'm very proud of this place. We're a small community, but supportive. There's lots of busy people who would love for you to join in their activities, but if you'd prefer to be alone, then so be it. We have nurses, a full staff of PSWs and housekeeping and a doctor who checks in every day."

"That sounds good," said Martha. "Dad really wanted a golf course."

Enid laughed. "We do have a small putting green but no one has used it in a while and I fear it might need a bit of work. There's a lap pool, a hot tub and a nicely equipped gym."

"It seems just about perfect, doesn't it, Dad?"

Nick reached for a cookie.

"Let's not rush your father into anything. I'm sure he still has lots of questions." Enid smiled at Nick. "Shall we do a quick tour so you can get a better look?"

Enid guided them through the building, a classic centre-hall design with four floors, each divided into suites of varying sizes. All the amenities were on the main floor, including a coffee shop with three small round tables, comfortable chairs and a large platter of donuts with a handwritten sign that simply read *Enjoy!*

The top floor was secure and Enid used a fob to both operate the elevator and allow them to enter through heavy double doors. There were a few people sitting in the lounge, most were in their rooms. Nick realized that these people weren't really residents anymore. They were patients now. How soon would June occupy one of these beds? Locked in time. He'd truly be alone then.

"This is good," Martha whispered as she nudged Nick's arm. "They'll take care of Mom here."

Nick stiffened, fighting back tears.

"It's okay, Dad."

As they walked back to the elevator, Martha slipped her hand into his. It felt warm against his clammy skin.

Next, Enid showed them a couple of suites, the gym and the pool, all good, maybe too good. Nick couldn't write this place off, but could he live here, full time, forever?

On the way home, Nick conceded that Whispering Pines was better than anything else they'd seen.

"It's nice, right?" pressed Martha.

Nick opened the envelope and scanned to the bottom line. "Nice and expensive," he said. Almost ten grand a month—more with the extra care."

Martha gasped. "Oh my god. I had no idea it was that much."

"Me either."

"There goes my yacht."

"What?"

"Well, it looks like you'll be spending my inheritance on Whispering Pines."

Nick laughed. "I didn't know you were into sailing."

"Oh, I'm not. Yachting. With staff to do all the work while I'd lie in the sun and drink margaritas all day."

"Oh, so you've thought this plan through?"

"Totally. I'll need a fifty-footer, at least." She chuckled and patted his leg with her free hand. "Seriously, Dad, don't worry about me. I'm solid—financially speaking, you know."

"But what about Jonathan?"

"Jonathan?"

"Your brother, he's—"

"I know who Jonathan is. It's *the where* that's the problem."

"Martha?"

"Look, Dad, I have no idea what's happening with Jon. The last time we spoke, like, three years ago, he was coming home. He didn't. I get the occasional text and I share those with you. That's it. Have you heard from him lately?"

"No. Your mother seems to talk to him a lot, you know, complete nonsense really. I assume he's still in Victoria, but we don't pay his rent anymore so I don't really know."

"Then, let's try and focus on one problem at a time. Whispering Pines just might be the right place for you and Mom. Let's work with that. Damn the cost. Damn Jonathan."

"Okay then." The colour had risen in Martha's cheeks. Jonathan had hurt her, hurt them all. But she was right. It was a problem for another day. "Um, you know I was kidding, right—about the money. It's not a problem. We have plenty to live out our years, even at the WP."

Martha chuckled. "Oh, so now you're throwing down nicknames?"

Nick grinned. "Just trying to be cool."

"Oh! The perfect man—cool and rich!"

Nick heard the click of the turn signal at the same time as he saw the Starbucks sign.

"It's your turn to buy," said Martha.

He involuntarily reached out for the dashboard as she steered quickly into the narrow drive-thru lane. "My pleasure," he said through his teeth. "I could use a real coffee."

Martha grinned as she moved the car forward and placed their order. For the first time he noticed her wrinkles; crow's feet, laugh lines, signs of maturity and strength.

"I love you, Martha."

She turned and smiled. "I know, Dad. Me too."

CHAPTER TWENTY-ONE

Nick opened his eyes and was surprised to see daylight through the edges of the curtains. He glanced at the clock on the bedside table. He'd slept almost seven hours straight. When was the last time that happened? June was still asleep, snoring softly. He turned onto his side, toward her and softly brushed back a few stray hairs from her forehead. Like many mornings, he fantasized that he'd been trapped in an endless nightmare. Maybe today it would end. He pressed his eyes closed and opened them quickly, willing his June to wake up and greet him with a smile, a kiss and a warm, *good morning, my love.* They could stay here together like that, maybe forever. She stirred, her fingers tightening around double handfuls of the cotton sheet.

He slipped out of bed before she woke completely. Sometimes it took several minutes, sometimes much longer before she knew where she was, knew him. He didn't want to witness it today. He dressed quickly in the clothes he'd left on the chair the night before, khakis and a blue polo shirt. He slowly pulled the bedroom door closed behind him and made his way to the kitchen. It was just past seven and Gloria was baking. June's recipe box sat open on the counter. Her *Mom's Best Scones* recipe card, handwritten by her own mother, was propped against the flour canister.

"G'morning, Mr. Walker." Gloria greeted him with a warm smile. She slid the baking sheet into the oven.

"Good morning, Gloria. It looks like you've been busy."

"I'm making scones for Mrs. Walker. She asked for them yesterday and I promised her I'd have some for her this morning."

"She won't remember," said Nick.

"Probably not, but she'll still enjoy them." Gloria set the timer.

"Hope so."

"You feeling okay today, Mr. Walker?" It was a friendly enough question but it irritated him.

"Yes, yes, I'm fine." He sounded surly. "Sorry, I think I'm just tired." It was an easier excuse than the truth. "And sad." He hadn't meant to say this.

"Sad?"

"Yes, but I'm okay. It's only…I can't seem to pull the trigger on that home—Whispering Pines. It's a decent enough place, but—"

"Are you worried about Mrs. Walker's care?"

"No, that shouldn't be a problem. It's me I'm worried about." He chuckled uneasily, feeling a little sheepish about admitting this to Gloria. "I'm not sure I want to live there or anywhere other than here." He shrugged. "Mighty selfish of me."

"Mrs. Walker doesn't want to leave either."

"I know. Once upon a time I made her a promise, but back then, well, I had no idea." Nick sat down at the table and took the pills Gloria set out for him each morning. They were mostly for his heart, but recently his doctor had added vitamin B to give him an energy boost.

"I don't know how much longer we can stay here."

"Mrs. Walker knows her own home. She's comfortable here, yes?"

"Yes, of course. But I'm not sure it's safe for her." Nick sighed. Gloria was right, but so was he. "How the hell am I supposed to know what's best?"

"You'll know soon enough."

"I don't know about that."

"You're a good man, clever too. You will make the right decision. I know."

Nick looked at her. "You know?"

"I do." She untied her apron and hung it on the hook with June's. "Is she awake now?"

"Maybe. She was starting to stir when I came down."

Gloria cocked her head toward the ceiling. "I think I hear her."

"You go. I'll take care of the scones."

"Ok, eight more minutes," she said. She pulled open a drawer and set a pair of oven mitts beside Nick. "Use these and don't let those scones overcook. They'll be dry as sand and hard as rocks."

"Yes ma'am." Nick chuckled. "I do know my way around the kitchen."

"Uh huh." Gloria clicked her tongue. "We'll see."

The kitchen was so quiet now that he could hear the rain trickling down the drainpipe. The gutters probably needed cleaning again. He scrolled through the pages on his iPad. He still missed the morning paper. The ding of the timer reminded him about the scones. He opened the oven. They looked pretty good, a little bigger than usual but the colour was right. He slid each one carefully onto the wire cooling rack, trying to ignore the voices from upstairs. Gloria was calm, June was getting louder, arguing, complaining about the colour of her shirt or an itchy sweater or not wanting to wear pants or refusing to brush her teeth or her hair or being frightened by the water swirling in the toilet. June was shouting, maybe crying now. He turned off the oven and headed back upstairs.

Tops, pants, socks and underwear were scattered around the room. The closet was a mess and June, sitting on the side of the bed, was still in her pajamas.

"We're getting dressed," said Gloria, clearly undaunted. "And we're having some trouble deciding what to wear."

Nick surveyed the mess. "Apparently."

Gloria was holding a navy and red silk shirt, one of June's favourites. "I tried to let her choose, but—"

"It's okay," said Nick, trying to reassure her with a shrug and a smile. "June, my love, would you like me to help you get dressed?"

June ignored him. He reached for the buttons on her pajama top, but she clutched her hands to her chest.

"Sweetheart. It's okay. It's me. I just want to help."

June started to rock back and forth; a low hum fluttered in her throat.

Nick sat beside her and slowly reached his arm around her, drawing her close. The rocking slowed. "Shhh. Shhh. You're okay." She leaned into him. "So, let's get you ready for the day, okay?" She nodded. "Ready now?" He held out a hand for the shirt.

"No. I don't want it."

He turned away to hide his frustration. "Shit," he muttered.

Gloria moved closer.

"No, I've got this." Nick placed a hand on June's cheek. He wanted her to see him but her eyes were empty, her face grey, slack, blank. Nick blinked back his tears. "Okay then." He grinned and feigned surprise as if he'd just come up with the best idea. "Let's make this a pajama day, like when the kids were little. You can stay in your pjs all day. Would you like that?"

June smiled and nodded. "Pajama…day."

"Well, it's a little chilly today, so I think you'll need your housecoat too. Are you alright with that?"

Gloria held up a white cotton dressing gown. June shook her head, stood and walked into the closet, shuffling through the jumble of clothes. She pulled her pink fluffy robe from the hanger and handed it to Nick. She slipped in her arms and, as he tied the final loop of her belt she leaned in and kissed him, a real kiss—soft and sensual. Surprised, Nick pulled her close, holding on until she jerked away.

"Okay then." He felt himself blush. "Now let's have some breakfast. I haven't had my coffee yet."

"That's not good," chuckled Gloria as they followed her down the stairs.

June was calm, settled for now. Nick brewed himself a coffee while Gloria prepared June's breakfast. He felt the tension slip from his neck and shoulders as the coffee steamed into his cup. June glanced at him as he sat across from her and took his first sip of the day. He smiled, hoping to elicit one from her. "It's good," he said.

She moved her head. It was barely a nod.

"The coffee, it's nice on this rainy morning."

June stared over his shoulder, out the window.

"I have a treat for you this morning," said Gloria, smiling as she set a couple of scones in front of June.

June looked down at the plate.

"Scones," said Gloria. "Like I promised."

"Jam. Strawberry jam."

Gloria chuckled. "No, they're jammy scones, like my mama's. The jam's inside."

"I want…mm…mom's scones." June shoved the plate away and muttered, "No, no, no."

Nick looked at Gloria in disbelief. "You changed the recipe?" He tried to swallow the accusation. "Damn it! You know you can't change things!"

Gloria flinched, turned away from him, then calmly spoke to June. "I can get you some jam, so you can add it—"

"No."

Gloria shrunk back. "I...I can cut one open, maybe scrape out the jam?"

"No! No!" June hammered her fist on the table. "No! No! No!"

Nick grabbed a scone from June's plate and took an angry bite. "Ummm. Delicious." He spat out the words.

Gloria looked close to tears. "I'm, I'm sorry—"

"Don't," said Nick, holding up his hand. "Just get her something else." He turned to June. "What about eggs?"

June pinched her lips together and shook her head in exaggerated defiance.

"Oatmeal? Toast? Yogurt? A banana?" Each word was louder, heavier.

"No! Scones!" June shouted, beating both fists on the table.

"June! Stop it." Nick could feel the fury building but his impatience overpowered his good sense.

"Scones!" June stared at him, her mouth set, her eyes full of hate.

"You're not a child. These scones are delicious. I want you to eat one."

June covered her ears and closed her eyes.

"Frosted Flakes?" offered Gloria. She'd filled a bowl with cereal and milk.

"Alright," exhaled Nick, acquiescing in the face of defeat.

Gloria set the bowl and a spoon in front of June.

"June." Nick was trying to control his temper. "Eat your cereal."

No reaction.

"JUNE!"

June opened her eyes. "No!" The scream left her lips at the same moment her left arm shot forward and, with the force of an angry toddler, she sent the bowl flying, stippling the wall with milk and sticky flakes.

"Stop it!" Nick yelled. He was furious, filled with fear and hatred—for himself, for June and for the whole god-damned world.

June slumped low in her chair; her pink fluffy robe soaked in milk. She placidly gathered bits of the gooey flakes on the end of her finger, then licked them off.

Nick wanted to absolve her, to forgive her. He wanted her back. He needed to love her, to hug her. June refused to let him near or even let him in. She rocked back and forth, doodling in the milk, calming herself as Gloria cleaned up the soggy cereal and the broken bowl.

Nick offered to help, but Gloria just shook her head. He mumbled an inadequate apology, then fled to his office along with the plate of culpable pastries. He'd treated Gloria badly, completely lost it. Shit. He closed his eyes, trying to alleviate the throbbing in his temples. He briefly considered a remedial Scotch, but it wasn't even nine o'clock. He opened his computer, scanned through the news, then printed off the day's crossword. He read through the across clues without filling in a single word.

At ten he called Enid.

CHAPTER TWENTY-TWO

Nick slammed his door, which rocked the car but did little to alleviate his frustration. He'd almost turned around in the parking lot when June declared she wanted to go home. He had arranged this visit after talking with Enid. She thought it would be good for June to see Whispering Pines and Nick knew Enid wanted to meet June.

"Come on, sweetheart. Let's go. They're waiting for us." He had held the passenger door open, willing June to move.

"No." June shook her head. "I don't like this—"

"Come on. You don't know that."

"Smells bad." June looked straight ahead.

"No, no. That was a different place, Green fuc—" *Stay calm. Be patient.* It wasn't fair to be so frustrated with June. "That place was called Green Acres. We went there a while back. I didn't like it either. But this one, well it's much nicer. Come on. I'll show you."

"Nope."

"June. Look at me, please." June slowly turned her head just enough so Nick, bending into the car, could see her face. "Trust me. It's nice here. Martha and I came a couple of weeks ago and—"

"Martha! She's trying to lock me up." June stared ahead again. This wasn't new. June had become paranoid lately, suspicious of nearly everyone, especially Martha and Gloria. It was unpredictable and arbitrary. The smallest thing could set her off. Ironically, suspicion seemed to enhance her ability to connect and communicate.

"No, not true." Nick curbed his anger with a long deep breath, closed the door and leaned heavily against the car. He was already exhausted. This might be a good time to take up smoking, long luxurious cigars. He had no idea how this appointment would go, assuming he could first move June out of the front seat and then into the building. He kicked a small stone with the toe of his shoe and sent it skittering across the pavement.

"Hi. Is everything okay? Do you need any help?" Nick looked up and saw a woman approaching. He started to shake his head.

"Are you the Walkers?"

"Yes," answered Nick. She was tall, taller than him. And very young.

"Welcome!" She extended her hand and shook Nick's firmly. "I'm Mel Gordon. I'm going to show you around today."

Although they hadn't been formally introduced, Nick recognized her from his previous visit. Like the rest of the staff Mel was dressed in smart, comfortable street clothes, solid colours, no uniforms here. "Hi, I'm—"

"Nick, yes. It's nice to meet you. Do you need some help?"

Yes, he did, but he wasn't ready to admit it. Before he could answer, Mel moved toward June. She tapped lightly on the window, waited a few seconds and then slowly opened the car door. She paused again and then squatted down, resting on her heels.

"Hi, June. I'm Mel." She held out her hand, not for a greeting, but palm up, a calm, peaceful gesture. "Would you like to see what we have planned for you today? June?"

June lifted her head. "Mel? That's a man's name."

"You're right." Mel laughed. "And that's what my mom says."

Nick smiled, relaxed by Mel's confidence.

"She calls me Melanie so you can too, if you'd like." She lightly touched June's hand then slowly took it in her own. "What a beautiful ring! Did Nick give you that?" As Melanie spoke, she gently but deliberately guided June from her seat, managing and supporting her as she set one foot and then the other on the ground.

"It's my wedding ring. Do you know Nick?" June looked at Mel suspiciously.

"Oh no," chuckled Mel. "We just met. Like you and me."

"Okay," said June.

"Would you like to see inside? I have so much to show you." Mel's euphonious voice was enticing. Even Nick wanted to see what she had planned.

June reached up and touched Mel's golden hair, which, loosely gathered into a messy knot, was bobbing in time with her words. "Pretty."

"Thank you!"

The two women walked into Whispering Pines, hand in hand. Nick followed, impressed but still worried. June's mood swings were unpredictable.

Mel guided them through the building, stopping to rest when June needed. They sat for a while with Enid and met the ladies who were in the lounge, knitting, but mostly chatting. June didn't say much, but she didn't complain either. Mel told them the names of some of the residents as they passed their rooms and pointed out the photos and keepsakes displayed in the shadow box frames beside each door. They stopped at an open door, an empty suite, the one Nick had tentatively chosen for them, two bedrooms, on the ground floor with a private patio. It was the only available unit and fortunately it had a view of the gardens.

"And this would be yours." Mel made a sweeping gesture towards an open door. "If you decide to join us."

June followed the motion of Melanie's hand and stepped just inside the doorway.

Nick trailed behind and nudged June a little further into the suite. He felt a tightening in his gut. What would they do if she hated it?

"It's nice, isn't it June?" Mel was speaking calmly, directly to June. "It's such a lovely place, quiet and in the morning you can hear the birds."

June stood still, stiff and unresponsive.

"June?" Nick took a few steps towards the patio door. "Look. There's a nice garden!" He sounded eager, too keen. "Well, what'd you think? It's great, isn't it? Do you like it?"

"No." June turned and shuffled out.

Mel was close behind. "Well then, let's go have a cup of tea and some cookies. Or one of those yummy looking cupcakes." She gently took June's elbow and steered her towards the dining room.

"Is there chocolate?"

The conversation faded as Nick surveyed the empty rooms. Could they really do this? They'd be right on top of each other, all day, every day. He stuffed his hands in his pockets. He felt like he was being crushed, packed in a slowly shrinking box. Dementia had first stolen their time and now their space was going too. This space, what there was of it, felt claustrophobic, airless. He moved around slowly, running his hand along the walls to confirm they weren't closing in on him.

The bedroom was small, hopefully big enough for their king-bed. The living space worried him more. No room for most of their stuff. The kitchen was tiny, utilitarian, but then neither of them would be cooking. He approximated the space for his espresso machine.

Nick moved to the windows, dragged his fingers across the cool glass and walked the few steps back to the centre of the room. He turned, slowly, until he'd completed a full circle. He felt his world spinning, spiraling down, down. "Home." It echoed back at him. *Home. Home.* He had to make it fit. Damn it!

**

Enid's call a few days later didn't surprise him. She couldn't hold the suite much longer, not without a deposit so Nick promised to go through the contract and get back to her that day. It was a pretty standard agreement. The monthly fee included all meals served in the dining room or delivered to the suite. Guest meals were charged to the resident. The monthly fee was set for a year but then increased with the cost of living. This seemed fair to Nick. A one-time upfront charge covered all the facilities, like the pool, the gym, crafts rooms, a minivan for field trips and the coffee shop. His parking space would be extra. Laundry, clothes and bedding, was done weekly and always on the same day. Pill monitoring and distribution were included. Prescriptions were refilled by the nurse. It was all pretty standard and mostly acceptable. The cost would rise substantially as June's care needs increased. Basic morning and evening care was included, but anything more was charged by the hour. And, if June needed to be moved to the extended care floor their costs would double. That was hard to swallow.

Nick used his red pen to highlight the sections that needed negotiating and clarifying: how many hours of care were provided? Would their laundry be done separately and not with the other residents? He refused to label all his clothes like a kid going to Boy Scout camp! When he questioned the unlocked door policy, *Jesus they wouldn't have any privacy,* Enid confirmed that, as per the Fire Marshall, all suites had to remain unlocked. Nick couldn't argue with that, but they had gone back and forth on a few things. The biggest being the cost of two suites if they had to be separated. Enid wouldn't budge on the monthly fees, but pointed out that Nick could move into a smaller unit just for him. Nick pushed back a little and Enid offered him a parking spot at no cost for two years. And she had agreed to let Nick bring his espresso maker. That was a win!

Enid had sent him the revised contract the next morning. He'd printed and filed it on the corner of his desk and hadn't touched it since. He needed more time. Time to settle some things. Time to get June used to the idea of moving and packing up a lifetime. And he had to sell the house or at least find out what it was worth these days. He could find more excuses if he tried, but he had to decide—one way or the other.

He slipped the Whispering Pines brochure out of the file folder. It was glossy and sophisticated. Picture-perfect granny and grandpa faces smiled at him. They all looked happy. He let the words seduce him, hoping to find his answer in the clever advertising, boutique residence, vibrant community, continuum of care, outdoor oasis, peace of mind. He could hear Martha telling him to take it. He turned to the back page. The rates no longer made him flinch. He'd accepted the cost, just not everything that came with signing the damned contract. He knew in his heart what was best. Even the doctors agreed. Then why the hell did he feel so guilty? Because he knew June. He'd thought he'd lost her once, long ago, but she'd come back and they'd made promises. They'd made plans, but they'd never imagined one of them fading away, living but lost.

The diagnosis, they now knew, was LBD, Lewy Body Dementia which, according to the doctors, could have been worse. Really? Yes, this was a slower, less aggressively debilitating form of dementia than say Parkinson's or even Alzheimer's, but Nick was having trouble seeing the silver lining. There were no magic pills, operations or chemical therapies on which to hang even a sliver of hope. The examinations, tests, and scans were of little value except to generate a guidebook, a ghastly roadmap to June's inescapable future.

Nick was angry at this fucked up world. June was an amazing woman, kind and compassionate, a good wife and loving mother. Oh sure, she wasn't perfect. He closed his eyes, trying to prevent the long censored images from invading his consciousness.

They'd moved on and he'd become a better husband. She didn't deserve this fate. What kind of God does this to a good woman? Maybe they'd backed the wrong God? He slammed the brochure down on his desk launching the computer mouse to the floor. It slid under the credenza.

"Shit." Nick bent to retrieve the runaway mouse and spotted the liquor bottles on his way up. A short shot would calm him, but no. He opened his Whispering Pines file and leafed past the *Residency Agreement* to the intake forms. He'd already filled them out, checked all the boxes except *move-in date.* Maybe he could pay for a month and buy some time to silence the debate in his head. He'd hate living there, but June would have good care. His life would be easier, but June would hate it. It wasn't big enough, but this house was too much for them. What about Gloria? What about June? What about him?

Intending to pace, Nick pushed back his chair and stood up. Instead, he filled a glass with a double shot of Scotch and set it on the corner of his desk. He sat down and watched the light catch the caramel liquid and reflect through the cuts of crystal. He picked up his pen, signed his name at the bottom of the last page, fed the contract into the scanner and attached it to the email he'd already prepared for Enid. He pressed *send* then logged into his bank account and transferred the sizeable deposit. No turning back now.

The sound of Gloria's warm deep laugh drifted through his open window. Nick turned and could see June and Gloria on the patio. It was a little chilly, but June needed the fresh air. The rain had kept her in all week. He stretched the muscles in his arms and shoulders, breathing in the smell of autumn. The trees they'd planted as saplings, one for each twin, towered over the house now. The pool was full of leaves and needed to be closed for the winter. He'd sure miss his putting green, June's roses. He picked up his phone and typed a quick text to Martha: *I've signed on the dotted line. Looks like we're moving.*

On the way downstairs he hurried past the photos, the memories they'd be leaving behind. Knowing the bang would frighten June, he held the kitchen door as it closed, then joined June and Gloria on the patio. June was eating the homemade cookies that Norah had brought yesterday. Mercury was home for a visit too. Nick sat down and rubbed Mercury's head. He'd be moving too, likely becoming a permanent resident at Norah's. Nick sat next to June.

"Hi Sweetheart. May I have a cookie?"

"They're good. Peanut butter." June chose one from the container and offered it to Nick. Her hand was shaking.

"Thanks." He took a bite. "Yes, very good."

June nodded and smiled. "Good," she said. The afternoon sun had tinted her cheeks pink.

"June, can you listen, hear me for a minute?"

"Okay." She set her cookie on the table and folded her hands in her lap.

Encouraged by her attention, he didn't allow himself to hesitate. "I've made a decision. We're moving to Whispering Pines."

June's eyes widened. "Whispering Pines?" She smiled, a sly little grin. "Mel. Cupcakes?"

"Yes. At Whispering Pines."

June held a finger to her lips. She leaned forward and spoke softly. "Trees don't talk. It's the fairies. My fairies are whispering there."

Nick sunk back in the chair. Taking this as compliance was risky but it was all he had.

CHAPTER TWENTY-THREE

Martha stood by the open dining room window, fanning herself with one of a set of eight woven rattan placemats. "My god it's hot. Can we turn on the AC?"

June rotated her head slowly from side to side and pulled her blanket up to her chin. "Cold," she whispered.

"Mom, it's like a hundred and fifty degrees in here." They were enjoying an unseasonably warm spring and knowing her mom's need for extra sweaters, Martha had dressed in layers. She was down to her tank top and running shorts, her hair tucked into one of her dad's baseball caps, which she'd turned backwards in a cheeky defiance of fashion.

"Warm for babies." June spoke sharply now.

"What?" It was becoming harder and harder to follow her mom's thoughts.

"Your babies. Keep them warm."

Dad shook his head in his *just go along with it* way.

Martha sighed but her mother persisted.

"Martha babies!"

"Oh Mom. No. There are no Martha babies."

Dad froze, a candlestick in each hand. Even from across the room she could feel his empathy. *It's okay*, she mouthed to reassure him, but maybe more to console herself. Martha stepped away and tossed the placemats into a cardboard box labeled in bold red letters, *Giveaways*. She was proud of her system: *Keep, Donate, Throw Away*. So logical and orderly. *Trash* was written in black on an optimistically large box and they'd leave it to the movers to pack up all the things they were keeping. She'd been forced to add a third carton which she reluctantly labeled *Undecided* in green. Martha tried not to argue every time an item was added to this box even though it violated her *Touch it once and only once rule*. But Dad had insisted, convincing her it was necessary to help her mom deal with all the changes.

"Consider it therapy, for all of us." He'd winked and smiled while

Martha counted to ten.

"You look...like a boy."

"What? You don't like the hat, Mom?" Martha laughed, but then realized her mother had spoken a rare full sentence. Her mind jumped in and out of reality these days. Strangely, in the last few months, since her father had finalized the move, she'd had bouts of near clarity, short but remarkably lucid. Dad stuck close to her now, admitting he couldn't risk missing her good episodes. He looked tired today. This was all too much for him.

They'd procrastinated the move as long as they could, celebrating both Christmas and Mom's birthday in the house as well as Valentine's Day when Gloria had introduced them to Filipino food. Gloria had helped them place an order from *Kitchen Manila,* a new local restaurant and all four of them enjoyed a variety of dishes that Gloria rated from *Good* to *Absolutely Perfect.* But now they literally had to get moving. The suite was almost ready. The new furniture had been delivered and in a couple of weeks, movers would bring a few pieces from the house. Martha wasn't sure how she was going to persuade her parents to walk out the front door, away from the house they'd lived in for more than fifty years.

"So, I look like a boy, do I?" Martha did her best impression of a cocky male. She rubbed her mother's boney shoulders, happy to have made her smile. "Actually, Mom, I'm dressed for sorting and packing. And I'd better get back at it."

Martha eyed all the crystal and fine China in the hutch and wondered if sorting through all of Mom's favourite things would keep her present for a while. Martha pulled open a drawer, expecting to find fine linen tablecloths and napkins, all carefully starched and pressed. Instead, the deep drawer was full of crayon drawings, glittery crafts, string art, and finger paintings.

"Mom! This looks like every piece of art we ever brought home from school. You kept all this?" She held up a stack of yellowed and crumbling papers. The top one was a Thanksgiving turkey, with painted feathers and obviously traced from the outline of a child's tiny hand.

"Treasures." Her mother leaned forward and pulled on a green ribbon. A long, articulated dachshund emerged from the pile. She draped the paper dog over her knees and read the barely legible words written on each section. "T-t-t-to...Mom...love...Jonny."

"That's cute. I remember those." Martha sifted through the artwork.

"Here's our macaroni self-portraits. I can't believe you saved all of these."

"And in the dining room," added her dad. He pulled open the bottom drawer. "This one is full of photos." He picked up a handful. "Family photos."

Martha shuffled through them. "These were all in albums. Didn't you sort through them years ago, Mom?"

Her mom sat straight in the elegant dining chair, composed and resolute. "Mine."

"Okay, the photos are yours, but where are all the tablecloths and the linen napkins? Those lovely damask placemats?" She knew by heart what should be in these drawers. She and Jonathan had been tasked with setting the table for family dinners every Sunday night.

"Gone."

"Gone?" Her mother had collected some exquisite pieces over the years, and Martha had planned to keep them. "Gone where?" asked Martha.

June pushed aside her blanket, raised her hands, palms upward and shrugged. "Dunno."

Her dad chuckled. "We can't argue with that, can we?"

"No, but…they were vintage and…I actually liked them." She smiled and shook off her disappointment. "Well at least there's a little less to donate now. Are we keeping your treasures, Mom?"

"Yes ma'am!" declared Mom, her face bright with the happiness that Martha remembered, and missed.

Martha bent and hugged her mother. "Well then, we're going to need a few more boxes."

Dad laughed and moved all the photos and artwork to the dining room table. They sorted quickly as it was clear which had to go, especially the artful creations made from edibles: macaroni creatures, Cheerio necklaces and pretzel reindeer antlers had all deteriorated beyond repair.

"I'm surprised we don't have mice," said Dad.

"No mice." Mom assured him.

Martha laughed. "That's good." She was trying to stay cheerful. Mom and Dad seemed happy, but she couldn't help noticing that Jonathan's artwork had a much higher survival rate than hers. Dad helped with the slow work of sorting the photos, adding pictures of her when it became clear that Mom was mostly choosing ones of Jonny. Luckily, she and her brother were twins so it was impossible to leave Martha out completely.

Martha could understand why Mom had hung onto these simple things for so long. Couples in her divorce cases often fought over the silliest things. But Mom had moved these things, crafts and photos, from the storage closet in the basement and chose to keep them all. When did she do this? Was she already too sick to realize what she was doing? Or had she known she'd never remember unless she had something to remind her? Of Jonathan, mostly. He'd been gone so long—maybe the photos and the coloured handprints helped her recall or relive the past that was slipping away.

Martha opened an envelope and pulled out a thin stack of photos. "Who's this?" She placed them on the table in front of her mother.

"Jonny...sss."

"No, it's not Jonathan." Martha picked one up and turned it over, looking for a name, or date. "It looks like a girl. And these pictures aren't that old." She held it up so Dad could get a good look.

"No idea."

"Can I throw them out, Mom?"

"No."

"Really?" Martha tossed them on the table, next to the pile of family pictures. Her mother stretched from her chair, slowly gathered the baby photos in her hands and pointed to the drawer.

"Okay then." Martha wasn't willing to fight over a few photos. "But that's it, Mom. We really must start getting rid of things."

Despite the smug little smile on her mother's face, Martha was happy to give her the victory.

Together they tackled the remaining things in the buffet. There were no more big surprises but instead several butter dishes, a collection of novelty mugs including ones from CN Tower and Niagara Falls and Martha's favourite, *World's Sexiest Husband*. Martha set this one in the middle of the table, causing her father to blush. Although her mom was tiring, nodding off every so often, they were moving along more efficiently now, donating things none of them had used or seen in years. Martha decided to donate a boxed set of eight gilded napkin rings, inexplicably shaped liked snails.

"Oh!" Mom revived with a start. "Ger…Gerr…tttt."

"Great Aunt Gertrude," said Dad. "A long-ago gift. We don't need them. Hell, I don't think we've ever used them."

"Once." Her mother pointed towards the napkin rings. "Hate 'em."

Martha grabbed the box and lined it up for a shot. With a perfect arc they landed in the giveaway box. "And just like that, they're gone."

Mom rewarded her with a tired thumb's up.

"How do you do that, Mom?" Getting no reply she turned to her father. "I don't get it. She remembers Great Aunt Gertie? And most days she doesn't know who I am." She'd had this struggle before but there wasn't time for a pity party today.

Martha felt her dad's hand on her shoulder. "I know. It hurts but that's why we're doing this."

"Yeah," murmured Martha. "Too bad we don't have more help, like from our missing link."

Her dad looked confused. "Oh. Jonathan?" he whispered under his breath.

"Yes. He could probably get Mom to dump all this stuff. She's always been on team Jonathan."

"Hmph."

"What?"

"Don't get me started."

Martha glanced at her mother. She'd closed her eyes again. "Still angry?"

"Yeah, he manages to get under my skin — even when he's not here." He shrugged. "Maybe even more now. I am angry, Martha, royally pissed off. He should be here. But no—not Jonathon." He lowered his voice. "He's busy, missing in action so to speak. Doing what exactly? Skiing? Partying? Drinking himself into an early grave? Jesus Christ!"

"Dad, I've tried but—"

"No, this isn't on you. It's him and when I think back to all those fights, the insolence. He was always such a smart ass. Your mother tried to keep the peace. But Jonathan and I were like oil and water." He picked up a wine glass and swaddled it in bubble wrap.

"Oh, Dad." Should she reach out to Jon again? Maybe she could get someone at the office to track him down or at least find his new number.

Gloria poked her head into the room. "Sorry to interrupt, but I think Mrs. Walker would be more comfortable in bed."

Martha nodded. "Do you need help?"

"No thanks, we're good," said Gloria.

Martha watched as her mother shuffled away holding onto Gloria's arm.

"That makes me so sad," said Martha. She busied herself with a new roll of tape, fighting back the tears. "I'm scared Dad. For Mom. For you. There's so much stuff here. And Mom's no longer capable of—" She choked on the tears. "I need Mom. I need you." She buried her face in her father's chest, surprised and comforted by the strong rhythm of his heart.

"I'm worried too, sweetheart." He hugged her tight. "I'm afraid this might be the easy part and that scares me because it's so damned hard."

"Geez, don't say that." Martha stepped back and surveyed the room. "I was just starting to feel like we're getting somewhere."

"We are! At least those damn ugly snail things are gone."

Martha laughed. "Gone forever. But Mom—"

"Look, none of this has been easy. There's been days when I just want to give up. But you've kept me going. And your mom, well, she's come through too, some days, somehow, in ways I just can't explain. We're doing the right thing. Once we've moved, you'll get a bit of a break. You've helped us so much."

Martha shook her head. "Not really."

"But you have and now you won't have to worry. Well, at least not as much."

"I guess so."

"You know, sometimes what I fear most turns out to be okay, not amazing or great but okay. And most days that's enough."

"Is it?"

"Well, it's all I've got right now." He cleared his throat. "And I do apologize for losing my cool about your brother."

"Your cool?" Martha laughed. "Oh, Dad, I think you lost that a long time ago." She wiped away her tears and loaded the new roll of tape in the tape gun. "Okay, let's get back to work." She opened the doors of the China cabinet and took out a dinner plate. "Can we give all this stuff away?"

"That's our wedding china!"

Martha stepped back, almost doubling over with laughter. "You're just as bad as Mom! You're a sentimental old goat." She pulled back her arm as if to whirl the plate in his direction, a classic frisbee toss. He winced. "Don't worry. I'm well aware that these are going into safe storage in my basement. I'm not about to break my mother's heart. Yours either, apparently."

Dad chuckled, relieved and amused. "If we work fast, we can get this room done while your mom's resting."

"Let's do it." Martha picked up a small but heavy glass bowl. "I might keep this pickle dish." She turned it over in her hands.

"That's an ashtray."

"Really? You smoked?"

"Back in the day, before it was unhealthy."

"Dad, it's always been unhealthy."

"There's a lot we didn't know back then. Keep it if you want. It'd make a decent pickle dish. Reuse and recycle."

Martha wrapped the ashtray in packing paper and put it in the donation box. "All this talk of pickles has made me hungry. Let's break for lunch."

"Good idea. Gloria might be a while. Would you like a bowl of soup and a sandwich? Ham? Tuna?"

"So, you've added chef to your resumé?"

"I make a pretty decent omelette too if—" The doorbell interrupted him.

"Chef's choice. I'll get the door." Martha took off her hat and used her fingers to comb through her hair, releasing the curls and some of the tension in her back. She pulled open the door expecting a neighbour, perhaps a parcel. Instead, she was face to face with her brother.

For a moment she couldn't take it in. Then anger washed over her— a flood of red-hot rage. Mom's precious Jonny, casually dropping by. She wanted to slap him. Hard.

"What are you doing here?"

He had the nerve to grin, going for the trademark Jonathan charm. "You invited me, remember?"

"Four fucking years ago!" she hissed and pushed forward, making Jonathan backup. "Dad can't see you." She stepped onto the porch, barefoot and angry. She pulled the door closed behind her.

"Uh, that's kinda the reason I'm here—to mend some bridges."

God what an idiot. Jonathan just showing up. It'd be like dropping a bomb in the middle of the calm she'd managed to put together. "More likely, you'd give him a heart attack."

Martha couldn't tell what was going on behind his sunglasses—Ray Ban Aviators no less.

"I can't believe you'd just show up here. Why didn't you call?"

"Yeah, it's not that I didn't consider it. But I figured I'd take my chances."

Martha snorted. She was furious, wanted to strangle him but she kept her voice low. "So, you thought an ambush was the way to go?" She pushed and prodded him across the driveway to the side of the house where they'd be concealed by the cedar hedge.

"Stop shoving me. I get it. You don't want Dad to see me. Jeez you haven't changed at all."

"Well neither have you." Martha looked into his face, never a mirror image of her own but now, suitably lined with the same signs of aging and even a few extra wrinkles. "Look, don't do this, not this way. We...no, I need to...prepare them." Beads of sweat trickled down her spine soaking the waistband of her shorts. "Meet me later, tonight. Then we'll figure out a better plan."

"Really? You're in charge now?"

Martha glared at him. "Just shut up and trust me." She poked her finger into his shoulder, two, three, four times.

"Okay. Okay." He slapped away her hand. "You come to me. I'm at the Marriott." They heard the front door open.

"Shit!" Martha gasped. "I'll be there at six. Just stay right here so I can distract Dad."

"Martha? Lunch is ready."

She turned to Jon and pulled an invisible zipper across her lips. "Coming Dad," she called out. "You stay here," she whispered. "I'll see you tonight, six o'clock. Sharp."

Jon nodded in agreement and leaned against the garage wall. "Nice to see you too, Sis."

Martha ignored him and hurried back across the driveway, suddenly aware of the hellfire radiating from the asphalt.

"Who was at the door?"

"Just a salesman. Can I interest you in some frozen steaks? Shrimp?"

Dad chuckled. "No, I'm good. But a ham and cheese on rye awaits."

Martha walked inside, closed and locked the door without looking back.

CHAPTER TWENTY-FOUR

Martha arrived at the Marriott just before six. Jonathan wasn't in the lobby or at the bar. She decided to wait where she could see the elevators and chose one of the armchairs that dotted the lobby. She was nervous, fidgety and annoyed for feeling anxious. It's just Jon, she reminded herself. *Stop fretting. You're the good egg. Jon has so many miles to go before—*

"Ahem—"

Martha jumped, startled by the hotel employee standing in front of her.

"Oh, I'm sorry!" His voice crackled with uncertainty. He was young, with stylishly cropped hair and a sparse neat beard. His nervousness was explained by his name tag: *TRAINEE*

"Yes?"

He glanced at the piece of paper in his hand. "Are you...ah...maybe...waiting for a Jon Walker?"

"I am," replied Martha with a smile he'd never see, as he seemed to be afraid to look at her.

"Oh good. He asked us—" The young man sighed and took a breath. "He's in the dining room."

"Thank you." But he'd already scurried back to the desk. So, Jonathan wanted to stretch this into a dinner. She smoothed out her jacket, set her shoulders, prepping and composing herself. It's just Jon, she repeated. Just Jon.

The dining room was surprisingly chic, modern yet warm, a rugged stone wall behind the bar was softened by the simplicity of the modern wooden tables and high-backed chairs. Only a few of the tables were occupied. Jon was seated at one with a leather banquette, the colour of Martha's morning lattes. She signalled the hostess, interrupting her chat with a waiter.

"Excuse me." The hostess looked at her. "I'm with that man, over there." Martha pointed out Jonathan who hadn't noticed her "And we're going to need a proper table. One with chairs." She didn't wait for a reply but walked toward her brother. "I don't think I agreed to dinner." Her voice bounced back at her, harsh, judgmental. She wasn't about to cut Jonathan any slack. He'd better have come prepared.

"Well, we all have to eat," he replied quickly. "And hello."

"Yes, but *you* wouldn't be on my list of preferred dinner companions." She stood beside the table, unwilling to sit down and making no attempt to hide her rising temper. Surely he didn't think she was here to make nice and forgive him. "What are you doing here, exactly?"

"Well, I tried to tell you this afternoon, but—"

"Look, Jon, we, and by *we* I mean Mom, Dad and I, can't handle any more problems or…" Martha searched for the right word, one that would make it clear he couldn't ask for their help, or anything else for that matter. "…or burdens. Things are hard enough right now and to me, you are just another problem."

"Jesus, that's harsh."

"And ignoring your family, your ailing mother for years isn't? So, what do you need?"

"No! I don't need anything. And…I won't…oh shit." Jon slid clumsily along the bench seat and stood in front of Martha. "Could we maybe call a truce? Just until you hear me out?" He extended his arms for a hug.

"Nope," she said, stepping back. "That's not happening."

A red blush rose from under Jonathan's collar. "Seriously? Okay, I get it. Persona non grata."

"What did you expect? Four fucking years, Jon. And you never explained why. A few cryptic texts don't count as staying in touch."

"I'm sorry."

Martha glanced around for the waitress. She wanted a table and glass of wine. "Sorry doesn't cut it, not by a long shot."

"Well, I am."

Jon stepped closer. He'd always been a lot taller than her and even in her heels she had to look up to stare him down.

"I've missed you, Boo Boo Bear," said Jon, surprising Martha with a quick kiss on the cheek. "Missed you a lot."

Martha wiped her cheek with the back of her hand "I think we can retire that ludicrous epithet."

"Okay, consider it gone." Jon chuckled. "Would you like a drink?"

She thought he'd be nervous, unsettled like her. But no. He looked different even from this afternoon—composed and confident. He had shed that sad, hangdog look that had branded him in his teens and every time she'd seen him drunk.

"Yes, please. But not here." She sounded petulant, but she didn't care. "I'm getting us a different table. I don't do booths."

"Fine by me." Jonathan shrugged as a smile spread across his face.

Was he mocking her? She ignored the reserved sign and dropped her purse onto an empty chair at a nearby table for four. "Here, this will be more comfortable. Sit down."

"Yes ma'am. You're still in charge, I see."

"Yes, only now I don't just follow the rules, I make them." She was willing to spar, if that's what he wanted.

Jon laughed. "Look I know you're pissed about today. I'm sorry. I didn't know you'd be at the house, but I shouldn't've just showed up like that. I thought it would be best, like ripping off a bandage. But you're right. I needed a better plan. I am really sorry, for what it's worth."

"Not much." She raised a finger to the waitress. "You've needed a better plan for quite some time. Like, one that didn't include abandoning your family."

"You're right," agreed Jonathan.

"Yes I am."

"Look." Jon smiled. "Can we *not* fight? Let's talk this out." He settled easily into the chair across from Martha.

"You're such a dumbass."

Jon nodded slowly, opened his mouth to speak, but stopped, as if suddenly remembering his request for a cease-fire.

She reached into her purse, set her phone on the table. "You really are, you know. A giant-sized dumbass." It sounded childish, but she seemed to have lost the loftier words. Just having him here, face to face, was eroding her defences. Would Jon ever acknowledge the hurt he'd caused? How could he? He had no idea how hard the last several years had been—Dad's heart, Mom's dementia, finding a place for them, all while surpassing her required billable hours. And then the divorce. She'd handled countless others but until she'd found herself single and alone, she'd never fully understood the longevity of heartbreak.

Martha looked up and studied Jon's face. A few deep frown lines crossed his forehead, but she could see the affable boyhood twinkle in his eyes. She'd loved him so much. Could she forgive him? Maybe. Now that he was here, letting go of some of her anger seemed more possible. Yet, all those years. She slid her hand across the table, almost meeting his. Her brother, her twin, divided yet connected. "I've missed you too." She wanted to believe it.

Jon squeezed her hand. She pulled free just as the waitress arrived at the table with two empty glasses and a bottle of water. "Could we order drinks, please?" Martha focused on the name tag pinned to her pocket. "Uh, Wyllow?"

"Yeah," the young waitress said. "My mom was kind of a hippie." She poured them each a glass of ice water and set the bottle on the table. "What can I get for you?" she asked, looking at Jonathan.

"A glass of red," said Martha as she studied the menu. "The Amarone."

Wyllow leaned in, peering at the small print.

Martha highlighted her choice with a perfectly manicured nail. "This one. The Masi."

"Great," said Wyllow. "That's a nice one." She scribbled on her pad. She'd likely never heard of the wine but now realized she might be getting a healthy tip. She turned back to Jonathan, pen at the ready.

"A Coke, please, large, diet, on the rocks, any vintage is fine." Jon winked. Wyllow rewarded him with a giggle.

"Cute," said Martha. "I'm sorry. I forgot. I guess you're not drinking?"

"Nope, alcoholism is kinda a long-term thing."

Wyllow chuckled as she walked away.

"Are you—? I ordered wine. Will it bother you?" What was the protocol for drinking with an alcoholic? Was he rehabilitated? Still recovering? She knew so little about his life now.

"No, of course not. It's fine. Lennon has a cocktail once in a while.

We just don't keep it in the house." He inhaled sharply.

"Lennon?"

Jon stared past her. He fiddled with his napkin, twisting it around his fingers.

She noticed the ring. "You're wearing a ring…are you…like committed? Together?"

It wasn't a difficult question, but it seemed to have silenced Jon. He ran his index finger through the condensation on the side of his water glass and clicked his tongue but said nothing.

"Jonathan?" She was curious, but willing to wait. Jon seemed lost in thought. The uncomfortable silence probably lasted just a minute or two but seemed like forever.

Jon leaned forward. "Well—"

Wyllow arrived with their drinks. She set down coasters then the beverages, making a bit of a production of Jon's.

"Thanks," said Martha, dismissing her. "So?" Martha swirled the red elixir, coaxing it up the sides of the glass while Jon slowly peeled the paper from his straw and worked the bits into a tiny white ball. She took a sip. Lovely. "Let's hear it."

"What was the question again?" Jon's tone matched his cheeky smile.

"Lennon? That ring?"

"Right! Well, yes, Lennon and I are married. Almost three years now."

Martha choked, almost wasting a delicious swallow of the Amarone. "Three years? Wow, that's a long time." Mom wasn't too bad back then, but Jon hadn't even told them. "Well, it's a bit belated, but congratulations." Martha raised her glass and clinked it against Jon's. "Details please. Did you have a big wedding? Lots of friends? No family, obviously."

Jon shook his head, sighed. "I know. You have every right to be upset, but—"

Silence again. Martha refused to fill it, waiting while it spread. She took a sip of wine then chugged it, emptying the glass.

"Well, the wedding was simple."

"Some details would be nice."

"Um, okay. Yeah, you might need another glass of for this."

"That bad?"

"No. Nothing bad, but—"

"But?" Martha had little patience for Jonathan's dramatics.

"No buts. I just wish I'd shared it with you a whole lot sooner." He signaled for another round of drinks.

"Me too." Martha allowed the edge to slip from her voice. "Me too, Jon."

Jon squared his shoulders and drew himself up. "Well, obviously, a lot has changed since I talked to you...after Dad's heart attack. I know. I ghosted you. It wasn't just the drinking. AA helped but I'd lost everything. I didn't come home at first because, well, apparently you can't leave the jurisdiction until you've satisfied the court ordered rehab and community service. And then when Dad got sick—look I screwed up. Screwed up big time. The night I called you, I had every intention of using the ticket and flying home. But I got into my own head and—well, I felt so guilty, useless and— I'm not making excuses but that night, I drowned my guilt and all my progress at AA in a bottle of vodka. I was embarrassed and ashamed and I couldn't imagine facing our formidable patriarch."

"Oh, I didn't know. Court ordered for what?"

"DUI." Jon sighed. "A car accident, at night, while driving home from the bar. It was late and the road was dark and narrow—sounds like a country song, doesn't it?"

"A bit," said Martha.

"Well. I swerved to miss a deer, not that the cops believed me." His attempt at a smile failed. "But I swear there was one—it was probably just a little Blacktail. I managed to miss it but I caught the gravel shoulder and skidded off the road, took out a mailbox and a hedge, then crashed into a panel truck that was parked in the driveway."

"Jesus."

'Yeah. It wasn't pretty. I was drunk and to make it worse, I had so cleverly stashed some pot under my seat."

"Double Jesus."

"Yeah, hence the DUI."

"Oh Jon." Martha whispered, trying to think like a sister and not a lawyer. "Were you hurt?"

"No. Too damn drunk to feel much of anything. I was pretty sore and bruised the next day, when I woke up in jail."

"Oh no!"

"Yup. So, you really didn't know about this?"

"Uh-uh."

"I guess I shouldn't be surprised. I did ask Mom not to tell you. She flew out right away to help me. Found me a place to live, made sure I ate properly and walked me to my mandatory AA meetings—like that wasn't embarrassing at all!"

Martha knew her mother used to talk to Jon, even visited him. She remembered once she'd stayed more than a month, but she'd had no idea why. Had she kept all of Jon's deepest secrets from her dad too? She had so many questions—*How long were you in jail? What were the charges? Do you have a record?* She settled for, "Was it horrible?"

"Yeah."

"But you didn't go to trial? Or serve time?"

"No, I got lucky—just community service."

"That is lucky," said Martha. "You got off pretty easy."

"Well, the night in a jail cell wasn't fun." Jonathan fiddled with the laminated *Happy Hour Specials* card that sat on every table; "But it was the wake-up call I needed."

"Finally."

"I'm a slow learner."

"It's a disease."

"Yeah, I know."

"And not an easy one to beat." She'd give him that.

"No, not easy at all." He finished his Coke in three long gulps. "But some good came out it. I got back into biking." He chuckled. "Fitness by suspended license. And I met Lennon while I was working off my time at the community centre. He volunteered there, still does, coaching kids' basketball. I was assigned to bathroom and garbage duty and mopping floors. We hit it off, dated and now we're together. The wedding was just a small city hall thing."

It was hard not to identify the lump in her chest as jealousy and the pain from her failed marriage. "That's all good news. I just don't understand why you kept it from us."

Jon shook his head. "I really don't know. Maybe because it was all mine and good and I didn't want to break the spell."

"You thought we'd ruin it?"

"No. It wasn't rational—just me hanging on to hope. Look, meeting Lennon was a fluke, loving and marrying him was beyond my wildest dreams. He's my husband, Martha!" Jon's grin said it all.

"Yeah, of all the things I'd pictured for you, married wasn't one of them."

"I know."

"Is he a good man?"

Jon blushed. "He is. Really good. I…probably too good for me."

"You might be right."

"Ouch."

"Sorry, I'm having trouble being happy for you and hating you at the same time," said Martha.

"It's okay. I hated me for a long time too."

"Uh-uh. That *poor me* shtick doesn't suit you anymore. It might work on Mom, but it's old and tired. You need a new routine."

"I'm trying to be honest."

"Honest? About what exactly? Why you left? Why you stayed away or why you suddenly needed to come back?"

"Jesus, you're—I don't even know." He tapped his finger on his temple. "Ah yes, you're just like Dad!"

"And proud of it." So much for the truce. But she was almost enjoying this now.

"Yup. You always were the Walker-in-waiting."

"What! What about you and Mom? You were her golden boy—still are apparently!"

Jon chuckled. Then he took a long sip of his Coke and chuckled again.

"Listen to us. We're too old for this shit."

Martha grinned. "I can almost hear Mom telling us to stop fighting."

"Yeah, when we were like ten."

"I could still take you, you know." Martha flexed her well-toned arm. "I work out."

"Ha! Is that a challenge?" asked Jon.

"No. Not right now, but let's see how the next few days go."

Jon shrunk back, faking fear. It might be the wine talking but Martha liked this Jonathan. He'd changed, maybe improved. Time and alcohol had tempered his boyish guise, but the dimples had survived. She tipped her glass to him. "You look good."

"You seemed surprised."

"I am. You were a bit of a mess last time we talked."

"Yeah." Jon slowly chewed a piece of ice. "That was then—I'm good now. Really good."

"Well, I'm relatively happy for you." She raised her glass. "Congrats Jon. I'm glad you found your way." She was or at least she was trying to be. She picked up a menu. "Shall we eat? I'm very hungry."

"There's more—"

Martha flinched, gripping the menu with both hands. "More than a gay, married, alcoholic twin brother?"

"Yeah. We have a daughter, Lennon and me. She's almost four."

The words barely made sense, but the fierce rush of nausea that overwhelmed her was proof that she'd heard him. No! This was so unfair. Very wrong and totally fucked up!

"Her name is Ruby. I have pictures." Jon thumbed through his phone. "Lennon had started the adoption process before—oh here's a good one."

He pointed his phone toward her. Martha blocked out the screen with her hand, a fiery anger robbing her of words. Why didn't he just shut up?

"Yeah—before we met and so when we got married it made things a little easier. He knew her mother. Ruby had been in foster care and then some crazy shit happened but her mother couldn't take her back. So, she agreed to let him adopt her and—"

"You're...a...a father?"

"Yes, it's crazy, right? Don't you want to see? She's really cute."

She waved him away.

"Martha?"

He seemed to take her silence as permission to keep talking.

"She's changed my life, well, her and Lennon. I can't believe how good things are now, almost perfect." He was leaning forward, perched on the edge of his chair.

"Almost?" She shivered; her fury had turned cold.

"Yeah. And it turns out I miss you guys, Mom and you — even Dad." He grinned. "I want you all to meet Lennon and Ruby."

"Jesus, you're a selfish son-of-a bitch!"

"Whoa!"

"It must be easy to build a new life when you don't have to worry about anyone but yourself."

"You're jealous? Of me?"

"Jealous? Now *you* sound just like our father." She chuckled sarcastically. "How could I possibly be jealous of your fabulous new life, when I've been having so much fun taking care of the elderly and demented?"

"Martha, I—"

"You? You think that it's alright to waltz back in here and drop this on us? Are we just supposed to welcome you back? Arms wide open, bear hugs and pats on the back?" Martha paused, fighting back tears, but they evaporated instantly as her mind, ahead of her emotions, arrived at the obvious. "They're here, aren't they? You brought them with you?"

Jon nodded. A small smile crept across his face. "Yup. They're upstairs in the room. Lennon would love to meet you. Ruby should be in bed but probably isn't."

"No."

"No? You don't want to meet them? Martha, Ruby is your niece." Jon reached out but she snatched her hand away before he could touch her.

"You, you're—You left, ignored us for years. And…and the few times you did appear you were either wasted or about to be. Then, when we needed you most, you disappeared completely. We tried to help you

Jon, but you wrote us off. How can you, even for a minute think this is alright?"

Jon's lips moved, emitting tiny unrecognizable sounds, no words.

"You sit there and expect me to be happy for you? You and your perfect little family? Have you asked about Mom or Dad? No! About me? No again. You want me to celebrate? Yay! Jon is finally happy." She drained her glass.

"Jesus Martha. Slow down. Let's get you some food."

"No, I'm leaving." Martha pushed back her chair and grabbed her purse, sending a knife clattering to the floor. She caught sight of Wyllow scurrying towards her.

"No. Not yet. We're not finished," Jonathan said. He turned to Wyllow. "Could we have some bread, two garden salads and steak frites, both medium rare. And more water. Please." He looked at Martha. "And another glass of the Amarone."

Martha sank back into her seat, too angry to leave, too wounded to crawl away, too...everything. She closed her eyes, willing Jonathan to disappear. "When did you get so bossy?" she finally said. "I don't remember you having a backbone."

Jon winced. "Go ahead. Take your shots. I deserve them all."

"Yes, you do."

Jon seemed calm and unlike her, composed. She stood up. Jon's eyebrows twitched into a skeptical arc.

"Relax, I'm coming back. I'm just going to the ladies' room." She walked away slowly, concentrating on each step, trying to steady her world.

Martha locked the door just as the first sob escaped—a riotous assault of emotions: hate, fear, anger, jealousy. God dammit, Jon. Tears burned her cheeks. The poorly lit mirror hid nothing. "What a mess." A couple of handfuls of water cooled her face. "I hate him." *But he's your brother. You're an aunt. Auntie Martha.* "But Jon's an ass." *Still your brother. Family.* "Shit! Shit! Shit!" Martha leaned heavily against the counter. A couple of glasses of wine and she was talking to the *mirror mirror on the wall.* She really did need something to eat.

She returned to the table, relieved to find the service had been quick. Jon slipped his phone into his pocket.

"Lennon?"

"Yeah, just wanted to let him know—"

"I don't care."

"Okay then." Jon picked up his fork and stabbed a tomato "Martha, are you okay?"

"Of course. I'm fine." She selected a multi-grain bun, split it and stuffed it with butter. Neither spoke, filling their mouths and the silence with greens and carbs.

"Saved by the food," said Jon. "Sorry, I'm not quite sure how to get this conversation going again."

Martha removed the thick cut red onions from her salad. "Let's just eat, maybe a little small talk? Nothing earth-shattering, okay?"

"Small talk. Sure." He carved off a few slices of steak. "Well. Ruby started school this year, JK. We were a bit worried about her socialization skills but—"

"You're just so damned…lucky to have…a child." Martha could feel the onslaught of a fresh batch of tears. She pinched her thigh, a previously successful way to prevent crying.

"I know. She's so—" He stopped, his fork poised in midair. "Oh my god. Martha. I just realized. I'm such an idiot. I'm sorry. You and Peter couldn't have kids. Mom told me you tried and even IVF…but you couldn't—ever…why…why…" He was stammering. "…didn't you try something else? Adoption or—?"

Martha held up her hand, rejecting his sympathy. "It's okay." She surveyed the dining room, worried people were watching, relieved to see it was still mostly empty.

"Do you also know about the divorce?"

Jonathan nodded. "I do."

"I guess I shouldn't be, but I'm surprised Mom shared so much of my personal life with you."

"Well, we stayed close. Mom refused to give up on me, all the visits and phone calls. Until she got sick. She really cared."

"And I didn't —or Dad?"

"Dad didn't seem interested."

"Interested? He hadn't heard from you for a long time, Jon. None of us had."

"I know and I'm truly sorry."

Martha shrugged. "I'm not sure if that's enough. The last few years have been hell for Dad. He gave up the law so he could care for Mom. Where were you when we—" This wasn't about her. "When Mom has needed you, Jon? She talks about you, dreams about you—"

"You could have told me."

"You're blaming me for this?" Martha pushed around the lettuce searching for the chunks of cucumber.

"No, but now *I'm* surprised Mom didn't talk about me. Like fill you guys in on—"

"Her golden boy?"

Jonathan grimaced. "Hardly."

"Well, she didn't. But then I didn't ask."

"No, but you or Dad could have reached out. I had no idea she'd gotten so bad until Norah called. *She* found me. I wasn't lost or in hiding."

"I'm calling bullshit, Jon. The last time I tried, if you recall, our father was sick, our mother was struggling with dementia and I sent you an airplane ticket which you didn't use and couldn't be bothered to explain why. Your phone went dead. And I wondered if you were too."

"I know. I wasn't in a good place."

"None of us were." Martha eyed her empty glass. No escape there. "But *we* didn't have a choice."

"Yeah, that's what Lennon said. He made me see how poorly I've handled things. I really screwed up. Actually, that's why we've come. I want to make things right."

"Easy peasy, right?"

"No, but—"

"Just stop. I need time to process all this…breaking news." She reached into her bag, pulled out her wallet and snapped her platinum card onto the table.

"Martha don't. Please don't go. Please."

"It's a lot, Jon. Too much. It's too late to meet your family now." She handed him a business card. "In case you want to stay in touch."

"Don't leave like this."

"Go see your parents tomorrow. Afternoons are probably best. I'll let Dad know you're in town."

"Martha, please."

She ignored him. "As for the rest of your story, well, you're on your own there." She collected her purse, jammed her phone into the front pocket.

"Come on, Martha."

She stood and picked up her card. "Dinner's on you."

The noise and bright lights of the hotel lobby seemed to intensify her wine buzz. She just needed some fresh air. Martha leaned on the heavy revolving door and moved with it, so dizzy that she missed the first opportunity to exit and went around for a second time before deliberately stepping back inside the hotel. She walked to the desk.

"I'm going to leave my car here. Could you please call me a cab?" Within minutes she was climbing into an oversized SUV, annoyed with herself about the time she would waste in the morning retrieving her car, but driving angry and drunk was never a good combination. She'd head home, get a good night's sleep and talk to Dad in the morning. That sounded like a reasonable plan. But what if Jon decided to just show up again? Could she trust him? Should she? God damn Jonathan! The car hurdled over a hotel speed bump. Martha groaned, the heavy red wine sloshing around in her nearly empty stomach. "Take the highway, please." The driver nodded. "It's fastest and I'm not feeling very well."

**

Martha chugged a tall glass of water and ate half a sleeve of soda crackers before calling her father. She'd set a container of *Cherry Garcia* and a tablespoon on the kitchen table, still trying to decide if she really needed its magical soothing powers.

"Hello?"

Martha pressed the speaker button. "Hi, Dad. It's me. Sorry to call so late."

"It's not even nine o'clock. Are you ok?"

"Yeah, I'm fine. It's just—" She pulled the cardboard lid off the ice cream container, a little disappointed that she'd already eaten half. Another day, another problem.

"What?"

"Now don't be upset." She heard her father sigh. "Jonathan is—"

"Jonathan? What's happened? Is he alright?"

"He's fine. Absolutely fine." She lowered her voice which added an unexpected touch of melodrama. "Jonathan has returned."

Dad laughed. "Have you been drinking?"

"Yes, but I'm serious. I met with him for dinner, well, sort of dinner, but—"

"Jonathan's here, in town? That's what you're telling me?"

"Yes." Martha scooped out a large spoonful of cherries and vanilla ice cream. "Yes, he has, at long last, returned. He's staying at the Marriott. He came to the house today, at lunchtime."

"What?"

"Yes, and I sent him away."

"Why? Why didn't he come in?"

"I wouldn't let him. He wanted to, but no way." She rewarded herself with a spoonful of ice cream.

"What the hell, Martha! Why in the world would you do that?"

Martha was surprised and a little hurt by her father's anger. "For you and Mom, of course. I didn't know if you could take the shock. I didn't want you to be...*traumatized*."

"What?"

"This afternoon, you were so angry with him—you know, like oil and water. You said it and then—poof, he was on our doorstep. I was only thinking of your heart and—"

"My heart is fine. But I am rather annoyed."

"At Jon?"

"At both of you. You're still acting like children."

"Oh, sorry."

"Is he really okay?"

"Yes, he's perfectly fine."

"Good."

"Dad, aren't you even a little upset? He's been gone forever, and well, he's done sweet all to help you and Mom. Like absolutely nothing." More ice cream, more cherries.

"Yes," agreed Dad. "It has been a long time. He's been absent, it's true. But he hasn't asked for anything lately." He paused. "Or caused us any trouble in quite a while."

Martha laughed. "That's damning with faint praise, isn't it?" Now she was annoyed. "We've been walking on eggshells for years about Jon. Mom—"

"Yes, your mother, that's why this is a good thing."

"Yeah, so good."

"I'm not a child, Martha. I can handle a visit from my son, and you know your mom's dying to see him."

"Okay then." Martha scraped the container, hoping for one last taste of sweet cherries.

Dad laughed. "It's just Jonathan."

Yes, that's what she'd thought. "Sorry, I was just trying—anyway, I told him to drop by tomorrow, in the afternoon, when Mom might be asleep."

"Okay. I'll be ready." He waited, then added. "It's been a long day. Maybe we should both hit the hay."

"Yes, I'm exhausted. But I'll stop by on my way home from work tomorrow. Okay?"

"Yes. Great. Good night, sweetheart."

"Dad."

"Yes?"

"Jonathan. Well...he's not alone."

CHAPTER TWENTY-FIVE

They were waiting for Jonathan and someone else—maybe a friend, maybe a boyfriend. Martha had been quite cryptic last night, but Nick had to assume that Jonathan was bringing someone special enough to subject them to his parents. Nick chuckled. It would be nice to find Jon settled, and God forbid, happy. He'd always been so moody and unsettled. He'd never really understood the boy or taken the time to. That one was always June's.

Nick glanced over at her, his beautiful broken wife. She sat in her chair, listening, maybe lost, in the classical music that drifted from the stereo. June was always so cold these days, so he'd lit a small fire for her, but it was starting to fade. He added a log and tossed in a few pieces of kindling to encourage the flame. June didn't seem to enjoy or even notice the flames anymore, but sometimes she'd react to the warm spicy aroma of the cedar logs that he'd ordered from the garden centre.

He wanted a coffee, but he'd wait for Jonathan. He settled on the sofa, put on his readers, opened his book, then set it aside. What if they had nothing to say to each other? He closed his eyes and saw the twins, ripping into presents on any Christmas morning. He pictured one of them, then both, covered in chicken pox, snuggled under the same blanket that was now comforting June. They'd been so close then, two peas in a pod, but it didn't last. He couldn't stand the teenage bickering, the fights about the car, tennis rackets, friends, stolen leftover pizza, anything and everything. They'd never outgrown it. Petty jealousies, M*om likes you best, you're such a daddy's girl.* He'd heard it again last night—the petulance in Martha's voice. Trivial grievances, lifelong grudges. June had tried for years to get them to hug it out, find some common ground. But they'd gone their own ways. Jonathan chose to run away without a plan. Martha went to university. He partied. She studied. She's a partner, he's an alcoholic. Nick had spent so much time with Martha, guiding and supporting her, but Jonathan didn't stick around long enough to take or even hear Nick's advice. It pained him to admit he'd let Jon slip away. And now he was nervous, anxious about seeing his own son.

Nick barely heard the tap-tapping on the heavy wooden door. He'd been anticipating the doorbell, so it took a minute and a couple more small erratic thumps for him to realize that someone was knocking.

He hurried to the door in his slippers, checking his reflection in the hall mirror. Something a bit dressier than this old cardigan would have been more appropriate,. He heard voices on the porch and opened the door, not quite wide, not yet.

"Hi, Dad." Jonathan met his gaze, smiling.

Nick gripped the brass door handle, hoping to steal a few moments to take him in. Jonathan. Nick noticed his eyes first, bright, clear, sober. He inhaled his relief. But not just Jonathan—two men, each holding the hand of a small child, a girl who was trying to free herself from their grips.

"Sorry, Ruby wanted to knock and then she wouldn't stop." Jonathan laughed softly, grasping the girl's hand to prevent her from breaking away.

"Jonathan." Nick stepped aside, allowing the door to swing open. He felt weak, no befuddled, old and confused. "Jonathan. Welcome. Won't you please come in?" He sounded too proper, stodgy. "All of you, please, please come in. Welcome, again…hello…hi." Now he was babbling. What he wanted to say was who's this? This man, this little girl?

Jonathan stepped into the house and instantly embraced him. It had been many years since Nick had been this close to Jonathan. Astounded, he returned the hug. His son was bigger than him now, taller and stronger.

"Oh, Dad. Thank you. It's so good to see you."

He could feel his son's pulse, his beating heart. Nick sucked in air, harnessing the breath, silencing a sob. He pulled back but held onto Jonathan's forearms. "Welcome home, stranger." He tried again, to get it right. "Son, I mean. Jonath…Oh dear, I think I'm a little—"

"Dad, it's okay. Sorry, I know. Yeah, it has been a long time—way too long. And I know this is a bit of a surprise."

"Yes," said Nick as he stepped back to make room for Jonathan's guests to enter. The other man was now carrying the child, her arms wrapped loosely around his neck. He was tall, robust with a genial face, his jawline trimmed in neat stubble. "Dad, this is Lennon and Ruby."

Nick moved to shake the man's hand. "Hello. Lennon, is it?" The girl shied away, burying her face. She was wearing a yellow dress and a pretty white sweater like Martha used to have.

"Hello Sir. Yes, Lennon, Lennon Gunn. Len is fine. My parents were Beatles fans so I suppose I'm lucky they didn't call me Ringo." His laugh was warm and good-natured. "And this is Ruby. Can you say hello Ruby?" She burrowed deeper into his shoulder.

"Oh, don't do that." Jon tried to get her attention. "Ruby, please? Can you just look at me?" She shook her head. "She should be fine in a few minutes. I think she's just a little out of sorts."

Nick nodded. Why was Jon so worried about her? Why didn't he come alone, so they could visit and talk things out? Nick moved into the foyer. "Come in," he said, almost wishing he could close the door, leave them on the porch. He was unsure, unsettled, at sixes and sevens, like his mother used to say.

"Is that my grandad?"

The little voice shot through Nick, suddenly pulverizing his thoughts and feelings, and whirling them into one gigantic possibility. He spun to face Jonathan. "What did she say?"

"Oh geez, Ruby!" Jonathan's face had turned red. "You weren't supposed to—Dad that wasn't the way—"

Nick leaned back against the wall, grateful for the support. His mind was racing. He felt lightheaded. His heart was pounding. What the hell was happening?

"Dad, you...you might need...I should have told you—"

"Jon...Jonathan?" Nick's voice quavered. Flustered, he took in a deep breath but then couldn't remember how long he was supposed to hold it. He'd learned how to calm himself in the hospital, a trick one of the nurses had taught him: breathe in and hold for—shit! He let the air escape slowly. The wall was still holding him up but thank God his heart wasn't pounding in his ears anymore.

Jon moved toward him. "Are you okay? Should I get a chair?"

Nick shook his head. "No, I'm fine." He pressed away from the wall. "Just fine, but what's going on here?" He swept a hand toward the strangers. Then moved in front of Jonathan. "Well—?"

"Well, Dad—"

Jonathan's nervous smile took Nick back many years, to a young boy with big ears who took too long to get his words out. He placed a hand on Jonathan's shoulder. "Calm down. It's alright."

Jon stepped back, closer to his friends. "Dad, you've already met Ruby, but what you didn't know, of course you had no way of knowing—I should have—" Jon reached for Ruby's hand. "Ruby is my daughter and your granddaughter and Lennon is my husband."

The words filled Nick's consciousness and silenced the world.

"Dad? Are you okay?"

The voice echoed from far far away. He nodded. He wasn't, but it was the easiest thing to do.

"Yeah." Jonathan grimaced. "You know, Martha thought this news might be the death of you."

Nick ignored him, slowly sorting through each new detail. Jonathan married. Grandchild. Son-in-law. Jon married. He pivoted back to that one. His gay son had a husband. The laws had changed—hell the world had changed. Granny Walker was no doubt spinning in her grave.

"Are you sure you're okay? Maybe you *should* sit down?"

Nick tuned him out. He wanted to investigate this child, who according to Jonathan, was his granddaughter. He stepped closer. "Hello, Ruby." She reached tentatively for his outstretched hand. He gently tickled her palm. She rewarded him with a giggle.

Nick gasped but stopped it from escaping. He didn't want to frighten her. He trembled with excitement. The possibility, maybe the reality that this little girl, this beautiful child was grandchild? The very idea filled him with joy, but what if he'd misunderstood, jumped to the wrong conclusion? He felt his cheeks heat up as Ruby examined him. He smiled at her. Ruby smiled back. Could it be true? Jonathan had declared it, called her his daughter, said he was married, to this man. By fact and by the law. Ruby was his—his granddaughter!

She clapped her hand on his. "Gimme five!"

Nick laughed, hoping to disguise his tears.

"Are you crying?"

Her angelic voice delighted him. He chuckled, tried to whisper *no*, then shook his head. She was beautiful—her dark eyes set off by spirals of light brown curls. He wiped his cheeks and then finally found his voice.

"Well Jonathan, you certainly know how to throw an old man off his game."

"Sorry Dad. Are you okay?"

"Yeah, yeah. This is good news. Happy news." Nick held out his hand to Lennon. "Welcome, again. To the family, I mean. Sorry. It's been—" He shook Lennon's hand, and held on, probably a little too long. How the hell do you greet a man who you've just learned is your son's husband?

Lennon finished his sentence. "A very confusing day for you, I'm sure, sir. I'm sorry if we've upset you."

"No, no. Not upset." He wasn't. "Just confused, and happy." He looked at Ruby again. "And if I'm being honest, a touch anxious too." How was June going to take this?

"I'm sorry." Jon and Lennon spoke in unison. Ruby giggled.

"No, I am fine, really. But let's move into the kitchen, okay?" He started along the hallway, but stopped, blocking the family room entrance. "I'm just worried about your mother, Jon. She's not herself anymore. Did Martha fill you in?"

"Yeah, I know, Dad."

"She's resting in here." He glanced into the family room. "— and...maybe...maybe I should go ahead, try and prepare her?" He needed some time for June but maybe more for himself.

"Sure, whatever you think's best." Jonathan motioned toward the living room. "We can wait in here. Come on, Ruby, let's bounce on the good sofa. I wasn't allowed to when I lived here."

Ruby wriggled in Lennon's arms. He let her slip to the floor. She tapped a toe on the hardwood and twirled.

"Come on, Ruby," said Lennon. "This way." But Ruby scooted forward, ducked under Nick's arm and ran into the family room.

"Wait!" Nick spun around, reaching out to grab her, but she was gone.

Jon and Lennon dashed past Nick.

"Ruby! Wait!"

Lennon's command didn't stop her.

Mesmerized, Nick watched Ruby tiptoe across the room. He'd wanted some time alone with June, to tell her, prepare her, help her—but Ruby had planted herself right in front of her new grandmother. June's eyes were closed. She was usually placid but easily startled. Nick bit his lip. Anything could happen.

"Are you sleeping?" Ruby said.

June opened her eyes.

Ruby smiled. June smiled back. Ruby reached out and placed her hand on the blanket covering June's legs. Nick strained forward, ready to intervene.

"I like your blankie." Ruby's tiny voice filled the room.

June clutched the edge of the cover and gathered it closer to her. She scowled at the little girl. Ruby stood tight. She petted the blanket. Jonathan moved next to Nick, a backup.

"Feels soft like my Bunny Baby."

June stared at Ruby. "Who are you?"

Nick was stunned by the clarity, the childish lilt in her voice.

"Ruby. Ruby." She repeated it, a bit louder, and took a step back. "Who are you?"

June scowled. She clenched her fists; Nick recognized her rising anger. He moved forward but before he could intervene June answered, "I am Junie."

Ruby nodded as if approving of this moniker. Nick watched, awed, as Ruby reached down and adjusted one of her white frilly socks. She lined up her feet, as if comparing her ankles. She quickly tweaked the other sock and then checked again. Clearly satisfied she took one deliberate step closer to June. "I have new shoes."

Nick held his breath.

June reached out her hand. Ruby met it and allowed June to take hold. She spoke slowly, deliberately. "Ruby Ruby. Ruby Ruby."

It was a juvenile chant.

Ruby frowned.

Nick started to move again but Jonathan shook his head and walked toward them. He knelt on one knee next to Ruby, placing an arm around her waist and extending the other to his mother. "Hi Mom."

June was fiddling with her rings; the small diamond and the wedding band clicked as she spun them around her boney finger. Nick could barely breathe. This was too much for her. "Careful," he whispered. He knew the pain of her blows. One wrong move and—

June turned her head slowly. "Jonny."

"Yeah Mom. I'm here." He turned to Nick and raised his shoulders in a *what do I do now* shrug.

Nick leaned forward, pleased to see that June had relaxed her fists. "Talk to her."

"Um, right—" Jon shifted on his knees. "Well, you look great, Mom."

"You are late. Ruby Ruby...we are playing." She spoke clearly, confidently.

Jon looked over at Nick again, obviously confused.

Nick walked over to June and placed, what he hoped would be a calming hand on her shoulder.

"Well now Junie, let's not be too hard on Jonny. He's a busy lad you know." He seldom called her this, but she was there again, a child somehow decades younger, but still recognizing Jonathan.

June leaned back, freeing her hands from both Jonathan and Ruby. She looked at Nick and smiled. "Wanna play?"

It felt like she was flirting. "I do. Who are your new friends?"

Jonathan lifted himself onto the ottoman and allowed Ruby to wriggle in between his knees, still standing, still watching June.

"Ruby Ruby."

Ruby shook her head. "No, I'm—"

"Junie," said Nick. "She is Ruby."

"Ruby," repeated June.

"Yes," said Ruby. Her curls bobbing in agreement.

"Mom, I see you've met Ruby."

Jon started to add more but Nick held up his hand. "Go slow," he said.

Jon nodded, but instead of waiting he spoke slowly. "She's my daughter. Your—grand-daughter."

Nick sighed.

Jon tried again. "Can you understand Mom? You're a grandma. Grandma June!"

Nick rubbed June's shoulder. She'd started with the rings again, twisting them round and round. Ruby watched in fascination. Jonathon exhaled impatiently.

"Don't Jonathan. She doesn't understand. Maybe later. This is a lot for her, probably too much."

Jon looked crushed. Nick realized it was a lot for him too—coming home and expecting, well he had no idea what Jon expected but Nick was certain it wasn't this.

Ruby squirmed between her dad's knees. She freed herself and scampered to Lennon. He settled her beside him on the sofa.

"Jonny's here," said June.

"Mom—"

Nick held up his hand. "Yes, Jonny is here. He brought some friends, special friends."

June looked at Nick. "Ruby Ruby."

"Yes," said Nick. "Ruby and Lennon."

Jon interrupted. "My daughter and—" Nick scowled at him. "Yes, Mom. Ruby and Lennon."

June was quiet for a moment. "Ruby red 'n lemon yellow." She laughed, full of delight. "Ruby red lemon yellow, ruby red lemon yellow, ruby red lemon—"

Jonathan stood up. "No Mom, Ruby and Lennon." His voice was too loud and sharp.

He's scared, thought Nick.

June stopped chanting. Her shoulders slouched. Nick covered her hands, stopping the spinning rings. He leaned in close. "Shh-shh-shush. It's okay. It's just Jonny." He nodded to his son, silently pulling him closer. "See, Jonny. He's come to see you today." To Jonathan he said, "Sit down again. Here, put your hands on hers and talk to her slowly, softly. Don't scare her again. Please. Stay calm—she might surprise you."

"Dad, I'm sorry. I didn't know."

"Yes, there's a lot you don't know," declared Nick, all at once feeling annoyed. He stole a quick look at Ruby, their Ruby. "But it's okay, Jon. Mom knows you and she's happy you're here. Just be patient."

"Sorry, Dad." Jon settled onto the stool again and placed his hand over his mom's. "Mom, I'm really happy to be here with you."

Nick nodded. "Perfect."

June turned her head toward Jonny and smiled. She grasped his hand and brought it slowly to her cheek. "Jonny."

Relieved, Nick exhaled. They should be fine now. But he'd wanted to up the odds by getting Ruby and Lennon out of the room.

"June, I'm going to leave you and Jonny now."

June said nothing. Jon answered. "Thanks. We're good now, right?"

"Yes, of course, just sit still and follow her cues." He touched June's arm. "And soon it will be time for your nap." He mouthed *fifteen minutes* to Jon and crossed the room to Lennon and Ruby.

"Ruby, would you like to help me find some cookies?"

"Yeah," said Ruby. "Come on Papa." She tugged at Lennon.

Had Martha ever been that little?

In the kitchen, Lennon said, "Will they, Jon, be alright in there, alone?"

Nick smiled, pretending to ignore the knot in his gut. "For sure. This is a good day for June. Her Jonny makes her happy. We'll check on them in a few minutes. How about some coffee?"

"And cookies!" Ruby reminded him.

"Yes, and cookies. I think there might be a bag of Double-Stuffed Oreos up here somewhere." He rustled through the pantry. "They're my favourite. I hide them way at the top so I don't eat too many."

The back door slid open just as Nick found the cookies. Martha stepped into the kitchen.

"Hi Dad—" She stopped. "Oh, we have guests. Hello."

"Martha, you're here." He looked at his watch. "Early. I thought you said after work."

"I did, but I decided you might need, I don't know, some help."

Lennon stepped forward, extending his hand. "Hello. Martha. I'm Lennon, Lennon Gunn."

"Hello." Martha met his gaze. "Yes, I figured that. You're Jon's—"

"Husband!" Nick announced with too much gusto. Steady old man, he chided himself, opened the bag of cookies and popped one in his mouth.

Martha laughed. "Yes, yes, I got that, Dad." She shook Lennon's hand, then pulled him into a quick hug. "It really is nice to meet you. Wow. This is a little awkward. Where's that capricious brother of mine?"

Nick chewed his cookie, swallowing quickly. *Did Martha just hug this Lennon guy?*

Martha turned and suddenly noticed Ruby. "Oh my!"

"Martha, this is Ruby, Jon's daughter," said Nick, adding and immediately regretting, "And I'm her grandad."

"Yes Dad. That makes complete sense." Martha rolled her eyes. "It's lovely to meet you, Ruby."

Ruby drew back, looked to her papa and then to her grandad.

Lennon sat down next to her. "It's okay sweetie, this is Martha, your Auntie Martha." Ruby stared at her.

Martha gasped. "That makes me sound old, very, very old! Let's stick to Aunt Martha or maybe just Martha, okay?"

Ruby said nothing and shifted closer to her papa.

"Where's Mom?" asked Martha "And Jon?"

"I'm making coffee. Would you like some?"

Martha sighed. "No, Dad. No coffee."

"Okay then. No coffee. Everything is fine Martha. We're good."

"Family room, then?"

Nick nodded. "Yes, they're getting reacquainted."

Martha turned and left the room.

"Sorry guys." Nick set the bag of cookies on the table. "Martha can be a little prickly sometimes."

"Like a hedgehog?" mumbled Ruby through a mouthful of Oreos.

"Yeah, kinda," chuckled Nick. "But deep down she's very nice—a real softie."

"So exactly like a hedgehog," said Lennon. "But without the furry tummy."

Ruby exploded into giggles, her cookie smudged face rippled with joy and Nick was smitten.

CHAPTER TWENTY-SIX

The sound of laughter, Ruby's playful giggles, followed Martha into the family room. She steeled herself, not sure what to expect, but even then, she wasn't quite prepared. Jonathan was sitting on the ottoman, his long legs splayed out in a V. He was holding her mom's hands, massaging her arthritic fingers. Her mom, their mom.

"Well, this is cozy, isn't it?"

"Hey Martha." Jon's grin was infuriatingly relaxed and still boyishly charming.

Martha ignored him, dropped her bag on the couch and focused on her mother "Hi, Mom," she said, deliberately avoiding Jon, no easy feat as he was almost wrapped around their mother. "How're you doing?" She touched her mom's shoulder, a point of connection that usually didn't startle her, and then leaned in to kiss her cheek. Mom turned her head, away. "Okay then," said Martha. It always stung when her mother rejected her. It's not her choice, she reminded herself. It's the dementia.

"Shouldn't you be at work?" asked Jon.

"You wish and yes, I should. But Dad specifically asked me to be here," she said, stretching the truth to make her point. "Just in case he needed help, or, you know, protection."

"Protection from me? Maybe Ruby. She does pack a mean punch." He laughed. Martha didn't. "Have you met them? Ruby and—"

"Yes, yes. Dad appears to be quite taken with Ruby. He's filling her up with Oreos."

"Great." Jon scowled but he seemed pleased.

"How did he react to meeting your hubby? Did you ambush him?"

"Sort of." Jon squirmed and sat up straighter. "Dad was surprised—confused and a little shaken, but he seemed to recover quickly. I was amazed at how well he took it. Ruby helped."

"I'm sure she did." Martha bristled. "I did brief him, you know. I told him you'd returned and wanted to come round for a visit. I didn't mention your entourage."

"Thanks." Jon pushed back the ottoman and stood up. "That explains a lot."

"I didn't do it just for you. I was trying to prepare Dad."

"I know, but thanks anyway. You've always had my back."

Martha shrugged. "It's nice that you still think that."

"Come on. I do. We're still the Walker twins, right?" She gave him a dirty look. "Come on Martha. I've paid for my sins. Surely you can forgive me." He poked her arm, like he used to do when they were kids.

"Sweet Jesus you're a pest."

A wicked grin crept across Jon's face. He stretched out his arms. "I'm coming in for a hug."

"Don't get too carried away," She ducked out of his reach. "Do you see this, Mom? He's still so annoying."

No response, not even a smile. Had Mom even noticed them squabbling? It used to drive her crazy. Martha remembered Mom's anger, rare, but when she'd finally had enough, she'd send them both to their rooms. They'd slam their doors, wait a few minutes and then Jon would creep into her room and they'd serve their penalty together. Did Mom know this? Martha felt a lump in her throat. Geez, what was wrong with her? Maudlin wasn't usually her style. This was the exact reason Martha had seldom spoke about her family or looked at old photos. Her *remember when we used to* memories soured when Jon effectively deserted them. The good old days just hurt too much.

Martha watched her mother, motionless except for her rings. She wished she could go back with her; reminisce, relive, remember, laugh and learn. She had so many questions. Now it was too late.

Jonathan had returned to the ottoman. "Don't listen to her, Mom. Martha is just whining, again."

June closed her eyes.

"Just leave her, Jon."

Jonathan leaned in closer. He spoke slowly, enunciating each word. "Mom? Can - you - hear - me? "

"No, don't. I think she's tired and if you startle her, she might freak out."

"I know. Dad told me." He stood up quickly, frustration clouding his face. He stuffed his hands deep into his pockets. "Damn, Martha. She's not even there. She's way worse than I thought. It happened so fast."

"No, it really didn't. It's been painfully slow, almost imperceptible at first, even after the diagnosis." Martha tugged on Jon's sleeve, leading him away. She spoke quietly. "Look, she's just really tired. But she can hear, you know, and process lots of things. Don't talk about her like she's the village idiot."

As if wanting to prove Martha right, Mom spoke, "Water." She smacked her lips and slipped her skinny arms under the blanket. Mom looked so cold, tired and cold.

"Where's Gloria?"

"Who?" asked Jonathan.

"Gloria," said Martha impatiently. "Just go get your mother a glass of water." Martha opened the fire screen before adding, "Please."

"Yeah, sure. I'm on it." He turned to leave. "I am sorry, you know. For everything." Martha nodded but he was gone.

"Do you need me to take Miss June?"

Martha jumped, startled by Gloria's sudden arrival.

"Oh, excuse me Miss. It's time. Your mother should rest now."

"Oh, yes, yes, I think so too, but check with Dad, okay? He seems to be in charge today."

Gloria chuckled. "Every day, Miss."

Martha could hear the voices in the kitchen: Gloria, Jon, Dad, Lennon and Ruby's sing-song cadence. It all sounded so jolly, too perfect. She felt left out, jilted. "Oh Mommy, the winds they are a changing," she said, not expecting a response.

But her mother looked at her. "Wind…blows the leaves—" She was trying for more, her dry lips moving but silent.

Martha pulled a stainless-steel water bottle from her handbag and handed it to her. "Here, I'll help you." She supported the container as her mother raised the rim to her lips and drank eagerly, noisily, water dripping from her chin. "Good girl. Don't worry. I'm here for you." Her mom slipped her hand over Martha's and squeezed, with a surprising amount of pressure. "Oh Mom, you're welcome."

Jon returned with a large glass of ice water. "Sorry. You were just a little too slow," Martha kidded him. "And Mom doesn't take ice anymore.

It's a choking hazard."

The colour rose in Jon's face. "Right. I'll add to the ever-growing list of *things Jonathan should know but doesn't.*" He sighed. "I'm, I'm…sorry. Damn, sorry, yet again."

"You didn't know." She sat down beside her mom. "Look Jon. We've been living with this a long time. We have routines. We've learned what to expect from Mom, even though the needle keeps moving, more like bouncing back and forth. It's hard to explain. And you can't just pop in, in the middle and expect to get things right, you know?" She heard Gloria approaching, her soft soled shoes making sharp staccato squeaks on the shiny hardwood. "Like that."

Jon looked confused.

"Those squeaks mean Gloria's coming. It may simply be the result of overly polished floors, but it has become a bit of a clue for Mom. She hears it, this familiar sound, and it comforts her. She waits for Gloria, even when she doesn't know her."

Jon nodded. "I get it. Mom stays calm."

"Yes, mostly. Mom's comfortable with her."

"So, Gloria is Mom's helper?"

"Yes, her nurse and a whole lot more."

"Got it." Jon smiled at Gloria as she entered the room. "Hello."

"Gloria," said Martha. "This is my brother, Jonathan. He's come from afar."

Jon nodded. "I'm very pleased to meet you. I hear you've been taking care of my mother."

"I have been helping. Yes," said Gloria. "And I have heard quite a lot about you!" She laughed, deep warm notes. "It's almost as if you were right here all along."

Jon chuckled. "Well, unfortunately, I wasn't but I'm here now. And I'm happy to help."

Martha grimaced. "Still a charmer, I see."

"Indeed," agreed Gloria, helping June up from her chair. "Up we go." She placed one hand on June's arm and wrapped her own arm around her back. "It's nap time." Her voice was strong and cheerful. "Steady now. Good work."

Martha watched her mom unfold herself and stand, her body crooked now, her shoulders bent forward. Her blanket slipped to the floor. She leaned into Gloria and pointed at Jonathan. "Nap time. Nap time. Jonny. Come."

Jon looked at Martha, his face a quizzical *what do I do?*

"Go with her," said Martha. "Play along. She'll be asleep soon enough."

Jon jumped forward and held out his arm. "At your service," he said. "Mom, I'm so glad you met Ruby. I've told her all about you and she's going to pre-school now and oh there's just so much to tell you."

Mom latched onto Jon and they ambled off, arm in arm, thick as thieves.

CHAPTER TWENTY-SEVEN

Thankfully Jon's chatter faded away as he headed upstairs with Mom, but the sound of Gloria's laughter, which usually felt like a warm hug, infuriated Martha. *Think happy thoughts.* She placed one hand on the back of a chair to steady herself, closed her eyes and sucked in a long deep breath. She exhaled and tried again—*happy thoughts, happy thoughts.* Unfortunately, none came to mind. *Jonathan!* Was it only yesterday that she'd opened the door to find him on the front porch, grinning like a fool? So much had happened since then. Mom was, as always, comforted by her Jonny; she'd forgotten he'd ever been gone. But what would happen when he vanished again? Martha stretched her back and then her neck to work out some of the tension. She was exhausted. Jon had brought a shit load of stress along with his little family.

Martha opened the fireplace doors and poked at the last glowing log, a simple distraction that had little effect on the quality of the flames. She startled at the sound of her father's voice.

"Here, let me help you with that."

"Oh, you scared me." She handed him the poker. "I think it needs less poking and more wood. It's dying."

"I see that."

He looked tired and sad again, as if the exuberant Oreo-eating grandfather she'd encountered in the kitchen, had been a pretense, a display of good manners. This all too much for him. Damn it, Jon.

"Dad? Are you okay? All this excitement—"

"Yes, I'm fine."

"Maybe if Jon had just reached out, emailed or something. At least gave us a bit of a warning."

"Martha, I'm good—great actually." He turned to face her, now looking happy and surprisingly relaxed "Of course, I'm still concerned about your mother. But, yes, I'm feeling good." He sighed. "It's been quite a day."

"You look tired. You should rest. Maybe go to your office and put your feet up for a while."

"No, I'm fine. And I'm sure Jon will be down soon."

Had she totally misjudged her father? He was stronger than she'd thought and surprisingly open-minded. Had he forgotten all the years, all the heartaches, the drinking and the lies? "But Dad—"

"Stop fretting, Martha."

Martha balked. "I'm not fretting. It's just that—he won't stick around, you know."

"Pardon?"

"Jon will leave again. He always does."

"Yes, I know. But maybe—let's just give him a chance, okay?"

Martha turned away. Her father had certainly risen to the occasion, hadn't he? Good for him. But she wasn't ready to forgive and forget—not by a long shot. She could accept that this whole *return of Jonathan* thing wasn't all bad. Afterall, her foolhardy brother was sober, healthy and settled. And on top of everything, he'd brought Ruby, the perfect little granddaughter. And like a magic elixir, Ruby was making Dad happy.

As if on cue, Ruby walked through the doorway cradling one of Mom's fancy cake plates in her chubby hands, deliberately placing each footstep so as not to challenge the balance of the cookies. Martha stared at the little feet, the tiny black shoes. Patent leather *Mary Janes*. She'd once had a similar pair for church, shiny black perfection. Ruby wore them well, daintily lifting her left foot behind her as she leaned in and carefully set the cookies on the coffee table.

"Good job, sweetie," said Lennon.

Ruby twirled, hopped and landed on the sofa. "See, Grandad, I told you I wouldn't drop them."

"Yes, your papa knew you could do it, didn't he?"

Lennon seemed pleased, taking in both Ruby and her grandad with his smile.

Well, well, Lennon and Dad had hit it off rather quickly, hadn't they? Martha watched as Lennon settled Ruby, smoothing her dress and spreading a napkin on her lap before handing her a cookie. With his attention diverted, Martha had just enough time for a quick appraisal. What kind of man could look so relaxed after being dropped into this powder keg of a family? He looked up and held her gaze; friendly, confident and good looking. The almost perfect man. A rare beast. Lucky Jonathan.

Jon's footsteps echoed on the stairs. It sounded like he still took them two at a time. He burst into the room. "You were right. Mom's out already. It's weird how fast she fell asleep." He motioned to Mom's chair. "Can I sit there?" He didn't wait for permission, allowing his body to collapse into the vacant seat. He still moved like a teenager.

"Really Jon?" Martha rolled her eyes. "I'm having trouble figuring you out. You're...different."

Jon raised his eyebrow and added a mischievous grin. "You mean like new and improved."

"No, that's definitely not it." She was here to help her father, handle Jonathan and his world of trouble. But she'd let him get under her skin. And now she was pissed off and cranky. Leave it to Jonathan to bring that out. She watched her father drop a log on the fire. The sparks danced, then faded. Mom used to think they were fairies—bonfire sparks, fireflies, even shooting stars—

"Martha?" Jon was waving his hand. "Yoo-hoo. Are you in there?"

She scowled, sending Jon her best *if looks could kill* side eye, while resisting, for Ruby's sake, the adolescent urge to give him the finger. "Well, you see, dear brother," she said. "I just can't decide if you're finally all grown up, or like Granny Walker used to say, you really are a 'feckin eejit'."

Dad chuckled. "Bless her soul."

Jon shrunk into the chair, just a little, but enough to give Martha a twinge of satisfaction.

"Geez, what's your problem Martha? I'm *sooo* sorry if I'm a little on edge and not meeting your high standards of behaviour. It's been a stressful couple of days."

"Grow up, Jon. We're all stressed."

"Yeah, like you're so mature."

"Stop! What's the matter with the two of you?" Dad sniffed his impatience. "Hell, you're not kids anymore." He glanced at Ruby. "Um, um whoops, sorry. I mean—heck!" He prodded the log into place and closed the brass doors. "Just be nice, okay? Ruby's here."

Hearing her name, Ruby leaned forward as if suddenly aware of the conversation. Lennon offered her a cookie but she ignored him.

Jon broke the silence. "Sorry, Dad. Sorry. Sorry. Geez! I just keep apologizing. Am I making everything worse? That's not why we're here."

Martha was surprised and a little impressed with his determination. She would have guessed he'd crumble under all this.

"Well then, why *are* you here?" asked Dad as he sat down next to Ruby. "Not that we're not happy to have all of you, especially you!" He leaned over just enough to scrunch Ruby against her papa. She giggled.

"Yes, yes!" said Jon. "See, that's exactly why we're here. To introduce…" He gestured toward the ceiling, to include their mom, Martha guessed. "…everyone to everyone. But as soon as Martha gets in my way I seem to fail miserably. Crash and burn." He extended his fingers as he added the sound of an explosion.

So, this was her fault? As if! Martha quickly drafted several sharp retorts. But remembering Dad's plea for civility, she countered as affably as she could. "Come on now. I can't possibly be to blame for all of your crimes and misdemeanors."

"No, no, you're not." Jon replied, serious now. "It's just that I'd hoped you'd be a lot happier to see me."

Martha bristled. "You're still here, aren't you? I could have sent you packing last night, you know."

"You did your best," said Jon.

"Ahem!" Dad interrupted, with a single clap of his hands, eliciting a bounce and another giggle from Ruby. "Well, I want you all to know, and I speak for both your mother and me, that we are very pleased with this reunion."

"Of course you are!" said Martha, attempting to leap up. She'd chosen the wrong chair for this confrontation; a Queen Anne style armchair, a remnant from Mom's grandmother's estate, too low and with a very saggy bottom. Having lost most of the intended dramatic impact, she hoisted herself out of the chair. "Why wouldn't you be happy? He's brought you a grandchild! Geez she's perfect, practically gift wrapped and tied with a shiny red ribbon."

Ruby adjusted the pink glittery headband that had begun to slip toward her forehead, pushing it back through her curls. Lennon pulled her closer, clearly using his body to muffle the conversation.

"Ah, I think maybe Ruby and I should go for a walk. Is there a park or something nearby?" Lennon asked.

"Right. Good idea," said Dad "The back yard is pretty nice and—"

Martha turned to Lennon. "There's a playground on the street just north of here, with swings and a slide, I think. That might be more fun."

Ruby jumped up, rewarding Martha with a toothy grin. She did seem very sweet and insanely cute. Lucky Jon.

"Thanks. We'll start out back then," said Lennon.

"Feel free to try out the putting green," said Dad. "But keep an eye on Ruby around the pool."

"Really Dad?" chided Martha. "I'm pretty sure Ruby's father will keep her safe." She moved to the coffee table and silently slid the cookie plate closer to Ruby, using her own body to hide the move, and adding a quick wink.

Ruby palmed a couple of cookies. She smiled and glanced at Jon. "Bye Daddy," she said as she skipped to catch up to her Papa.

"You guys have fun," said Jon.

"We always do," replied Lennon as he ushered Ruby out of the room.

Dad turned to Martha. "So? Was all that necessary? Really, I'm a little surprised by your behaviour."

Clearly, he wasn't referring to the cookies, but he seldom spoke to her like this. She shrugged, trying to look indifferent. "I'm tired, exhausted. I didn't mean to be unkind."

"It's okay," said Jonathan. "I know this is a lot. I feel like I've created a shit load of trouble here. I didn't mean to."

"Really?" Martha said. "Did you think you'd come back here, say *howdy-doo* and everything would be perfect? You've been gone for years! And if you recall, things weren't that great when you left!" Was he really that self-centered? So insensitive that he hadn't even considered them?

Jon shrugged. Just about the answer she'd expected. He seemed so content. Was it an act or was he just that happy?

Jon leaned back into the chair and crossed his legs on the ottoman. He stretched his arms, interlocking his fingers behind his head. "I always liked this room. You know, this place is exactly the same. It's weird, but nothing's changed."

Martha felt her father stiffen, harnessing his emotions as she'd seen him do so many times at the office.

"No son. Everything has changed."

"I don't see it." Jon leaned back, taking in the whole room. "The photos, the books, the dreaded chess board. I'll bet you still put the Christmas tree in that corner. Is the eye screw still there?" He laughed softly.

Dad's voice was controlled, but thick with emotion. "Well, we haven't needed to anchor the tree with fishing line for quite some time. But maybe this year. If you're staying 'till then, Christmas, I mean. Are you?"

The question seemed to surprise Jonathan.

"You have no idea, Jonathan. No idea at all."

"But—"

Dad didn't wait for a defence. "Yes, I'm sure the house looks the same to you, however so much has changed, we've changed. But how would you know? You gave us up a long time ago."

Martha watched as Jonathan squirmed. Dad wasn't pulling any punches now.

"I'm pleased you've come home. I'm glad you've found happiness, a family, but please don't dismiss our struggles. I'm not saying things would have been easier if you'd been around. But your mother has been ill for a long time now and Martha has done a damn good job helping us out."

Martha felt the warm glow of his praise.

"Oh, Dad, I'm—" Jonathan's voice cracked. He was still, as dazed as the bunnies Mercury used to ambush in Mom's vegetable garden.

Martha was worried about her dad. His face had turned a blotchy red and again showed all the pain of the past year. She sat down beside him, hoping to comfort him—and herself.

Jonathan finally stood up, rolled back his shoulders and cleared his throat as if priming for a formal speech. Martha half expected him to pull notes from his pocket.

"Look, I'm sure it hasn't been easy for you guys. I am really sorry for upsetting you. I think I need to explain some things, about my life."

"I'm listening," said Dad.

"I'm not sure where to start. But I'm not completely in the dark about the situation here. I know some things, a bit about you guys. Your heart problems, the surgery, I know it was serious. You might not believe it, but I wanted to come home. I know Mom's been sick for quite a while now. Martha says it's dementia and the prognosis isn't good. I think the term is neurodegenerative, right?"

"Actually, it's LBD, Lewy Body De—"

Dad cut her off and spoke directly to Jon. "Oh, so you know all about us? Do you? So, you know how much we've missed you, worried? Speculated? Did you know that your mother has been broken, crushed by your disappearance—nearly every single day? For years?"

Jon flinched. "Jesus Dad. I—that's just not true."

"No, it's true. And how would you know anything?" Dad grumbled, browbeating Jonathan like the old days.

Martha felt a pinch of pity, until she realized that Jon wasn't backing down.

"I tried," said Jon

But Dad wasn't finished. "Did you know how sad she was? How she worried that you'd die in the streets or get arrested or end up in the drunk tank?"

Now, Jon's face turned red, but Dad couldn't seem to stop. "She gave you money, our money, which you wasted. But your mother kept trying. She hated those trips, never sure if—"

"No! She didn't!"

"What?" Dad inhaled deeply, gasping, catching his breath.

"Mom didn't hate coming to see me. I won't accept that. I wasn't always on my best behaviour, but not all drunks end up on the street. And…I…I know that *you know* that Mom had other…other…reasons to visit!"

"Jonathan!" Dad slammed his hand on the arm of the sofa. "Don't!" he shouted, stood up and walked toward the doorway.

"Dad, wait," said Jonathan. "I'm sorry—"

But Dad shook his head, his shoulders slumped. He didn't look back.

Martha turned on her brother. "What the hell, Jon! What was that?"

Jon wiped his face with his palm. "It was me being cruel. And none of your business."

"What? You've really upset Dad. What's going on?"

"Back off, Martha." He held up a hand. His expression was enough to silence her.

They waited, the room heavy with secrets, as Dad's angry steps faded. Martha tensed, expecting the slam of the back door, instead, espresso beans clattering against the blades of the grinder. "Looks like we're all getting coffee."

"Huh?"

"It's his go-to ritual—for stress. We drink a lot of coffee these days."

Jon leaned over and picked up the blanket that had fallen off his mother's lap earlier. He folded it and placed it over the arm of the chair. They sat for several minutes, Martha unwilling to engage and Jonathan completely silent.

"Well, I can't change the past." Jon paused. "And I don't really know how to apologize any more, or any better. I didn't want to make things worse. I'm a screwup. I get it."

"Self-pity is it then? Poor Jonathan. We all have scars." Her own seemed to be taking a long time to heal. Between Peter, Mom and now Jon, she was getting kicked in the ass on an almost daily basis.

"I really want to lay everything out for you guys. No secrets, no more hiding," said Jon.

"I like that idea." Dad returned, carrying a silver tray with three glass demitasses, each one filled with dark coffee and capped with a perfect line of crema. His mood had lightened, the magic of the espresso machine. "Cream and sugar are in the kitchen. I put brandy in mine." He took a long satisfying sniff.

Jon stood up and selected a cup. "I'm good with black." He took a sip. "That's really good Dad. When did you learn to make coffee like this?"

"Oh, don't get him started," said Martha.

Jon chuckled. "So, I'd like a chance to explain, to set the record straight so to speak."

"Okay, but…proceed with caution," Dad said quietly.

Jonathan nodded. "I don't know how much either of you knows about this, but here goes." He licked the coffee foam from above his lip and sucked in a trembling breath. "I'm an alcoholic."

"Okay, now this just sounds like an AA meeting," said Martha, confused by the enigmatic edges to this exchange.

"Martha, please," said Dad.

'Yeah, a little," chuckled Jon. "I'm in recovery now, sober more than four years. That's why I didn't—couldn't come home when you were sick, Dad. A couple of years before that, I got a DUI and court ordered community service, so I couldn't go anywhere then." He stopped and drained his cup. "And then when you were sick, in the hospital, well, I was pretty low. I'd started drinking again and I couldn't face myself, let alone all of you. I…I—"

"Go on," said Martha.

"You knew about the accident, didn't you, Dad? I've always suspected you intervened somehow, called in a favour or something. I didn't go to jail."

"You can thank your mother for that," said Dad. It was almost a whisper.

So, Dad knew. He'd helped Jonathan. But he'd kept it from her.

"But, son, that doesn't explain why you—"

"I know I know," said Jon. "I'm getting there."

"Slowly," muttered Martha, earning her impatient glances from both men.

"It took me a long time to get clean after the DUI and then when I relapsed and—I was too ashamed to tell you why I couldn't come home." Jon swallowed. "I've done a lot of work since then."

Was he expecting praise or understanding? Martha held her tongue.

"But we're your family," mumbled Dad.

"Well, I couldn't live up to the Walker standards. I never wanted to be a lawyer and I'm gay."

"So?" Now Dad sounded impatient. "We never—"

"Yeah, I know that too, Dad. But back then, I felt all alone. I wasn't

- 192 -

one of you. I convinced myself that it was me against the world. I felt like such a failure so I left. Such a stupid kid. I thought I knew everything."

"That's not true." said Martha. "Except the stupid kid part."

"Yeah, I know, but it's how I felt." The colour had drained from his face. Jon turned to his father. "I wanted you to care about me, to talk to me. To help me figure things out. But you were always so uninterested and too busy."

Martha wanted to come to her father's defence, but she was speechless. Was Jon seriously blaming Dad for everything? She could say the same thing about Mom and her Jonathan devotion. Martha had often felt excluded from their little world, but she hadn't run away or become an alcoholic. She opened her mouth to point this out but was stopped by the look on her father's face. He loved Jonathan. End of story.

Dad stood, pulled Jon into a hug and added a couple of manly back pats. "We both have a lot to account for, don't we? I wish we'd talked more, been more open with each other."

Martha watched as the tension between them evaporated. It seemed so unfair. "Oh geez. You're really getting off easy," she said, forcing herself to sound flippant even though she was really upset. It didn't matter, neither of them noticed. She was tired and confused. She needed to go home, curl up in her empty king-size bed and sleep, or maybe have a good cry.

"I hope you know I love you." Dad hugged him again. "I...I failed you. I didn't know how...your mom was always so...Shit! I have no idea what to do about any of this now." He stepped back. "Bottom line, you're home. That you're healthy and sober is more than we'd hoped. Married, with a husband and a child, well, that'll take some getting used to."

"Yeah, and good move, bro, bringing Ruby. She certainly sweetens the deal, especially how you coached her—Grandad, Auntie Martha. Come on!"

Jon looked hurt. "Not coaching. We've taught her about her family."

"Right," said Martha, trying to sound less bitchy. "But really, she's off the charts, cuteness wise."

Jon smiled. "Yeah, she's great. We were so lucky to get her. The circumstances were a bit unusual. Her birth mother is still in the picture, but Ruby's ours, legally adopted and all that. Mom was really happy when it was finalized. She said she always knew I'd be a father one day."

"Excuse me? Mom *knew* about Ruby?" Martha spit out the words. "What about Lennon?"

"Sure. I sent her baby pictures of Ruby. And the last time she came out west, she met him—we weren't together then. He was coaching when she picked me up from work at the rec centre one Saturday. She thought he was nice." Jon stopped. "Jesus. Okay, one more news flash."

"What?" They asked, together. Dad's tone was kinder than Martha's.

"Last one, I promise."

Martha watched his Adam's apple bounce up and down slowly, steadily.

"Okay. Mom knows—knew we got married."

"What? No way." Martha tried to figure out the timing, but she couldn't.

"Impossible!" Dad's voice had risen. "Your mother certainly would have told me if she knew you were married."

"She didn't want...I sent photos to Norah. Mom loved the excitement, the intrigue of...a secret." He flopped back into the chair. "Jesus, I just assumed she'd told you by now—or Norah had. I knew she was starting to lose it but, I can't believe she didn't say anything."

Baby pictures? Martha jumped up and ran into the dining room. She ripped the packing tape off the box she'd labelled *Mom's Secret Stash*. The envelope of photographs was near the top. She dashed back to the family room and thrust them at Jon. "Is this Ruby?"

He looked at the pictures and smiled. "Yeah. But before I met her. Her mother—"

"Jesus Christ, Jon. I can excuse Mom, but why didn't *you* tell us?"

Jon laughed nervously. "Well, when I told Mom and then heard nothing, well, I just figured you didn't care."

Martha fired back, "How the hell could we care when we didn't know?!" Without looking at him she challenged her father. "Dad, did you know about this?"

Dad shook his head, "No. Apparently she shut us both out."

"Really?"

"Yes, really. I didn't know." He sat beside her again, hunched over, elbows on his knees.

"Dad?" Martha handed him his coffee. Caffeine laced with brandy couldn't hurt.

Her father set the cup on the table without drinking any. "I...I guess I wasn't paying close enough attention...to any of you." He covered his eyes with his hand.

They all sat quietly for a while. Martha could hear movement in the bedroom above, the flush of the toilet and muffled voices. Her mother was, no doubt, asking for Jonny, her Jonny. It was just so unfair. She'd been here the whole time. Had Mom even noticed or cared? Unfair, but Jon, despite all his screw ups, had always gotten so much more from her. For a moment Martha missed Peter. He always made her feel better. Well, he used to.

Her father cleared his throat. "Look Jon. I'm going to need time to process this. Your mom—she should have told me. But I guess this isn't all on you. Norah's got some explaining to do too." Dad's voice trembled. "But it changes nothing...about the way I feel...about you. You're here, you and your new family. And I would really like to spend some time with them, real time, you know?"

Martha could tell he was trying hard to hold on. So was she. She'd been wrong about so many things the last few days. But mostly about her dad. He'd really surprised her. He wasn't outraged or shocked by Jonathan's homecoming. She was struggling with this new Jonathan, but Dad, not so much. He'd found a way to accept and maybe even forgive Jonathan's mistakes. He was a better soul than she. Could she get there?

"Thanks Dad," said Jonathan.

"So, what are your plans, son? Are you going to stick around for a while?" It was a question full of hope. "We'd like to get to know you all a little better."

"Yeah, especially Ruby," said Martha, but no one was listening to her.

CHAPTER TWENTY-EIGHT

Nick set the phone on the kitchen counter and laughed. "That was Martha," he said. "She's stuck at the office and worried we won't have everything ready for tomorrow."

Jon chewed and swallowed the last bite of his chicken sandwich. "We're almost done, aren't we?"

Nick nodded and picked up a piece of paper, a spreadsheet. They'd spent the morning finishing up the last of Martha's list and had stopped for lunch. It was important to eat with June. She was so different since Jon and Ruby had arrived—happy, engaged, well more so than she had been for a long time. He couldn't imagine life without Ruby, and Jonathan, of course. It had been almost a month now, since he'd first heard himself called Grandad. It hadn't been hard to get used to it. Grandad just seemed to fit. He looked at June, *Grandma*. She sometimes smiled when Ruby said her new name.

"We're almost there," said Nick, forcing himself to come back to the task at hand. Martha had been organizing things for weeks. They'd decided to move into Whispering Heights and leave behind what they didn't need or couldn't fit into the new place. They'd worry about selling the house later. It was a big undertaking, but Martha had created to-do lists for them. "We've checked almost every box. See." Nick slid the paper across the table towards Jon but Ruby grabbed it.

"Mine." Ruby stuck out her lip.

"Ruby, stop it. We don't grab things," scolded her dad.

Ruby looked from Nick to Jon and back to Nick, grinning, as if calculating the exact temperature of the hot water she'd just gotten herself into. Nick returned her smile and patted her back, releasing her from further reprimand. They hadn't had much time for her today.

Ruby turned her attention to the paper, her nose nearly touching the printed rows and columns. She picked up Nick's pencil and added some cockeyed letters. "Smarties, Goldfishes, almonds, the salty ones. The plain ones are yucky and—" She pushed the paper towards her dad, then pulled it back. "Whoops! I forgot." She grinned and added a few more scribbles. "Cookie dough ice cream!"

June laughed, full and hearty, the laugh that made Nick's heart swell, then hurt.

"Chocolate chip."

It was the first thing she'd said for hours. She'd sat quietly while they'd worked, watched Ruby flitter about and even ate her lunch without objection. But she had remained silent.

Nick patted her hand. "My favourite too," He knew saying too much might overwhelm her, block the path that was temporarily clear.

"Where exactly do you see that?" Jon leaned in close to Ruby, his cheek touching hers, as if looking for the magic ice cream order. "This isn't a shopping list Rub, but nice try."

They'd been working hard all week. Getting ready for the movers— Nick had called it a family affair, but Martha had scoffed, still unwilling to forgive Jon. Nick worked hard, cleaning out his office, collecting books and movies and selecting the art and photos. He hadn't counted down the days, hoping ignorance would make it easier but now—tomorrow—the truck was scheduled for nine o'clock. The time had gone so fast. He looked around the kitchen, still fully outfitted, the little they'd need for the suite packed into two plastic bins, cutlery, plates, glasses and cups for two in one bin and some food— snacks, crackers and cereal in the other. This would be their last night here, he and June moving for the first time in forty years, no, almost fifty—when did they buy this place? Martha and Jonathan, not even a twinkle in this old man's eyes.

Ruby interrupted his thoughts. "I miss Papa," she declared. She was filling in the remaining empty spaces on Martha's to-do list with uneven letters to spell *Papa.*

Lennon had returned to Victoria several weeks ago, unable to be away from his work any longer. He and Jon had worried about Ruby staying here. She'd be missing pre-school, which Nick thought not to be important at all, but Jon insisted that the benefits of early education and socialization could not be ignored. Nick worried more about exposing her to the family chaos, but she seemed to be doing just fine.

"I miss Papa, too," said Jonathan. "But we'll be going home soon. And let's *FaceTime* today, Okay?"

Nick knew they couldn't stay, but still a part of him hoped. "You know, Ruby, I was just thinking about when this house made me happy, when your daddy and Aunt Martha were little, like you. I'm really going to miss living here."

She nodded, her bouncing curls expressing either empathy or boredom. Either way, Nick just liked having her around. She exchanged the pencil for a crayon. Martha had given her a vintage style tin box with twenty-four hand-picked colours.

"What's this one?" Ruby flung her hand at her dad.

"Whoa, slow down." Jon tried to read the jiggling label, finally steadying Ruby's hand with his own. "Granny Smith Apple."

"I like it," said Ruby as she added bright green scribbles to the *to do* list.

"Um Ruby, Auntie Martha made that list for the grownups and she may not appreciate your artistic skills." Jon passed the list to his father, pushed aside the empty plates and handed Ruby an alphabet colouring book "Let's try this instead. Okay?"

Ruby shook her head. "Grandma, do you want to colour with me?"

"Ye...yes," June nodded. "Ru...by." Her head continued to bob. "Happy."

"Usually," chuckled Jon. "Until she isn't."

Ruby slid off the chair and marched to the small desk built into pantry wall of the kitchen. June's cookbooks, recipe box, her day planner and mother of pearl pen were still arranged on top. Ruby pulled open the bottom drawer, licked her fingers and extracted two sheets of paper, seemed to reconsider, and then took another, leaving the drawer open, a threat to all their shins, thought Nick. She returned to the table and placed the paper in front of June.

"I brought two for you," Ruby said. "In case you make a mistake."

June steadied her trembling hand on the pages.

Ruby climbed back into her chair, chose two new crayons and waved them at Jon. "Huh?"

"Use your words, Ruby. What would you like?"

"Colours." She rolled her eyes. "These colours? What are they?" Her annoyance was lost in the magic of her smile.

Nick suppressed a laugh—grateful he wasn't in charge of discipline.

"Please," reminded Jon.

"Pl—eeea—se," drawled Ruby, adding another eye roll.

Jon sighed. Nick wasn't sure if he was giving in or giving up. But it was obvious that June was delighted by Ruby's theatrics. Her face was animated, bright, the soft pink blush a welcome change from her usual ashen pallor. Her eyes darted quickly, wittingly, from Jon to Ruby and back to Jon.

Jon rolled the crayons through his fingers. "Well, this one is *Jazzberry* Jam and this one, *Mulberry*."

"Thank you," said Ruby, sweet and hopefully genuine. Surely she was too young for sarcasm.

Jon scratched his head. "I may need help with this little monkey, Dad. Len is much better at the discipline thing than me."

"Sorry, I think I'm probably in your camp. I've become a bit of an old softie," said Nick.

Jon dropped his head into his hand, spreading his fingers just enough to be able to glare at his father.

"I know. I know." Nick bent his head, acknowledging the irony, accepting the censure.

"Here, Grandma. Which one do you want?" Ruby shifted closer to June, nearly tipping a water glass, and showed her the crayons. "This one is *strawberry jam* and this one is *grumpyberry*."

June slowly reached into Ruby's hand and selected the Jazzberry.

"Good," said Ruby. "I like the other one better."

They bent their heads to concentrate on the work at hand. June drew lines, scribbles, focusing as the colour transferred to the white page.

"I'm drawing Barb," stated Ruby without looking up.

Nick smiled, oddly pleased with himself for knowing that Barb was the rock-and-roll troll from the latest Troll movie.

"Purple," exclaimed June.

"No pink," said Ruby.

Nick marveled at their connection. Ruby never seemed bothered by June's outbursts. Or squirmed when she touched her curls, twisting them in her stiff fingers. They'd grown close; Wii bowling, puzzles and now colouring together.

"Purple." June insisted.

Ruby held out her crayon, they traded and carried on colouring.

"Purple," said June.

Ruby took the crayon back from her grandmother, put both, side by side in her little hand and scribbled a thick, dark tornado across her paper. "Purple! They're both purple! Grandma's right!"

June laughed again, took back the crayon Ruby offered and added some wiggly purple lines to Ruby's drawing.

"Hey," said Ruby. "Grandma and me are croperating."

Jon looked up from his phone. "Co-operating."

"More," said June. She reached for the tin and chose a new colour.

Jonathan and Ruby should live in this house. The idea burst into Nick's head, simultaneously striking him as both brilliant and ridiculous. They were already staying here. They'd left the hotel the day Lennon flew back to Victoria. There were so many good reasons. He began to list them in his head. Gloria would be happy to keep her job. This was a big one for Nick. He'd written her a glowing letter of recommendation, yet, other than temporary agency work—she hadn't found another placement. He planned to pay her until the end of the year, and Martha had suggested gifting her a trip home to the Philippines, but that wasn't nearly enough to thank her for the care and kindness she'd given them. So, he was still working on it. But, if they just cancelled the move—they wouldn't have to sell the house. And June would benefit from living with Ruby, keeping her Jonny close. Lennon would have to relocate of course, but he seemed like a good guy. What if they just all lived together? He could cancel the suite at Whispering Pines, forfeit the deposit. Not a problem. His mind flooded with visions of domestic bliss, as it catapulted right over reality.

"Ruby! Not in your mouth, please! Crayons aren't food. They're full of germs," said Jon.

The words startled Nick but had no effect on Ruby. She playfully licked at the crayon, teasing, her pink tongue just missing the waxy tip.

"Mom, don't!"

Jonathan's tone startled them all. June was mimicking Ruby, nibbling at a neon orange crayon "Mmmm." June's cheeks were flushed, her eyes bright. The orange crayon slipped between her lips.

"Grandma, you can't really eat that!" Ruby plucked the crayon from June's hand. "Here, Grandad." She stretched her whole body across the table. "Grandma was going to eat this one!" She shook her head with dramatic disapproval.

Nick was staring at June, captivated, her energy, her spirit bolstering his daydreams.

"Grandad!" Ruby waved the crayon at him.

"Right! Thank you, Ruby. But I think Grandma was just pretending, like you."

"Pre...tend," said June, still grinning.

"Well, I didn't know," Ruby said, full of childish righteousness. She remained sprawled across the table.

Hoping to coax her out of her huff, Nick balanced the offending crayon upright on the table in front of her. She giggled and blew it over. Nick caught it before it rolled to the floor.

"Hmm, I wonder what this one is called?" he said playfully. He checked the wrapper and burst out laughing. "No wonder Grandma wanted to eat it. It's Macaroni and Cheese!" Everyone laughed. Nick tried to freeze the moment, hold onto it. He wished Martha were here too.

June patted Ruby's bottom. "Mmm..mac n sheese." She struggled with more. "Jonn-y likes."

"I sure do. Grandma used to make the best. None of that boxed stuff for us, right Mom?"

"I-like-it-too," said June, her voice surer, stronger.

"Yes, we both do," agreed Nick. "It's not just for kids you know. Sure, we use fancier cheeses these days but always elbow pasta. Can't mess with the classics too much, can we?" He rubbed June's shoulder, hoping she could feel his happiness, his amazement at her contribution, her determination. "Come on, Ruby. Off the table now. Come and help Grandad pick out which books to pack up and move."

Ruby rolled over and slipped down, feet first.

Jonathan groaned. "Not too many. They're heavy."

"Books! Books!" chimed Ruby.

"Yeah," said Jon. "My father has a lot of books."

Ruby laughed. "Books books. Too many books!"

"Never!" chuckled Nick tickling Ruby's side. 'Can you help your mother now, Jon?" He bent to June. He was still picturing them all here, living together. "I'm sure you're tired now, aren't you?"

June nodded.

"Well, we've had a very busy day," added Jon. "Upstairs to bed or in your chair?" He took her arm to help her up.

"No. No." She shoved him away with both hands. "No!"

Jonathan stepped back quickly. "Mom!"

"June. June, it's okay." Nick felt Ruby recoil behind him. "Jon, take Rub and get her out of here. And find Gloria, please. I think we've lost your mom again." The fantasy of staying on in the house imploded. Well, it was a nice dream, thought Nick. As fanciful as June's fairies, still, there was no reason he couldn't hold onto it, even after they moved.

CHAPTER TWENTY-NINE

Nick looked around at his surroundings, his new home. It hadn't sunk in yet but then the movers had finished only a few hours ago.

"Well, that went pretty well, didn't it?" Martha was unpacking groceries, ones she'd picked up, so likely veggies and rice crackers.

"Much better than I thought it would," Nick admitted as he jiggled his Scotch over small round balls of ice. Definitely not rocks, but they were cold and frozen. He'd have to remember to fill the tray.

Nick settled into his new recliner, soft brown leather, slimline to fit the new space. He pressed the remote and felt the footrest rise to support his legs. Nice.

"Is it comfortable?"

"The chair? Yes. Excellent. You did good, Martha. I'm glad you talked me out of that beast of a recliner."

"Well, it was much too big. And the beer cooler in the arm rest was a little much."

Nick chuckled. "Yeah, maybe." He watched as Martha arranged some fresh fruit in a bowl, bananas, apples and pears, and placed it on the small kitchen island. How had she found the time to put this all together for them?

He looked around, recognizing a lot from home, pillows, photos, books, fresh yellow roses, June's favourite. So much was new and scaled down, smaller than their old furniture but comfortable and practical. June's chair and ottoman looked a little dated next to all the new things, but it was familiar and necessary. It was placed at an angle, a bit awkward in the room, but it faced the window so she could see outside and enjoy the plants and the birds. They should get a bird feeder. Was it allowed? This place had seemed a lot bigger in his mind's eye, but he'd probably been skewing it out of self-preservation. "Are you sure this is the same suite we looked at last fall?"

Martha chuckled. "Of course it is. Why? Doesn't it seem like it?"

"No, yes, I mean I know it is, but it seems different, smaller." He sipped his drink and let the liquor soothe him. "I suppose I'll get used to it."

"Mom did well today, didn't she?" Martha was stocking the tiny fridge—milk, yogurt, hummus and baby carrots.

"Did you get the smoked gouda?"

"Yes, under protest. It's not good for you Dad, so eat it sparingly."

"Oh, of course." He flashed her a smile. "And yes, your mom was much better than I'd expected, for the most part. I was worried. She slept well last night so that helped."

"It's Ruby."

"Ruby?"

"Yes, whenever she's around, Mom is checked in, more present. Haven't you noticed?"

"Hmm—" Nick thought back on the last few months. It had been a bit of a dance, working through the highs and lows. The hallucinations had become more frequent. Sure, June had had her good times too, when she was lucid, playing with the Wii or when Norah dropped by, but the lows, the silences had been growing longer, spreading through the day. "And Jonathan. He's helped her too."

"For sure, but Ruby, she's like some kind of happiness whisperer, even more so than Jon."

"We'll keep her then." Nick raised his glass to his lips, hiding his face so Martha wouldn't pick up on his ridiculous fantasy.

"Dad, you know they can't stay forever, right? Lennon must really miss them already."

"Of course." He swallowed the smokey Scotch.

Martha slipped on her sweater and took a long look around the suite. "I gotta go. I'm really tired."

"I know. Thanks for all your help. We couldn't have done this without you." She waved away the praise.

"No, it's true," he insisted.

"Jonathan helped."

"He did, but he just picked up the slack. You did the lion's share."

"You did too."

"Martha!" Nick pretended to scold her. "Take the damn credit."

Martha laughed. "Okay Dad, thank you and you're welcome. I'm going to check on Mom again before I go."

Nick knew she was asleep. She slept like a baby these days. Some nights he woke up and checked if she was still breathing. It was her waking hours that were tough. Martha was right, Ruby had changed things today—her excitement about the big truck, the moving day donuts and even helping Jon dismantle their bed, dropping each nut and bolt into a small plastic bag. She'd had lunch with June. Ruby had helped Gloria *smash* the eggs for the sandwiches while June watched. When Nick walked by the kitchen doorway, he stopped short, surprised to hear June taking part in the conversation. He'd asked June about it later, but she'd forgotten it all, so he was glad he'd eavesdropped on the simple discussion about eggs and donuts, June agreeing that the sandwiches were really good, but that raw eggs were disgusting, icky and gross.

"Gross," June had repeated, mimicking Ruby's expression of distaste.

"Let's have a donut, Grandma," said Ruby, forming her crusts into little tents.

"Honey."

Ruby peered into the box that had held a baker's dozen. "Oh, there's only one left. And it's got chocolate." She looked at June. "We'll go share-sies, Okay?"

June smiled, which was approval enough. Gloria cut the donut in half and Ruby let June choose first. June smacked her lips, making Ruby giggle. Both took big bites.

"Boston Cream!" June declared. *Had June really said that?*

Ruby had worked her tongue around the thick custard while Nick had watched in wonder.

Now, recalling their delight, he smiled and emptied his glass, savoring the warmth of his finest Scotch. He would always be confused and awed by June's jumbled mind—memories saved for years, like coins in a piggy bank, hidden, safe until shaken free. Boston Cream. He was sure they hadn't had donuts in a couple of years, and even then, when they used to treat themselves at a local coffee shop June always chose a honey cruller. The magic of Ruby.

Martha collected her purse and bent to kiss the top of his head. "All good in there, Dad. Your pjs are in the bathroom so you won't wake Mom. Don't forget the nurse will be here at eight tomorrow. Are you okay until then?"

"Yes of course. Just like at home. We'll be fine."

"You can always call downstairs, you know."

"I'm aware. Now go. You're exhausted. You've done enough." He waved her out.

The door clicked shut, prompting Nick to consider another Scotch. He looked around, forgetting where Martha had stored the bottles. No more liquor cabinet. Where were his decanters and the glasses? They'd been a gift from his partners—Baccarat crystal that June had always washed by hand. The new furniture confused him a bit. Nothing looked quite right to house his collection of whiskeys. He opened and shut a few kitchen cabinets with no luck. Maybe the credenza, the sideboard Martha had called it, such an old-fashioned word, now apparently back in style. He ran his hand along the smooth mahogany finish. It must have cost him a fortune. He slid open the left door and discovered photo albums, puzzles, small purple weights, stretchy bands. June's stuff. The right side held his whiskeys. He bent low, careful not to kneel as he might never get up, and made his choice. He spied the edge of a carton, a familiar label, slid his index finger along the shallow top shelf and discovered a box of cigars. He laughed. Martha had vetoed these, but Jon had intercepted them before they hit the garbage. "I'll take them for Lennon," he'd fibbed. Nick returned them to the shelf, pushing them as far back as he could. He put the Scotch back too. He'd had enough.

Nick walked through the suite, locking the main door and then checking the patio slider. He watched the wind move the trees and spotted a raccoon, seeing mostly its eyes as they caught the lights from the path. He opened the door and stepped into the night. Martha had been busy out here too. He sat in a wide wicker chair; the high back cushioned his neck and head. It rocked. June would like that.

Not much to do before bed anymore. He'd put the big house to sleep so many nights. Hopefully Jon had remembered to set the alarm. Had he given him the code? Ruby would be asleep by now. She'd had a busy day. But Martha was right. June engaged with her, more than Jon or Martha, even more than him.

Today had gone much smoother than he'd ever imagined, because of Ruby. He closed his eyes. Rewound the day.

They didn't have to coax June into the building. She'd held Nick's hand under hers on the walker as they'd followed Ruby and Jonathan to the pool, the gym, the cafe and finally the suite. She'd clearly lost any memory of her previous visit, but that was okay. She seemed more interested, if only in Ruby's excitement.

The rooms had confused June a little. But when she sat in her chair, Ruby snuggled beside her and spread the blanket over both. June's shaking hand rubbed her back. Nick heard her whisper, "little girl." Ruby didn't sit long, of course. Martha had organized dinner and they all ate from the takeout containers. The excitement of the day had taken its toll. Jon took Ruby home and the nurse arrived on time to help June get ready for bed.

He'd worried for nothing. June had done so well. But Nick was unsettled. He felt stiff, tired from what? He hadn't done anything physical. Maybe just the anxiety. His family had surprised him. They'd really come together. He rocked and studied the stars, remembering how June had told the kids that each one was a fairy, dancing across the sky with the fireflies. Jonathan had been wonderstruck but had Martha ever been convinced? She was wary, demanding proof. June had concealed fairy houses in the hedges and trees, left clues and tiny notes but still Martha questioned the evidence.

He was lonely. It hit him like an electric shock. Now, with all his family together, everyone nearby, he suddenly felt alone, forgotten. Silly old man. He was fine. But he was having trouble seeing forward. What was he going to do with himself? He knew June's future all too well. That's why he was here, for her, to make the best of the life she had left. He'd given up a lot, for June. He felt sullen, whiney. "What about me?" he wondered aloud. He'd been too caught up in everyone else's problems to figure out his retirement—caring for June, Martha's divorce, finding this place. And then, the Jonathan saga. Yes, he'd definitely had his hands full. But now what? What was left for him? He missed work, the challenges, the wins, and truth be told, he'd felt good in those bespoke suits he'd left hanging in his closet. He missed his partners, Sylvie, his golf buddies. He hadn't seen anyone in months. Christ, maybe it had been years. It sure felt like it. Jonathan and Ruby would head back out west soon. A little pang went off in his heart. He *couldn't* lose Jonathan again. But he might. So, it was going to be him and Martha.

"Oh Martha," Nick sighed. Could he maybe hook her up with a nice guy? Maybe not. But he'd better warn her not to end up old and angry like him. Angry? Jeez he was! And why the hell not? He was royally pissed off. At the universe? At June? At himself? Jesus, what kind of man was he? A hell of a lawyer for sure, but he had failed his family. His son had run away from home and his wife had deceived him. Both too scared to trust him. He knew June had loved him. They were in love, lovers. He'd forgiven her but an unwelcome anger swelled in him.

Nick closed his eyes, a futile attempt to block the memory. He'd taken her for granted for so many of their years, mistaken optimism for happiness. Maybe they'd just been living next to each other for too long, forgotten how to stay together. Sure, he'd been tempted, even gone too far a few times. But he'd never— "I had a lover," she'd said. Just like that, completely out of the blue. She'd come into his office and sat on the only chair not piled with books. He'd laughed a little. "Really?" She'd been surprised, offended by his skepticism and then she'd told him about her west coast lover. He hadn't understood, dismissed it as a cruel joke, her illness, a bad dream. But no, it was true. This lover, Mateo, had made her feel special. Fuck! All those trips out west. Jonathan knew. Nick had been too busy to notice.

She'd wanted him to know her secret, just in case he found out later, when it was too late to tell him that she'd always and only loved him. The recovery had been painful—fueled by anger, accusations, confessions and helped by time, a luxury they no longer enjoyed. There was too much to lose, so they had steered their way back on course, using all the years behind them to build the ones ahead. And in the end, forgiveness, because he knew he would disappear if he failed to love her.

Nick shivered in the night air. He shook off his anger. He missed June. The few sparks of her that remained were not enough. He wanted her back, all of her. Shit, they had, no *he* had wasted so many years. He'd counted on more time.

The wind blew through the trees, *Whispering Pines*. They seemed to be mocking all he'd given up. But no, this place wasn't to blame. June's life was fading and his would have to shrink to fit. He'd figure it out. That's what he always did. He'd really miss that putting green, though and—where the hell were his crystal decanters?

Nick went back inside. This was their home now. He locked the door and pulled the curtains. He turned out the lights and walked the few short steps to their bed. He sure didn't miss the fuckin' stairs.

CHAPTER THIRTY

Another day, another—well not a dollar. Was there a saying for those who idled away their days? He'd leave it to the poets. Nick stepped out onto the patio and slid the screen across. It was a little chilly, but he liked to have his first coffee of the day outside, out of the way, while the nurse, no, he'd been corrected many times, while the personal support worker, whose name was Shirley or Nelly or something, helped June get ready for the day. There seemed to be a different one every morning, even though he had asked for some consistency. But the substitutions didn't seem to bother June at all. She called them all Gloria. They were pleasant enough, helpful and efficient, patient and kind. Nick found them annoying.

It was a little ironic, really, one of life's little jokes. According to all the nursing reports, June was adjusting quite well to her new life at Whispering Pines. But Nick was not. It just didn't feel like home. He was trying. Every day for almost six weeks he'd gotten out of bed, full of drive and determination which routinely disappeared by mid-morning. It all boiled down to privacy and independence, and the fact that he had neither. He woke up very early to shower and dress before the first intrusion. Naps had become routine but then he didn't sleep well at night. He was unhappy with the mail system. His newspaper often went missing. And the towels came back from the laundry feeling crunchy. Sympathetic, but a little impatient, Martha tried to make light of his complaints, declaring he was much too set in his ways. Besides, Mom was doing so much better here.

Yes, but he wasn't.

Jonathan and Ruby were coming this morning. Ruby would be joining June in the pool again, for her aqua therapy. Nick had been unsure about the swimming, June hadn't been in the water for a few years, but on the first day, Ruby had helped to coax her into the pool and now they swam together twice a week. Just yesterday the doctor had added Parkinson's Disease to June's growing list of problems, not really a surprise given her uncontrollable shaking. Nick had spent enough time on Google to understand that Lewy Body Dementia and Parkinson's often went hand in hand. Having a name for the shaking didn't make it any better. But the water did. June relaxed in the warm pool—buoyant, bobbing, floating, sometimes humming softly to herself and, Nick hoped, free of pain. She had always been a good swimmer, teaching the twins herself, doing lengths in the morning and now Nick liked to watch her float on her back, arms extended, calm and untangled. She seemed whole again, as if time and disease had not fractured her mind and body. His beautiful June.

"All done, Mr. Walker." Today's Gloria called from the kitchen.

Nick collected his cup and newspaper.

"Thank you," he said to the young woman.

"Will you be needing anything else, then?" Her smile complemented her lilt. "Are you comin' down for breakfast?"

"Oh no," Nick replied. So, this was another new girl. "We always take care of our morning meal ourselves thanks."

"Oh, good on you. Have a lovely day then, the both of you."

Nick closed the door behind her, locking it, notwithstanding the commandment against doing so. Knowing that nearly all the staff had a master key annoyed him plenty. Nope, he chided himself, releasing the lock. Loud sounds, like knocks, scared June, so he'd have to live with the invasions.

"Good morning, June." He sat down across from her, waiting to see if she would know him today. "You look lovely, sweetheart. I like how this girl fixed your hair."

June nodded. It was early, but a nod was a good sign.

Nick prepared two bowls of cereal, healthy whole grains with bits of nuts and some kind of dried fruit pellets. He poured a little in June's bowl and topped it with a generous helping of her favourite sugary loops. Martha disapproved, but sugar was the least of their worries.

Nick tucked a napkin into the front of June's shirt to catch the drips. "Did you sleep well?" She studied her bowl. "I know, it's just cold cereal. Eggs would be nice, right?" He'd been indignant when told he couldn't use the single burner hot plate he had ordered online. And he refused to go to the dining room for breakfast, not without June, and mornings were too complicated to go with her. "I'd love bacon and eggs—even some toast. I'll find out if there's any rules regarding toasters." He gestured toward the kitchen where his espresso machine had taken over much of the counter space. "But no stove. That microwave thing is useless, you know?"

"Pandas are here… outside, baby ones, rollin', rollin'…"

Nick knew June saw fairies but the pandas were new. He wanted to point out that, of course, this couldn't be true, to remind her that she and Ruby had been watching the live panda-cam a few days ago, but he knew better than to try and change her reality. He'd been coached—he'd even attended a seminar on dealing with hallucinations. He knew what to do but still felt lost. "Should we go look at them together?"

"Gone." Her face was expressionless.

He changed the subject. "Ruby and Jonathan are coming today." He waited as June used her spoon to push the colourful circles under the milk and then watched them pop to the surface. "June." He gently touched her cheek. "June, look this way." She followed his words. "Jonny is coming today, with Ruby."

"Ruby...likes pandas." She returned to her cereal. Eating slowly, avoiding all the whole grains and fruity bits.

Nick gave up. He'd been instructed to go with her during her hallucinations. But this one was over, and it was a good one, positive, not scary, so he let her be. He checked his watch. Not even nine and he was already exhausted.

**

Nick startled at the sound of a quick knock, the door swooshing open. He'd just drifted off. His first cat nap of the day.

"Morning, Mr. Walker! Oh sorry. I didn't wake you, did I?"

Nick shook his head and automatically checked on June. "No. No, just resting my eyes." June was still in her chair, seemingly unaware of the intruder. "You startled me. That's all."

Holly was a geriatric physical therapist, thoroughly vetted by Martha, who came three times a week. She was very expensive and not covered by insurance but her work with June in the pool was impressive. She was cheery, vivacious, bubbly, like a cheap bottle of champagne. That's unfair, thought Nick, checking himself. June liked her, so he could endure her exuberance.

Why couldn't he get used to this place? The days seemed long—interminable really. Nick had started counting them, like a prisoner, until Martha chastised him for being petulant. He'd known it wouldn't be easy, but he really thought he'd be able to adjust to living here; less space, less worry, more help. But he had sorely underestimated the value of privacy and space. His usual mantra, *for June's sake,* wore thin some days, fraying his nerves, making him feel like a fraud, a hypocrite every time someone praised him for his devotion and patience. "June is so lucky to have you," they'd say. He'd smile and wonder if whiskey would soften the lump in his gut.

"Sorry," said Holly. "I did knock before I came in."

For some reason Holly annoyed him the most. She was always chipper and cheerily British. Was it her optimism and enthusiasm or maybe June's affinity for her? He just wanted to silence her, maybe with a resistance band or one of June's weights. *Jesus. That's a little harsh.*

"No, it's fine," said Nick. "Just sometimes—no worries." He forced a smile, but Holly had moved on.

"Mornin', M'lady," said Holly. She held out her hand and helped June stand up. "Come on then pet, which bathing costume should we choose today?"

Nick watched them walk to the bedroom, frustrated by his own resentment. He closed his eyes and tried to continue his nap. Swoosh—the door swung open again.

"Sweet Jesus." Was there no peace?

"Good morning!" Ruby bounced into the suite. "I'm here!" Ruby had arrived in her swimsuit and unicorn cover-up, another gift from Aunt Martha.

"Hi, Grandad."

Nick braced himself and put on his best grumpy bear face. Ruby jumped into his lap and he ambushed her with hugs and tickles.

Ruby giggled. "More please." She wriggled in next to him.

"Settle down, Ruby. You're going to crush Grandad." Jon was carrying Ruby's knapsack, her new favourite stuffy and a bag of groceries. "Here you go, Dad, as requested, even the chips and dip. But if Martha asks, I will deny everything."

Nick laughed. "Don't worry. I can handle Martha."

"Yeah, in your dreams."

"Daddy bought our favourite cookies too. Can I have one?" She jumped out of Nick's lap.

"Sure," replied Nick. "But after swimming. Grandma's almost ready to go to the pool."

Ruby's face slid into an exaggerated pout. "Hmph." She crossed her arms.

"All ready!" cheered Holly, leading June from the bedroom.

"Holly!" Ruby skipped toward them. "Hi, Grandma." She wrapped her arms around June's waist. June rested her free hand on Ruby's shoulder, fingering her hair. June looked happy, Nick thought, ashamed by his earlier thoughts.

"Hello, wee luv!" Holly's enthusiasm seemed to redouble for Ruby. "Are you swimming with us today? I love your shirt. Unicorns are the best!"

"I know." Ruby beamed and jumped to meet Holly's high five.

"Hi, Mom." Jon moved slowly toward June, smiling.

"Jonny?"

Nick could read the confusion on her face. She tugged at her swimsuit.

Jonathan took her arm, lightly steering her. "We're going to the pool, Mom."

"Pool?" Her eyes darted from person to person.

"Yes, swimming," said Jon.

"Jonny?"

"Yes, we're going to walk to the swimming pool. Okay?"

"I'm coming too," said Ruby. "See I have on my bathing suit." She lifted her coverup over her face and giggled.

June giggled too. She shuffled forward and grasped the handles of the walker Holly had set in place. Ruby tried to pull open the heavy wooden door but her tugs and grunts weren't enough.

"I'll help with that," said Nick. He opened the door and stood back. "And I might as well join you."

"Dad," said Jonathan. "Could you wait? I'd like to talk to you."

Nick nodded

"Holly," said Jon. "We won't be long. Are you okay with both of them? Even Ruby? She's a little wired today."

"Sure, no problem. We'll be fine," Holly assured Jon.

Jon bent down to meet Ruby eye to eye. "Do not go in the pool until I get there. Okay?" Ruby nodded. "I mean it, Rub. You can sit on the side, put your feet in and watch Grandma. That's all. Got it?" Her head continued to bob. "Say it, please."

"I got it!" Ruby spun around and ran ahead. "I'm ready!"

"Come on, ladies," said Holly. "We're off to the pool!"

Nick closed the door. "What's up, Jon. You look mighty serious for a Wednesday morning."

"No, not really. I just wanted to…to let you know. We have to leave, Dad, go home, you know back to Victoria. Lennon—"

"Oh. No." Nick sat down in his leather chair. "I know, I knew—"

"It's just that we've stayed a lot longer than I'd intended. And now, it's really hard to leave. Ruby has gotten so attached."

"Yes, that goes both ways for sure." Ruby was such a force in their lives now. "Your mother will…geez, I don't know what this will do to her. It's not like we can prepare her or that she had any idea that this wasn't going to last. I just don't know…." His voice trailed off as he pictured his days without Ruby. A searing ache churned slowly through him, sadness, regret, grief. Was this how a heart broke?

"Dad? Are you okay?" Jonathan moved forward, as if ready to catch him.

Nick touched his arm.

"Yeah, yeah. Fine. It's just that…" He paused. He had so much to say. So much to explain. He'd thought about it. He'd even made notes one night. But now, he couldn't remember. He blurted out his regrets, sharpened to a fine point. "I'm sorry. I was such a shitty father."

"Whoa! Where did that come from? And don't go there. It's ancient history. Right?"

"Right." Nick slowly nodded. "I just needed you to know how sorry—"

"Dad, can't we just leave it as, I don't know, mistakes of the past? Lord knows I have a bucket full of those."

"But I think we need to talk this out. I just don't want you to think I'm ignoring or avoiding things."

"I don't think that. And for the record you weren't a totally shitty father." Jon grinned. "My deep-rooted teenage angst may have contributed to our problems."

Nick nodded. "Not a good fit back then, were we?"

"No, kinda like bulls locking horns."

"Yeah," said Nick.

"Look, we can't go back, Dad. I'm a father now and guess what? It's not as easy as I thought!"

Nick laughed. "Just wait until Ruby hits puberty."

"Oh, that's when we'll send her to live with you."

"Yeah, because teenagers are my forte."

Jon chuckled.

 Nick needed to say more. "Jonathan, I don't want to lose you again."

"Oh Dad. That's not going to happen. I'll stay in touch. And we'll be back soon, I promise."

"With Ruby?"

Jonathan laughed. "Yes, she'll insist on it." He reached out and pulled his father into a hug. "I love you, Dad."

Nick fought back tears, surprised by his rising emotions. "Love you too, son." He held the hug a little too long, but Jonathan didn't seem to mind.

"So, you're heading back home, are you?" Nick used an old lawyer trick, ignore the emotions and get back to business. "When?"

"Friday. Lennon booked the tickets last night."

"This Friday?"

"Yeah, the day after tomorrow."

No. this couldn't be right. Not so soon. Nick was suddenly irritated, maybe angry. "Did you know?" His mouth seemed to have disconnected from his brain.

"Know that Len was booking the tickets?" Jon laughed. "Of course I knew. Do you think he's kidnapping us? He has the credit card we use for travel. The one with the points."

"Oh, of course." Nick shook his head, sorting out his thoughts. Had he somehow come to believe that Lennon had—what? Ceased to exist? Disappeared? Split? They were married, he reminded himself, with a daughter. "Yeah," Nick conceded. "I'm sure he misses you both."

"He does and we really need to get back to our normal lives, you know. I'm glad I was here to help you and Mom. And that we managed to straighten out some things. But, you know, it's time."

"We'll miss you."

"I know. I'm not sure Ruby will ever forgive me. She's fallen in love with all of you."

"Did you tell Martha yet?"

"No, but we're having dinner with her tonight. Pizza and a movie at her place. Ruby is very excited. I'll tell her then."

"That should be interesting."

Jonathan laughed. "Martha won't really care that I'm leaving but she won't want to give up Ruby."

"Indeed." Nick stood. "Well, maybe we should head to the pool, join the ladies. Okay?"

"Sure. You know, I'm really going miss you guys."

"Yeah. You sure you can't leave Ruby here?"

"Yes, Dad, very sure." Jon chuckled as he pulled the door behind him.

But Nick wasn't kidding.

CHAPTER THIRTY-ONE

"*F*riday?! Are you fuc—" Martha looked over her shoulder at Ruby, who was watching Trolls for the umpteenth time. She leaned into Jonathan's face and, making no effort to hide her anger, whispered, "Are you fucking kidding me?"

Jonathan took a step back, then another. "No. Look I know it's a bit sudden, but we've been here like for forever."

"And?" Marta waited.

"And what? We don't actually live here, you know."

"Yes, I am aware of that. This is just so typical!" Martha scolded herself for being surprised. Wasn't this just like Jon—parachute in, get into Dad's good graces and then take off again?

"Martha," said Jon. "I know you're still pissed at me but—"

Martha turned and walked into the kitchen. She yanked a bottle of the good cabernet from the wine fridge and set it on the counter. Yesterday's glass was still drying by the sink. "I'm having wine."

"That's fine," said Jonathan.

"I don't need your permission."

"I wasn't—" His words were cut off by the pop of the cork. "Martha, please don't be mad. I thought we were, you know, okay."

"Yeah, I know you thought that."

"So, we're not?"

"God, you're dense."

"But we're here. You invited us."

"Ruby's here, you're just a necessary evil."

"Hey!"

"We've made a start, but that's all."

"A start?"

"I'm not Dad. I can't just—" She snapped her fingers with a flourish. "And pouf, I forgive you. You screwed up, Jon—for years and years. That's a lot of damage."

"I'm sorry, I really am."

"I know. But—" He'd probably never understand. She didn't have the time or patience or the strength to try and make him see that while he was *finding himself,* they were hurting. After all, he was still Jonathan.

"Can I have some water?"

"Help yourself."

Jon filled a glass with tap water, took a slice of cold pizza from the box and sat down.

Martha peeked in at Ruby before she sat at the table.

"She's asleep," said Martha.

"Ruby?"

"No, one of the trolls. Yes, Ruby."

Jon sank into a kitchen chair. "Jesus, you're really wound up."

Martha contemplated her wine—sniffing, sipping, swirling it around and around. Jon had been here, like what, six, seven weeks? They'd never really talked. Oh sure, lots of casual bits, but nothing important. He'd betray her trust, hurt her too many times, disappeared again and again. At one point, she'd thought he was dead! Arm's length was safe; but then Ruby happened. Martha couldn't lose her.

"Martha?"

"Does Dad know?"

"Yeah, I told him this morning." Jon chuckled softly. "He took it pretty well, but he wants to keep Ruby."

"So, yeah, you two are just like buddies now. Dad and Jonny. Forgive and forget."

"It's not like that."

"But it is, isn't it?" She could feel her resentment swelling. She downed her wine but it was offering her nothing. She could feel Jon watching her as she took a bottle of Perrier from the fridge and filled her glass.

"We talked. Dad feels bad and we're—"

"Buddies."

"No, not exactly, but—"

Martha leaned forward. "What's the big secret?"

"What?"

"The secret," she said impatiently. Martha had been stewing about it for weeks—wanting to know, afraid to ask. "The one you and our father share. The one that nearly blew the top of his head off when you alluded to it."

Jon still looked confused.

"When you first got here!" Martha hissed. "About Mom's trips—"

"Oh!" Jon blushed. "Right, got you now. So, you really don't know?"

Martha glared at him. "Don't make me beat it out of you."

"It's not my secret." Jon screwed up his face. "I shouldn't—shit, I should've kept my mouth shut."

"But you didn't. And—"

"Mateo."

"What?"

"Mom found a friend, in Victoria. Mateo...and—" His face had turned hot red.

"Wait! Are you saying our mother had an affair?"

"I am."

Martha was shocked, trying to imagine such a thing, but pushing away the images that were too gross to imagine. "Like a lover?"

"Yes," Jon grunted and started choking. "Pepperoni," he mumbled, catching his breath.

"Our mother?"

"Yes, Martha. Our mother. June Walker. Wife. Mother. Church auxiliary and garden club member." Jon pushed back his chair. "Hang on, I just want to make sure Ruby's really asleep."

"Holy shit." Martha's mind was racing, searching for clues. Trying not to picture her mother in bed with someone other than her father. "Holy shit, shit, shit." There'd been office rumors, fights overheard at home, so she had suspected her father, but never ever her mother!

"Out like a light," said Jon, sitting back down.

"Did Dad know, I mean does he know. Or how does he know?" Martha's mind was doing summersaults.

"Yeah. That's the strange part. Apparently Mom confessed."

"Really?"

"Yeah. I think it was when she knew she was getting sick, but that's just a guess. As far as I know, he'd never suspected a thing. Too busy working, I guess."

'Yeah, some of us have real jobs."

"Ouch."

Martha flashed him an insincere grin. She had so many questions. "So how long? When? Who the hell is Mateo?"

"Really? You want the details?"

"Yes!" Of course she did. She had to make sense of this. "Wait, just the, I dunno, *facts*. Nothing vile or God forbid, lascivious."

"She's my mother too, you know."

"Yeah, it's just—"

"It's not a horrible story."

"Except for Dad," said Martha. Had Peter cheated? She'd wondered but there'd been no real evidence, other than his apathy. "Spill it."

"Okay, as far as I know, it started innocently enough—"

"Well, good to know our mother wasn't walking the streets!"

"Do you want to hear this or not?"

"Yes."

"Well, Mom joined a bridge group—at the community centre."

"Where you met Lennon?"

Jon sighed impatiently. "Yes."

"Seems like a remarkably good place to meet people."

"Martha!"

"Go on."

"She'd come for like six weeks or so, back when I crashed my car and got arrested—you do know that story, don't you?"

"Yeah, as much as I want to know."

"Well, Mom was there, basically to keep an eye on me—to make sure I did what the court order required, just like every grown man wants and needs."

"If the shoe fits—"

"Anyway, she got bored. I was busy with AA meetings and trying to hold onto a piece of my business and my dignity—" He stopped and inhaled and let the breath escape slowly. "I was trying to find work, so she started playing bridge in the afternoons. Mateo liked bridge too."

"Apparently."

"They were just friends at first."

"Of course they were."

Jon stopped talking. He waited. "You done?"

Martha nodded.

"They met for lunch a few times, moved onto dinners and then one evening, Mom texted me, something like; *Don't worry. I'm fine. With Mateo.* She came home in the morning."

Martha gasped. "Holy shit! What did you do?" She could hardly imagine what she would have done if her mother had pulled this on her. Confronted her? Maybe. Asked for details? Definitely not!

"Nothing. I left. Went to an AA meeting. I figured I needed one." He toyed with his pizza crust. "Honestly, we never talked about Mateo—not ever. She spent several more nights away and then went home."

"End of story?" asked Martha. She sure hoped so.

"Nope."

Martha tapped her wine glass. "Top me up."

Jon handed her the bottle of sparkling water. "So, that was the year when Mom visited more often. I guess Dad never questioned it because I was her excuse."

"Yeah, that's what she told me too."

"Well, she didn't spend *all* her time with me. And once, I wasn't even there."

"Are you kidding?"

"Really. She told me she was coming but I had booked a climbing trip for the days she wanted to come. But that didn't stop her." Jon shrugged. "She knew what she was doing alright."

"Mom." Martha wasn't sure if she was angry or in awe. "Who is this woman?"

Jon shrugged.

"Did you know him? This—Mateo?" She spat out the name like it was sour milk.

"Met him a few times at the centre. But once they'd started, you know—"

Martha cringed, put her hands over her ears.

"Yeah, once they hooked up, he stayed clear of me."

"And Dad?"

"I don't know much." Jon crunched that last of the crust.

"But he knows, right?"

Jon nodded.

"And—" Martha was trying to sort this out. "He knows that you know *and* that you know that he knows."

Jon chuckled nervously. "Yeah, I think that's right. So, out of the blue, like months later, he sends me a text, after midnight—the middle of the night for him. I remember the exact text, every word. *Mateo. Is it true?"*

"That's all?"

"Yup. I was gobsmacked. I didn't know what to think. How to answer. I left it until the next day." He stopped.

Martha impatiently waved him on.

"Wait, I need to back up a little. It's gotten a little confusing." He tapped his finger on his knee. "Right, Mom hadn't visited in quite a while. We still talked on the phone, and I knew she trusted Norah, because that's where I sent letters and pictures and stuff. Mom told me she was having trouble remembering things and Norah told me it was more serious than that. So, I kinda figured that for some strange reason, Mom had confessed and Dad needed to know if she was imagining it or if it was, you know, true."

"Yeah, it's sometimes hard to tell what's real."

"Exactly," agreed Jon. "So, I texted back, like the next day. *Yes. I'm sorry.*"

"Succinct." Martha shook her head. "You Walker men are an enigmatic breed, aren't you?" Perhaps this was the root of all their problems.

"I guess so. But that's it. End of story. Not exactly a fairy tale, is it?"

"No. Not a fairy tale."

Jon yawned. "You know, when I was still angry, with Dad or life or whatever, I was glad she'd had a fling. That she hadn't used up her whole life on us and the great Nick Walker." Jon waved his arm in the air as if orchestrating a grand introduction.

"She didn't waste her life," Martha protested. "Except maybe babysitting you."

"You're not going to forgive me, are you?"

"Nope."

"Mom talked to me, when she visited. She was like—a different person—not Mom, but different, honest, free."

"So, she hated Dad, her life, everything here?"

"No, of course not. Don't be so damn dramatic! No. She blamed herself. She had regrets." He paused. "But apparently Dad does too."

"Don't we all?"

"Yeah," said Jon. "Plenty." He stood and placed a hand on Martha's shoulder. "We'd better go. There's lots to do before Friday."

Martha watched from the porch as Jonathan carried Ruby to the car, Mom's old car, and buckled her into the booster seat. A wave of sadness was tempered by her rising anger. Jonathan was leaving again. She turned away and closed the door. There was absolutely no way of telling when he'd be back.

CHAPTER THIRTY-TWO

Nick woke with a start. The sound—a wail, a thud, a whimper. A bad dream? He reached across the darkness. "June! Oh June!" She lay crumpled on the floor, still, her eyes wide, pleading. Nick crouched next to her. "Are you alright? Where does it hurt?" No words, just fear and tears. He was afraid to move her. They needed help. The red button by the door. He leaned closer. "I'll be right back," he whispered. "I love you."

June moaned.

"Don't move, sweetheart. I'll get help."

"No," June reached up an arm to him. "You…help."

Using the bed for support Nick faced June, slid his arms around her and counted—one, two, three. They rose together, somehow sliding June back onto the bed. They didn't let go, cradling each other until their racing hearts slowed.

Her nightgown was wet, soaked through to the sheets.

"I'm going to turn on the light now, just so I can find things." He took a large towel and a clean diaper from the bathroom, "Arms up."

June raised her arms and he quickly swapped her wet nightgown for a dry one. He spread the towel over the damp spot on the bed and gently guided June back onto her pillow, then lifted her legs. He changed her quickly, then tucked the covers around her. He turned out the light and slipped back into bed.

"Thank you," said June, her lips barely moving.

Nick reached for June's hand and squeezed it, held it until she fell asleep.

In the morning, Nick dressed quickly, careful not to wake June. He was tired and needed a coffee. He still wasn't sure if June was hurt, but she didn't seem to be in any pain. With any luck she'd be fine. He hadn't slept much, maybe not at all after the fall, worried June would try and get up again. He'd decided not to tell anyone, not the PSW, not Martha. It was an accident, an isolated incident. He'd taken care of it. He'd do it again, if he had to.

Nick brewed his coffee and steamed the milk to perfection. Was it too much to hope that his paper had arrived? Damn. Mrs. Babchuk, from across the hall, must have *borrowed* it again. Nick sighed. She'd bring it back later, drop it in front of the door, the sections completely out of order. She hadn't been right since her husband passed and Nick didn't have the heart to reprimand her.

Nick scrolled through the news on his iPad and had brewed a second coffee before today's Gloria arrived. Rita was a regular. He followed her into the bedroom, eager to check on June and ready to explain away any questions.

June seemed fine, awake and uncomplaining as Rita helped her from the bed. Rita lifted the towel. "Uh, she had a little accident, so I changed her last night," said Nick.

"So, you need clean sheets?"

"Yes, please." Relieved, Nick returned to his coffee.

"Mr. Walker?" Rita was standing in the doorway. "Mrs. Walker has quite a nasty bruise on her right side, the hip and thigh area. Do you know how this happened?"

"Oh yeah. She sort of slipped out of bed last night. But we were fine."

"Like she fell?"

"No, more like slid off the edge. You know, I'm not exactly sure. I was sleeping."

"Hmm," Rita stood beside him now, then pulled out a chair and sat. "You know we're here to help. Anytime. Even at night."

Nick nodded. "Yeah, I know. It just didn't seem necessary."

"Well, I think it probably was necessary. It could have been a lot worse, like if June had broken her hip."

"I would've called."

"You shouldn't've moved her."

"She moved first." Nick felt like a delinquent teenager. "Just leave it alone. We're fine."

Rita nodded and went back to June. *Just do your job,* thought Nick, fully knowing that she was right. He gave up on the iPad and readied himself for the next invasion. June's physiotherapist would be here soon. She'd have questions too.

**

In the next few days, June's bruises grew, melded from black to yellow and green. No one else asked Nick about it, but he had to presume they knew. So, he wasn't too surprised when Helen, the Memory Care Coordinator came to see him. She billed it as just a friendly visit but he figured she had an agenda relating to June's fall. He didn't offer her a coffee.

"You know," said Helen after a few quips about the weather, "it might be time to start thinking about finding a bed for June, on the sixth floor."

"No," said Nick.

"Well, there's one available now. I can assign it to June, but—"

"No." He didn't want her help. She didn't know him or June. She didn't know what was best for them. "Look, Helen, this was an isolated incident. That's the very definition of an accident. I'm not moving June upstairs. Not now, not yet."

"This isn't the first incident. She hit you, didn't she?"

"No! She did not hit me. She doesn't have good muscle control. She clipped me on the lip. She didn't mean to."

"But—"

"No buts."

"Should we maybe speak to your daughter? See what she thinks?"

"Absolutely not!" Now he was angry. "I am perfectly capable of making my own decisions and looking after my wife. When we need your help, we will let you know. Just leave us be. We're fine."

Later, when June was sleeping, he made his way to Helen's office and apologized for his ill temper, but again, turned down her offer, at least for the time being. As much as he hated to admit it, he knew he would need her help eventually.

**

Nick had gotten used to the routine, the constant flow of people in and out of their home. It was Thursday, swim day. He had even gotten used to Holly. Nick pushed June to the pool, while Holly talked, she barely stopped for a breath. How was Ruby? Still swimming? Sweeter than ever?

Nick showed her a photo on his phone.

They'd opted for the wheelchair because it was easier, faster than the walker. June had changed into her swimsuit without much push back. But now, as Nick watched from the poolside bench, she refused to get in the water. None of Holly's cheerful optimism was working today.

"Let's just go back to the suite," suggested Nick. He tried to hide his frustration.

"No, no," insisted Holly. "I have her for two hours. We'll figure this out. You find something else to keep you busy." He started to shake his head, argue, but she wouldn't budge. "You look like you might be needin' a wee bit of a break, Mr. Walker. Go for a walk or something, anything to take your mind off things."

He stood slowly. "Thank you, Holly." He didn't have the energy to fight and June would hardly notice.

He wandered out of the pool area, feeling relieved, guilty and a little lost. He still hadn't taken the time to really explore things around here. He'd been lazy of late, holed up in the suite, being grouchy and stubborn according to Martha. But mostly he was anxious about June, and really tired.

The sound of laughter and the smell of fresh baking lured him down the hall. A small group of ladies were in the kitchen, seated around the large granite island, watching as a tiny woman wearing a long white apron, pulled a hot tray from the oven. They all leaned forward in anticipation. Nick stopped, inhaled deeply. Cookies, the sweet aroma of warm sugar and chocolate, immediately transported him back home. June used to make perfect chocolate chip cookies, soft and chewy. The twins especially loved them warm from the oven, delighting in the gooey mess.

"Would you like one?" A light cheerful voice interrupted his recollections "Fresh out of the oven!"

Nick shook his head. "Oh no, no thank you. But they smell delicious."

"Oh, come on," urged one of the other ladies. "You look like you could use a bit of sugar."

Was she flirting with him? No, she was probably just reacting to what seemed to have become his *permanent grumpy face,* so called by Martha.

He smiled. "Well, okay, then. You've twisted my arm. And how could I resist, given such a charming baker?"

One of the ladies pointed to an empty stool. "Come, take the load off awhile."

"Oh no," said Nick. "Thanks. I would, you know, but I'm headed to the gym." It wasn't exactly a lie—he just wasn't sure where he was headed.

The ladies looked disappointed. Had he broken some mysterious unwritten retirement home rule? He accepted a cookie and took a bite. "Delicious. My compliments to the chef!" The baker glowed, her cheeks flushed, but from the heat of the oven or his attention he couldn't tell. "Have a good day, ladies." He returned to the hallway and headed towards the gym, at least he hoped he was going in the right direction.

He passed a craft room and slowed enough to peek in the door. Another group of ladies, almost indistinguishable from the kitchen group, were knitting and a tall, gaunt man was humming as he painted a birdhouse. He looked up and nodded at Nick, a friendly, silent hello. Nick nodded back, wondering how he'd ever fit in here. He felt like an alien who had wandered too far from his mothership. Nick liked to golf. He'd never had any interest in hobbies like woodworking or painting. Maybe he could learn? God, next he'd be considering jigsaw puzzles. He chuckled.

The hallway opened onto a glass wall fronting the gym. Right. He remembered this from their initial tour. Martha had tried to set up a workout schedule for him at some point. He'd forgotten or maybe he was just too stubborn to follow Martha's orders. He pulled open the door and breathed in the smell of rubber, steel and stale sweat. Ah, finally something familiar. He looked around. The gym was empty, save for one heavyset man on a stationary bike.

"Hello there. Come on in."

Nick hesitated, preferring to explore on his own. He was dressed in a tee shirt and pants stretchy enough to try out the machines if he wanted to. And he'd worn his runners. He'd come to enjoy their comfort even though they lacked the weight of his oxfords and seemed to scream *old man*.

"Come on, come on, don't be shy. You need some help?"

Nick was irritated by his officiousness. "No, I'm good," he said with a bit of annoyance.

"The rules are on the far wall, next to the water cooler. Instructions are on each machine. Towels, over there." He pointed to a clean white stack.

The voice was friendly, but still Nick resisted.

"I'm Tony. You come for a workout?"

Nick felt like it was the first day of summer camp and this guy, an overzealous councilor.

He sighed without trying to hide his irritation. "Nope, but I'm good. I know my way around a gym."

Tony laughed, ignoring or not even noticing Nick's derision. "Great, most of the new guys who wander in here are lost or scared off by all the new-fangled equipment. Just give me free weights any day. But my knees are shot so I'm stuck with this bike to nowhere. But I'm not going under the knife. No way. I watched it on YouTube. It's all saws and hammers and stuff. It's just carpentry if you ask me. No way. How 'bout you? Your knees okay?"

Nick gave up. He'd either have to engage or avoid the gym forever.

"Not too bad, most days. I used to play a lot of golf. Maybe that helped."

Tony huffed. "Golf. Never saw the point of it. A good walk wasted, right?"

"Spoiled." Nick corrected him and then felt like a shit. "Some days it can feel that way." He chuckled, trying not to be a total jerk. "I've always liked the walk. It's usually pretty peaceful."

"Yeah? Really?" Tony laughed; his belly jiggled under his singlet. "Y'know, I might try walking one of these days. Check out the trees and all. Not much to do around here, right?"

Nick nodded. Yeah, he knew exactly what Tony meant. He moved towards the bike and extended his hand. "Nick Walker."

Tony stopped peddling, wiped his palms on his shorts, took Nick's hand and shook it firmly. "Antonio Rossetti, but my friends call me Tony."

CHAPTER THIRTY-THREE

Martha mixed a second spoonful of fresh raspberries into her plain Greek yogurt and slipped two slices of sprouted wheat bread into the toaster. She inhaled the wonderfully sweet yeasty aroma, so much better than that anemic bread Peter liked. Damn. Even after all this time he could still get in her head. Those last terrible months, he'd refused to eat anything remotely healthy. She'd been furious when he'd come home with a squishy loaf of Wonder Bread and parked it on the kitchen counter. He would eat it, two, three or sometimes four slices at a time, smothered in peanut butter and high fructose strawberry jam. She felt a bit queasy just thinking about all the arguments they'd had over bread. God, they'd been so stupid. Martha jumped when the toast popped up. It's only bread, she reminded herself, as she covered each slice with melting butter.

Martha sat at the table and checked her phone for new emails and then the latest headlines. Nothing very interesting, or very new for that matter. She watched a short trailer for the latest Disney movie. She was still surprised when these ads popped up with her newsfeed, a direct result of having searched through the classics to find a movie that wouldn't give Ruby nightmares. Jon and Ruby had been gone for almost six months now and despite almost weekly FaceTime chats, Martha missed Ruby. At least Jon was doing better at keeping in touch now, but she figured that was thanks to Lennon.

Martha opened her Amazon app and started searching for some books to send Ruby; nothing says *please don't forget me* like a gift, right? She'd added a couple of cute easy readers to her cart when her phone buzzed. The caller ID jolted her attention from unicorns and superhero puppies to *X Husband*. She'd texted Peter last night but for some reason he always called. Martha preferred texting—more efficient and less emotional. She could even add a sarcastic emoji without being too incendiary.

She pressed the speaker option. "Good morning. You got my text?"

"Yep, that's why I'm calling. Hi, Martha. How're you doing?"

His composure was so annoying. She hadn't the need nor the patience for chit-chat this morning. "Oh, just super! Feeling stressed, overworked. Mom's no better and now my father is depressed." She could hear her acerbic tone—she just couldn't stop it.

"I'm sorry your parents are not doing well."

"But really I'm missing Ruby." She bit her tongue. Why was she sharing this with Peter?

"Who's Ruby?"

Martha hadn't told him that Jonathan had reappeared, or about Ruby. They weren't exactly talking back then.

"Jonathan's resurfaced?" Peter knew the story, just not the sequel.

"Yes, he was here when Mom and Dad moved. And Ruby is his daughter."

"What? Are you kidding?"

"Yes, um, no. I'm not kidding." She just couldn't stop. "And he's married."

"Holy shit! Like—to a guy?"

"Yes, Peter. Jonathon doesn't care much for women, remember?"

Peter chuckled. "I know your brother is gay. I'm just a little surprised, that's all."

"Yeah," agreed Martha. She looked at her watch. She needed to get a move on. "Sorry, as interesting as it is, I don't have time to go into details. I only texted you to remind you that your boxes are still here, you know, all the heavy ones. Your squash and tennis rackets too. Hockey sticks. And of course, your canoe." That damned canoe had been a rare impulse purchase by Peter. She hadn't approved. They'd used it often enough, years ago when they could paddle together without arguing. Now it hung over her car in the garage, silently judging her. "When are you coming for all your shit?" She pictured herself chopping the canoe into tiny little pieces and sending it to him, payment due on delivery.

"Jesus, Martha. I thought we'd moved past this. We're divorced, no longer adversaries. Let's be nice, okay?"

Martha nodded but said nothing.

"Okay, then." She heard the frustration in his voice. "Look, just leave the rest of my *shit* on the front porch tomorrow and I'll pick it up after work." The line went dead.

"What the hell! Peter!" But of course he couldn't hear her. See, this was why they should text. She stared at her phone, waiting before realizing he wasn't going to call back. She picked up her phone and stabbed out

Tomorrow! and pressed send. She took two angry bites of toast, then tossed the rest of her breakfast into the sink, rinsing it out through the garburator. The grinding noise, usually satisfying, grated on her nerves. She didn't hate Peter. He just annoyed the hell out of her. She started the dishwasher and washed out the coffee pot, vigorously scrubbing at the calcified coffee stains. What an ass. Clink! Shit! A long thin crack ran up the side of the pot. Shit. Shit. Shit.

Why was she in such a bad mood today? She wasn't sleeping well. She hadn't gone for a run in a while. And she'd cancelled last week's visit with her parents. And then there was work. She'd somehow missed a deadline—a filing. Fixable but unacceptable. But no need to take it out on Peter. She dried her hands and ran through the conversation in her head. Yup. It was all on her. She could try blaming work or her parents. But no. Jonathan? Still no. Just Martha being bitchy.

She took a picture of the cracked pot and dropped the phone into her leather tote. She'd find a new one online. Next, she ran through her checklist, computer, phone, water bottle, keys. She set the alarm—a necessity now that she lived alone, and headed for her car. She glanced at her watch. Six minutes behind schedule, but that really was Peter's fault. He should have texted.

**

The office was unusually noisy. Was everyone in the office meeting in the hallway outside her door? The ongoing construction across the street rattled her office windows.

Martha managed to feed off the chaos and worked right through lunch. She was surprised and pleased when Sylvie set a large green smoothie on her desk.

Martha had inherited Sylvie from her father. Sylvie was just a couple of years older than Martha, taller and more athletic. Her round gentle face never looked angry and she greeted everyone with the same warm smile. She was dependable, efficient and affable. Clients loved her. She had a highly developed assistant's instinct and was not easily distracted, except by golf. She was an avid fan and a very good player, willing to rehash weekend tournaments and trade tips and tales of legendary shots with anyone, which explained why Sylvie had been Dad's secretary/assistant for more than twenty years. Martha had resisted taking her on when Dad retired, but now she had no regrets.

"Oh Sylvie. You're the best. Thanks." Martha took a long sip through the oversized straw. "I'm starving."

"Yes, I figured you'd be hungry." Sylvie smiled. "It's baby kale, strawberries, oat milk and some cashew butter."

Martha, mid-sip, gave Sylvie a thumbs up.

"You have a meeting with the Richardson-Brown people at 2:15," Sylvie reminded her.

Martha nodded. "Yes, it won't take long. They just need to sign off on the final agreement. The documents are ready, right?" Martha took the lid off the smoothie and took a swallow. "This is delicious, by the way."

Sylvie smiled. "Of course. Everything will be waiting for you in the small conference room."

"Thanks." Suddenly feeling quite hungry, Martha pulled open her drawer and found a protein bar. "I'm leaving early today. After the meeting I'm going to visit my parents. It's long overdue."

"Great," said Sylvie. "Please say hello from me." Sylvie had sent them flowers and a bottle of Scotch when they'd first moved in.

"Of course." Martha tore open the snack bar and remembered, not for the first time, the gossip that she had once overheard about her dad and Sylvie. Peter had laughed, nearly choked, when she'd recounted the rumour to him.

"Nope, not possible," he'd insisted. "Not Sylvie! Your Dad's way too smart to risk losing such a good assistant." Martha had agreed and laughed along with him. But it really wasn't until Sylvie brought her girlfriend to the firm Christmas party one year that Martha truly believed him.

The meeting went smoothly, as expected, and Martha was packing up for the day when Mark DeLuca tapped on her open door.

Mark, a young looking fifty-something, was one of the finest corporate lawyers in the city, hardworking, easy-going and handsome too. Still considered a catch, according to office gossip. He was one of those rare straight men who had never been married. Many had tried, and now he had a lot of baggage—two ex-fiancées, a son and a penchant for big adventure. He was a serious rock climber, a backcountry skier and even spent a few weekends a year paragliding. Eligible but hard to catch.

Not that Martha had ever tried. She'd had a huge crush on him when she'd worked as a summer student the year she finished high school. He was friendly, well dressed and gorgeous but at least five years her senior.

She was married when she joined the firm. He'd flirted a little in the early years, teased her about being her father's daughter, but there were never any hard feelings. He'd worked alongside her father and was made a partner on his recommendation. When she became a partner, he'd sent her an expensive bottle of champagne along with a cheeky note about being one of the *named* partners, not true of course. Mark's quips about nepotism were always clever and often funny. They had an easy friendship, one Martha valued.

"You aren't leaving, are you?" Mark looked confused

"I am. But don't worry, my bag is full of billable hours."

Mark laughed. "Why doesn't that surprise me? No, it's just that I thought we were going to discuss the students today." He looked at his watch, an understated yet stunning Tag Heuer, which Martha had often admired. "Like now."

"Geez, I forgot. I'm sorry Mark. I can't today. I promised my father I'd stop by—for a real visit. I haven't spent much time with them lately."

"Hey, no worries, tomorrow maybe?"

"Tomorrow works," Martha agreed.

"Breakfast?"

"Sure." It would be a nice start to her day.

"That bistro on King?"

"Perfect, 5:45?"

Mark groaned. "I hope you're kidding."

"Too early?" Martha grinned. "Seven, then?"

He laughed, flashed his perfect white teeth. "You are a formidable woman, Martha Walker. See you there." He turned to leave. "Please give my regards to your parents. They're good people." He saluted, an exaggerated flip of his fingers off his forehead.

Martha smiled as he walked away. She leaned out her door just enough to sneak a slightly unprofessional gander at his very nice behind. Must be the climbing.

**

Martha opened her sunroof and turned up the music. She pressed down on the gas pedal, sped along the country roads and sang along to *Destiny's*

Child. She no longer listened to break-up songs, vetoing them in favour of strong female anthems and singers. Today she belted out the words to Survivor; *I will survive. Keep on survivin'.* Martha sped past the poorly marked turn into Whispering Pines. Shit.

"Siri, stop music." She did a quick three-point turn and followed the winding lane up to the main building. Spring and the rain that had persisted for the last week had worked their magic. The maple trees, not pines, that lined the driveway were just starting to bud. She inhaled the smell of raw damp earth and freshly mowed grass. She drove slowly, for once minding the cautionary *SLOW* signs. She chose a parking spot next to a garden of bright spring flowers: tulips, daffodils, hyacinths. Mom used to plant hundreds of spring bulbs.

Martha glanced at the incoming messages on her phone, all work related. She'd read them later. She paused for just a second and then typed: *Sorry for the black mood this morning. Not a good idea to leave boxes on the porch all day. How about Saturday morning? 8:30? Coffee?* She sent it before she could change her mind. She closed the car roof, grabbed her bag and headed inside.

Her timing was almost perfect. Mom should be awake now and Dad would be sitting with her, but no doubt grumbling about something—the inadequacies of today's caregivers or the absurdity of eating dinner at five o'clock. She worried that Dad would never pull out of this funk. Was it depression? Should she have him assessed? Moving into The Home had really aged him. *The Home.* They'd all taken to calling it this now, it was easier than *Whispering Pines*, but Dad always enunciated the words as if he were saying *the haunted house of horrors*. Ruby had loved his spooky Dracula voice, but the truth behind it bothered Martha. They had spent so much time finding the right place and Dad had wanted it, liked it, until they'd moved in. He grumbled all the time now. He'd all but given up on driving, not of necessity, but because he just didn't want to do anything anymore. "No, your mother needs me," he'd replied when Martha had suggested he get out, go for a drive. Or more worrisome, "Where would I go?" He'd always been so active, engaged, and now Martha barely recognized him. His spark was gone.

Martha wished she'd paid closer attention, spent more time with him, and Mom. She'd been stretched thin lately, taking on so much at work, new clients and student matters, and trying to settle things with Peter. Visiting twice or even once a week had become a practical and emotional challenge. Dad was always crotchety and Mom so quiet, or worse, angry. She steeled herself, hoping for a good day.

Martha tugged on the door, twice before she realized it was locked. She rapped on the glass and peered inside, using her hand to focus her vision. A young woman jumped at the sound and scampered from behind the desk. The metal deadbolt shifted and she pulled open the door, standing aside for Martha.

"I'm so sorry Ms. Walker."

"That's okay," said Martha. "It's not usually locked."

"Right, yes, well we don't lock this door, except at night of course, but well, we temporarily misplaced a resident earlier and—"

"My mother?" asked Martha, alarmed by the word *misplaced.*

"Oh goodness no! June ah—Mrs. Walker is not one of our wanderers. And don't worry. All is well now, just a little misunderstanding." She patted Martha's arm.

Martha, fearing a hug might be imminent, took a step back. "Okay then, thank you." She walked to the reception desk and signed in, another policy that annoyed her father. A basket of cut daffodils caught her eye. "Are these available? For sale?"

"Yes. It's daffodil month! They're for charity—cancer research, I believe."

Martha pulled a fifty dollar bill from her wallet and picked up several bunches. "They're perfect," she said. "Thank you!"

"But that's too much—"

"It's a donation." She smiled and walked briskly through the lobby, eager to deliver the flowers to her mom. It usually seemed too quiet in here, eerily peaceful, but today she could hear conversation and laughter.

"Martha!"

She stopped short at the sound of her father's voice.

"Martha, over here."

She turned toward the little café and was surprised to find her father sitting at a small round table with two other men. "Dad, I didn't expect to find you here!"

Her dad laughed. "Just having a cuppa with the guys." He stood and took Martha's arm. "This is my daughter, Martha."

"Hello," she said, but was flabbergasted by her father's demeanor.

"Martha, this is Tony." He nodded toward a stocky man with a friendly, ruddy face that was dominated by a bushy white moustache. "And this is Arty." Arty, thin and frail, his shoulders bent with age, used a cane to rise slowly and reach for Martha's hand. Both men were cordial, chatted briefly and returned to their coffees when Dad and Martha excused themselves.

"New friends?" Martha asked.

"Just a couple of guys I met in the gym. Well, I see Tony in the gym. Arty spends a lot of his time here, drinking coffee. He'd not a big talker, but he seems to like when Tony and I join him."

Martha chuckled. "So yes, new friends. I'm glad, Dad, really." She tugged his sleeve and touched his bicep. "And you're hitting the gym?"

"Yes, I am. I just got tired of doing nothing all day. When your mom is napping, I sneak off."

"She's alone then? I can arrange—"

Nick held up his hand. "It's done. I asked at the desk and there are a few women who volunteer to help. They live here and one of them sits with your mom whenever I go to the gym or café or when I go out. I leave bonbons for them, as a thank you."

"Bonbons?"

"Yeah, you know, chocolates. From the Italian bakery, with Tony."

"Wait. What? You go out?"

Dad laughed. "Yes, Martha. Tony and I have gone out for lunch a couple of times. He doesn't have a car so I drive. There's a decent diner not too far from here. Good cheeseburgers."

"Really?"

"Yes really. I may be old but I'm not helpless."

"Oh Dad, I never meant to suggest—" She didn't finish because her dad was holding the door for her, grinning ear to ear. *Bonbons?!*

**

The daffodils were a hit, fussed over by Mom's chocolate loving sitter who left quickly to secure her own bouquet from the front desk.

Martha took several rapid pictures of her mom holding the bunches of daffodils. "Smile Mom." Her face was glowing.

"A smile brighter than the morning sun," said Dad.

"Yell...ow...flowers," said Mom, searching but not finding the word.

"Daffodils, Mom."

She nodded slowly, methodically.

Martha snipped the stems and set them in a large crystal vase filled with tepid water.

"That was a wedding gift," said Dad. "From the Wilkinsons, I think. They were friends of my parents and a bit weird. He always wore a bow tie."

Martha still couldn't believe the change that had come over him. "Seriously? You sure don't have any memory problems, do you?"

"Not yet." He crossed his fingers.

"Daffodil," said Mom as Martha set them on the table.

"That's right Mom, daffodils." Martha smiled and settled herself on the ottoman next to her mom. She grasped her mother's hand, the skin now paper thin, and she tried to calm her shaking fingers. "Mom doesn't fidget with her rings anymore?" Martha wanted to believe this was progress, a small improvement, but she knew better. She glanced at her dad and realized her question had saddened him.

"No, I think she shakes too much now," he said quietly. And then, louder, "Your rings are good now, right June?"

"...rings ..." She shook her head. "...don't...don't...don't..." She tried to pull the rings over her gnarled knuckles. Her face was twisted, her voice was low and raspy.

"Are they stuck?" Martha placed both her hands on Mom's knees.

Mom nodded, holding Martha's gaze. "...rings for...Martha rings..."

Martha gasped. "Oh no, Mom!"

"Martha's," repeated Mom. "Martha...Martha..." She was almost shouting now.

"Okay, okay, I get it Mom. You want me to have your rings, right?"

"Ye...yes," she said, settling back in her chair.

"Thank you. But you keep them. They're yours for now, mine later. Okay?"

Mom's face settled. She smiled and closed her eyes.

"She'll probably rest now, for a little while at least," said her father.

"You know, I haven't heard her speak for a while. Her voice has changed. She doesn't sound like Mom anymore."

He nodded. "I know. Good days and bad. Some days she says nothing at all."

Martha stood and moved to the small sofa, closer to her father. "I'm sorry," she whispered, fighting to hold back tears.

"I miss her."

"Oh, Dad."

Martha could hear the birds pecking at the feeder, a distant lawn mower, footsteps in the hall. Both of her parents were so strong, her mother fighting to hold on and her dad struggling to help her. Both refusing to give up.

"Would you like to join us for dinner tonight?" asked her dad. "Only if you have time, of course."

"Sure." Martha replied quickly, surprising herself. She usually resisted eating in the dining room, pleading work or tiredness and once a fictitious massage appointment. She knew it was weak, deceptive, but she'd felt so uncomfortable at previous meals in the communal dining room—a sea of white hair, canes and walkers, all reminders of the inescapable deterioration of life. But now she wanted to be with them. "Yes," Martha confirmed. "I'd like to join you tonight."

Dad called the desk and had Martha added to their table.

They walked to the dining room together, Mom in the middle, clinging to the walker, her velvet slippers shuffling with each slow step. Martha was surprised to see that she was now several inches taller than her mother. She placed her hand over her mom's, absorbing her frailness, the shaking and pain. How much longer would she last? They entered the dining room together and were warmly greeted by several of the diners.

They settled at their table. Martha focused on her parents, peppering Dad with questions about his new friends, all to avoid the clamour of the room. She was relieved when their meals arrived.

"So, Martha—" Dad leaned towards her, grinning like a Cheshire cat. "We, well I, met a doctor the other day, not your mom's doctor, but Arty's son, and he's available and—"

"Available?"

"Yeah, as in single."

"Dad! Are you setting me up?"

Dad chuckled, even blushed a little. "I guess I am. I met him, good looking, tall, seems like a nice guy and I told him you were divorced now."

"Dad, you didn't!"

"I did. I thought maybe you'd like to meet him."

"Geez, Dad." She hadn't a clue what to say but for some reason she blurted out. "I'm having breakfast with Mark tomorrow."

"Mark? From the office?"

"Yes, Mark DeLuca."

"Is that a good idea? He's a bit of a Casanova, Martha."

Martha saw her mother smile and nod, a choppy head bob that migrated into her hand, spilling a forkful of mashed potatoes onto the white linen tablecloth. Martha waited while her father cleaned it up. He used a spoon to help her with the next bite. "Seems like your mother agrees with me."

"It's just business, Dad. We're reviewing the students. That's all."

"Okay, well what about the doctor then?"

"No. Definitely not. I'm not ready."

Dad sighed. "But you will be ready, at some point, right? I don't want you to be alone, sweetheart."

"I know. But right now, alone is just fine with me. Honestly."

Dad nodded and turned his attention back to her mom, resting one hand on hers and feeding her with the other. She smiled as she ate mashed potatoes and peas. He tried to cut through the chicken with the fork.

"I can cut that for you," offered Martha.

'No, we're good," said her father, wiping a spot of gravy from her mother's cheek. He cut the remaining chicken in to small bites. "Would you like some more, June?" he asked, holding the fork to her lips. "Come on, just a couple more bites. I think there's butterscotch pudding tonight."

Well, thought Martha, her parents were getting along just fine without her. She'd felt so guilty about a few missed visits and her father's apparent depression when really everything was just hunky-dory here. Martha rested her chin on her hand, fighting the urge to pout. Geez, what the hell was wrong with her?

"Dessert, Martha? Martha? Penny for your thoughts."

"What?"

"Would you like some pudding?"

"Oh no, thanks. I'm good." And she was good—happy and proud of her parents. "Thanks for this," she said.

"What," said her father. "Dinner?"

"No. I don't know. Everything, I guess." She watched as her mother slowly spooned the caramel desert into her mouth. "Is it good, Mom?"

"Yummm," she hummed through a messy, toothy grin

On her drive home Martha wondered about Arty's son, the doctor, and handsome Mark DeLuca, men just on the edges of her peripheral vision. Someday. Soon. Maybe.

CHAPTER THIRTY-FOUR

Martha kicked off her running shoes, slipped her AirPods into their case and downed the large glass of ice water she'd left on the kitchen counter. She'd shortened her route today, just to be sure she'd have time for a shower.

She slipped out of her soggy running bra, peeled her leggings down to her ankles and then used her feet and some carefully timed hopping to free herself from the sweaty spandex. What had possessed her to invite Peter to come for coffee? He made her so angry, and sad. She'd try and do better today.

Martha turned on the shower and stepped in, not waiting for the water to warm up. She showered and dressed quickly, pulling on skinny jeans and a hoodie, checked the mirror and yanked off the sweatshirt, then chose a pale yellow linen shirt just back from the cleaners. She combed through her curls and then painstakingly arranged her hair into the perfect messy knot. It had taken a whole year, but her hair now stretched to just below her shoulder blades. The longer hair made her feel younger. Embracing change had never been one of her strong points, but this one was good. She checked the time and grimaced in the mirror. Peter was sure to be a little late. He always was.

She'd decided, after changing her mind a couple of dozen times, that they'd sit in the kitchen. The mediator and her therapist would have advised a coffee shop or a park bench, a neutral space for their first post-divorce meeting. But that wouldn't work today. How had this become such a big deal? She'd just wanted him to pick up his stuff. Maybe she should have had it delivered, or junked. Well, she only had herself to blame.

Martha opened the basement door and peered down the steps. Could she move it all to the porch before he arrived? Pretend she hadn't invited him for coffee? She shut the door. No, that would just accelerate things in the wrong direction. This was an olive branch. Martha was tired of feeling hurt and angry. She could do this.

At first she didn't care that Peter had left some things behind. Initially, he'd moved in with his parents, but then, once they'd managed to reach a settlement, he'd purchased a place of his own. With the help of a very patient mediator, they'd been able to avoid both the cruelty and the cost of a contested divorce. Martha had been able to keep the house. It was all that really mattered to her. Peter had pocketed a major chunk of their investments in return. His executive condo in a new boutique building downtown was predictably small and short on storage space so, in a very weak moment, she'd agreed to let him leave his stuff for a while. But she'd grown tired of it cluttering up her basement, a reminder of things past.

Martha surveyed the kitchen, checking for—she had no idea what. A couple of deep breaths steadied her nerves but she was hungry. She pulled open the freezer drawer, looking for something besides spelt bread. She peeled the foil from a frozen block that looked promising—Gloria's lemon poppy seed loaf. How long had it been in there? No freezer burn and it smelled okay. She microwaved it for fifty seconds then shaved off a thin test slice—still yummy. Did it matter that it was Peter's favourite? *Stop dithering!* She carved off several more slices, cut them in half, arranged them on a plate then turned on the coffee maker. Instead of replacing the cracked carafe, she'd had Sylvie order a sleek new machine, not as fancy as Dad's, but it did produce freshly ground beans for each pot.

The coffee was still dripping when she heard the knock on the door. The doorbell hadn't worked in years, which was more than fine with Martha. When they'd first moved in, they'd discovered that it played a full thirty seconds of *Pachelbel's Canon* every time it was pushed. Peter had disconnected it.

"Good morning," said Martha as she opened the door. Peter stood before her, balancing two large coffee cups stacked in one hand and a bakery bag in the other. So, he'd finally upgraded his wardrobe, from baggy weekend sweats to a classic white pocket tee and trim fitting chinos. He looked good. "Oh Peter, I've made coffee."

"But you asked me to bring coffee—in your text."

"I didn't, at least I didn't mean to. I was offering you coffee. Sorry. Come in." Her cheeks grew warm. She stepped back, stumbled over her sneakers and steadied herself on the wall. She avoided Peter's eyes, hiding her embarrassment in an oversized smile. "So—how are you?"

"Good, good, real good," said Peter. He seemed nervous too.

He walked toward the kitchen, but hesitated, just long enough to check out the living room. "I love what you've done with the place."

"What?" she asked, suddenly on the defensive. "What do you mean? I've been so busy. I haven't changed anything."

"I'm kidding Martha."

He was teasing her. His smile seemed genuine, boyish, a little humble. But she didn't know how to take him anymore. He was definitely being friendly, maybe flirty? No, definitely not. "So, you brought coffee?"

"Yup, an almond milk latte, extra hot, and muffins."

"Oh! Thank you." Her cheeks betrayed her again. She opened the brown paper bag and inhaled. "Cranberry walnut?"

"Yeah, you still like them, right? Whole wheat?"

"Yes." She tried to stifle her delight and accidently snorted. "I have something you might like too." She set the plate of lemon loaf on the table and slowly sat down. They were still tenuously connected. The kindness they'd lost over the years had resurfaced—in coffee and baked goods.

Peter slid into his old chair, directly across from Martha. He swallowed a long slow gulp of coffee, then rose, and took two small plates from the cupboard, adding a couple of napkins from the drawer. "This is strange, isn't it?"

Martha nodded. They hadn't been together, outside of the mediator's office for a long time. "It's a bit unsettling."

"I'm sorry," said Peter. He fingered his coffee cup, pulling at a loose edge. "I didn't mean to upset you." He looked sheepish, a little wretched.

"No, no." Martha inhaled shakily. "I'm fine. This just feels so weird. I didn't think—" What? That this wouldn't be uncomfortable for both? She took a muffin from the bag, peeled off the paper liner and took a large satisfying bite.

"Yeah," said Peter. "I know what you mean."

They laughed at the same time, low, rueful tones. They occupied themselves with the food and talked about nothing for as long as they could. How's work? Fine. Busy? Always. Rained a lot lately. Sure has. Small talk, idle chatter. It was so strange, awkward, having so little to say to the man she'd lived with, slept with, fought with for so many years.

"What happened to us, Peter? I mean, why or maybe how."

"Yeah, I was wondering that too." He picked at the skin on his thumb and then tried to remove it with his teeth. Martha tried not to cringe.

"We were so angry, I was mean, downright hostile," she said. Cruel words were hard to forget, whether spoken or heard.

"Me too."

"No, Peter, you were quiet, much quieter than me. Uninterested maybe? Just so damn complacent."

Peter chuckled. "Guilty as charged, but that's because I wasn't particularly unhappy."

"Really, so I blew us up? It was all my fault, then?" Martha dropped a second muffin onto her plate, causing it to wobble and rattle until it finally settled. She closed her eyes and sucked in as much air as she could. She could hear her therapist. Don't go there, Martha. It's old news, destructive and irreversible. She exhaled slowly. "Sorry."

"No, no," said Peter. "I gave up on us. I was boring and dismissive. Probably insensitive. You know, I think we just got used to being alone, together. Does that make sense?"

Martha shrugged. "I think so. Like we were just living next to each other."

Peter nodded.

"I'm not sure I ever thought of marriage as something to work at," admitted Martha. "I took us for granted too."

"Yeah, and I think we changed. We were young when we got married, maybe too young. Young and in love." He chuckled softly. "We were happy, at least I was."

"Me too."

"But time, life changed us. We're different people now. You know? Like you're champagne and I'm beer."

"Oh Peter, really?" Martha looked at his kind gentle face, noted the new wrinkles and greying hairs at his temples. "I guess we can't expect to be the same forever, can we? I wasn't good with the hard times or the sad times." She couldn't stop herself. "If we'd had kids—do you think that would have held us together?"

"Come on. You know that never works." He shook his head impatiently. "Honestly Martha, the universe, or some mysterious higher power decided we shouldn't have kids. I dunno. Maybe the universe got it right. But either way, we can't change it."

"I know. I know. I've given up blaming myself, the doctors and karma." She grinned and bit her lip. "Even you."

He chuckled. "Thanks. I'm glad for you." He helped himself to more lemon loaf. "Delicious."

"Thanks," she replied, but couldn't help noticing the few crumbs that had settled on his chin. She resisted the urge to wipe them away.

"So, dare I ask about your family?"

Martha rolled her eyes and chuckled. "Sure, but it will have to be a recap, or we'll be here all day."

"Okay, fill me in."

"Well, we're all pretty good, except for my mother. As I told you the other day, Jonathan came home. He shocked us all. Just showed up, clean and sober."

Peter's eyebrows shot up. He'd heard this before. They all had.

"No, really. He's done the work. He's like a new man." Even she had to admit it.

"And?" Peter, still eating, mumbled. "You said something about a family?"

"Yes." Martha chuckled softly. "Ironic, right? Jon is married. Lennon. He's a social worker, works with children, I think."

Peter laughed. "Well, that seems about right, for Jon, I mean."

"Right?" She laughed. "But that's a little unfair." Martha felt strange defending her brother. Peter had always supported her when she didn't. They'd shared many a cruel laugh. "He's—Jon's changed. He's different now. Let's call it maturity. He has a daughter too. Ruby."

"Like a baby?"

'No, she's four. Cute, precocious. Mom and Dad adore her." Martha grinned. "I'm Auntie Martha now."

"Wow." Peter let out an exaggerated breath. "Your father—how did Nick—? There must have been some kind of fireworks."

"Well," Martha chuckled quietly. "It was interesting, stressful for sure, but not as bad as you're imagining. Dad was surprisingly—" She paused to think. "Conciliatory. He loves little Ruby and we all approve of Lennon. He's a really good guy. Dad has mellowed a bit."

"A lot I'd say. Time really does heal all wounds then?"

"Yeah, maybe." Martha lifted her coffee cup, took a sip, to avoid looking at Peter.

"And your mom?" The concern in Peter's voice was real. He'd had a great relationship with her mom; mutually friendly, playful, loving.

"She's not great. Awful really. She's very weak now. She has a walker, sometimes a wheelchair. And mentally, she's fading, failing." Martha stared out the kitchen window which was streaked with dirt. "Dementia is really cruel, Peter. Relentless."

"I'm sorry. Is there anything I can do?"

"Nope." Martha leaned back and smiled. "Well, it's not all bad. My father is the good news. Up until this week I'd have said Dad was falling apart too, grumpy and depressed, but he seems to have found a couple of friends. That's helped. Oh, yeah—they're living in a home now."

"Yes, I knew that. Christ, you've had your hands full."

Martha peeled the paper from the second muffin and severed the top, the caramelized, crispy bits were her favourite. She was eating her feelings. She'd have to go for a longer run tomorrow to work off the extra calories. "Yup. Busy as a bee. But I'm fine." She suddenly felt exhausted, vulnerable. "How's your family? Are your mother and father well?" Her former in-laws were younger than her parents and they were serious church goers, Sunday services, choir, weekly bible study. They were always kind to her, but Martha had never felt close, unable to crack their stoic, resolute veneer.

"They're good, same as always." He grinned. "But, not happy that I'm a bachelor again, that I'm shamefully divorced."

"Oh, I can imagine." Martha could almost hear the tongues wagging in the Armstrongs' evangelical circle. "Sorry, that's not easy for you, I'm sure. But, if it makes you feel any better, you're a bachelor, but I'm a divorcée." She shook her head. "Horrible word."

"Hmm, you're right."

Peter leaned back in his chair and drank the last of his take-out coffee.

"Would you like another? It's fresh." She had wanted him gone quickly but now she felt like talking.

"Sure," he said, adding another slice of lemon loaf to his plate.

Martha set the steaming mugs on the table. "So, are you dating yet?"

"Whoa." Peter sat up, wriggled slightly in his chair. "I didn't see that coming." He chuckled.

"So yes?"

"I was, I have, a couple of times, dates. Nothing serious."

Her face crinkled into a playful smile. "I sense there's more."

Peter shifted again. "Do you remember Lola?"

"Lola?"

"Yeah, you know, Alex, from the office, his sister."

"Alex's little sister? She's quite young, isn't she? And married?"

"She's close to forty. And she's divorced too, almost." Peter blushed.

"Are you still—?"

"Martha, it's really—" The colour had crept up his neck and into his cheeks, even his ears were crimson.

"Oh god, I'm sorry Peter. It's none of my business. And I'm making you uncomfortable. Sorry. I guess I was just wondering, because, well, I haven't—"

"Oh." He was examining his hands, flexing his fingers as if they were new and fascinating. "No, no, it's okay. We're not dating, not anymore. We were together, but just for a couple, maybe three months."

Martha nodded.

"It was good—well at first anyway. Nice to have someone to go out to dinner with, movies, drinks, that sort of thing, you know?"

Dinner? Drinks? Movies? "Sure."

"Yeah, she even liked watching hockey, at least she said she did. But she was tireless. And she wanted to do everything together. Jesus, she signed us up for *CrossFit*. I'd never even heard of it. And a couple's massage at a spa!"

Martha laughed, trying but failing to smother it in her hands.

"And yes, she was young, too young for me. Some of it was good, really good, but she had way too many expectations." He looked at her, held her gaze. "It didn't last long."

Martha forced a kind, understanding smile. *Oh god, he'd slept with her, they'd had sex.* Yes, of course he did. Why was this so much easier for men? "Well, I'm working on things, dating and such." Not quite a lie. "Apparently, Dad's found me a nice doctor."

"A doctor," Peter nodded. "Impressive."

"Very." Martha pushed back her chair and stood up. She was done comparing lives. Peter had clearly beat her to the restart line. "Well, then, as nice as this has been, it's time to move on and out."

Peter looked confused.

"Your stuff. The point of this visit. It's all in the basement, right where you left it. The boxes are too heavy for me."

"Right. Okay then." He hesitated, as if he had more to say, but headed toward the stairs. With his hand on the doorknob he turned. "Martha—"

"Don't forget the rackets and that black plastic bin. It's full of your..." *worthless boyhood nostalgia* "...medals and trophies."

He made a few trips up and down the stairs while Martha cleared away the cups and plates. She leaned against the door jamb while he stacked the boxes in the front hall. His squash and tennis rackets, both gifts from her, rested against the wall.

"There's a couple of your coats in the front closet too." Martha tried to sound casual, but she wanted them gone. "The tweed and the leather."

Peter slid open the mirrored door and sifted through the coats. He pulled out his brown tweed overcoat, dropped it on top of his boxes and turned back to the closet. He slid the hangers along the metal bar. "You should keep the leather jacket. It always looked so good on you. You know, *Martha-from-the-hood*." His laugh was muffled by the coats and sweaters as he dug deeper. "But—it's not here."

"I'm sure it is." Martha reached in around him, nudging him slightly with her hip. "Near the back—ahh, here." She pulled the soft black leather jacket off the hanger and handed it behind her. She turned to step back and they were suddenly face to face. He ignored the coat and leaned in for a kiss. "Peter! No!" Martha ducked and retreated. "What the hell? What are you doing? Fuck Peter!"

"Me!? Shit, what's wrong with you? You've been sending me signals all morning!"

"No, I haven't! What signals?"

"You invited me here, the lemon cake, cross examining me about my dating life. You're all dressed up. And—and hell Martha, you were so damn nice to me today!"

She huffed impatiently. "Nice yes, but that doesn't mean I want to sleep with you!" She was shouting.

They stared at each other, frozen in a face-off.

"Well, this is quite the fuck-up," said Peter. He looked pissed off and embarrassed; more like a naughty little boy than a lustful ex-husband.

Martha burst out laughing and was relieved when he started to chuckle too. "Oh Peter, this explains so much about us, our marriage, about everything! I was being nice because I don't want to be angry with you anymore. It's not good for me. I don't want or need all that negativity in my life." Martha paused. Peter seemed to be listening to her for a change. She inhaled deeply and softened her voice. "Look, I'm not saying we have to be friends, well not yet anyway. We both know our marriage is over. Right? I was hoping we could just learn to get along, be nice, you know like in a *we used to be married but now we're not,* kinda way. I don't want to have to cringe every time I hear your name or be angry when someone tells me that you're dating some sexy young thing."

Peter scoffed and shifted uncomfortably.

"No, I mean it. Life is too short to—" She exhaled, exasperated, unable to find the words. "Life is just too short for this bullshit!"

Peter smiled. "Yeah. That's for sure. Look, Martha. I'm sorry, for the—for jumping to conclusions."

"It's okay." She smiled self-consciously. "It's just that, well, I've known you for most of my life, we've had years and years together, mostly good ones. Can't we just find that place where there's peace and respect—and no bullshit?" She couldn't read his face. Was he thinking about her proposal or planning his escape?

"I like it," said Peter. "No more fighting? Yeah, we can do that, right?" He nodded, as if convincing himself.

"Yes, definitely. It might take a bit of getting used to, but I think we can make it work."

He reached out and took her hand, clasping it between both of his. "I just want to apologize again, for my earlier assumptions or—um—let's go with brain fart."

"It's fine, Peter, almost forgotten."

"Thanks, but, just so you know, I never meant to hurt you. Jesus, that's a shitty cliché."

"Sure is," said Martha, extracting her hand from his.

"You're still important to me. I was never happy about losing you.

I'd say you're my soul mate but I'm afraid you'd slug me!" He laughed and took a deep breath. "So, let's just move on, okay? No hard feelings, no strings attached and certainly none of that *friends with benefits* stuff." He winked.

She laughed softly. "Definitely none of that!" Martha closed the closet door and caught their reflections in the mirror. She was flushed but Peter was too.

"Well, I think I'd best be on my way," said Peter.

Martha nodded and handed him the leather jacket.

"Nope, you keep it. I'm willing to bet it still smells like you—your perfume."

"Thank you." Martha set it on the bench. "Should we risk a friendly hug?"

"Sure, but just a hug." His face twisted into mock seriousness. "Don't go getting any ideas." They embraced politely. Peter ended it with a couple of buddy pats on the back.

Martha watched, didn't offer to help, while Peter moved his things to the porch and then out to his car. She handed him his rackets. "That's it then."

"Yup." Peter nodded. "Guess so."

She watched from the doorway as he hurried down the steps, stopped and turned back. He took a long look at Martha and the house.

"See ya." He waved.

"For sure." Martha moved out onto the porch, just as Peter slammed the trunk of a bright red, surprisingly sporty car. "Nice car."

"Yeah." Peter reddened, coming close to matching the car. "I treated myself. It's a bit of an indulgence, but it drives well and has a lot more room than you'd think." He folded himself into the front seat, started the engine and opened his window. "And my parents hate it."

Martha laughed. "So, I'm guessing you're not taking your canoe today?"

"Oh shit." He shrugged and then smiled broadly. "Next time."

CHAPTER THIRTY-FIVE

Martha slipped into her long black cashmere sweater and scrutinized herself in the mirror on the back of her office door. She liked how it made her look and feel taller. She inhaled deeply, sucking in strength and courage. It was just lunch with her father. It sounded easy, but after her conversation with Helen, she knew it wouldn't be. The call from the Home had surprised her. Her parents had been doing so well lately, but the Helen had not minced words—her mother had taken a couple of falls and her father had covered them up. Helen and her dad had argued over moving her mother to the care floor.

She was running a few minutes late, so no time for even a quick trip to the ladies' room. She wished, not for the first time, that she'd been able to snag Dad's old office with its very own powder room. She'd requested it during the last office shuffle but had been turned down based on fairness, seniority and most of all appearances. After all, she wasn't *the* Walker on the letterhead. So much for nepotism. She fluffed her hair, pinched her cheeks like Mom had taught her decades ago, even though it had no obvious effect, and decided against lipstick. It made such a mess on a wine glass. She scowled at herself, collected her handbag and left her office.

"I'll be back by 1:30. Two at the latest."

Sylvie removed her headset. "Your afternoon is clear, if you need more time."

Martha nodded. She'd shared today's mission with Sylvie and was grateful for her support. "Thanks, I might need it. Dad's not going to be happy about any of this."

Sylvie raised one eyebrow. "Your father's a smart man. He'll see it your way—eventually."

"Yeah, maybe but he's awfully proud."

"And stubborn," added Sylvie.

Martha laughed. "*That* runs in the family."

Martha arrived at Syd's just before noon. The posh but dated steak house was nearly empty so she had no trouble spotting him. "Hi, Dad. I take it you approve of my choice of restaurants?" She kissed him on the cheek. He smelled of Polo Green, his *serious business* scent. She loved the smell. The hostess, almost as old as her surroundings, pulled out her chair and placed a crisp linen napkin on Martha's lap.

Dad grinned. "Indeed I do. As soon as you suggested it, my mouth started watering for a nice thick steak and a loaded baked potato. But I am a little curious about the purpose of this meeting." His tone was cheery but he seemed tense. "In my experience a free lunch always comes at a cost."

"That's a bit cynical, isn't it?" She dug into her handbag and pulled out her phone, setting it face down on the table. "How's Mom?"

"She's good, 'bout the same."

"Will she be okay, while you're here, I mean? I guess she has physio and stuff to keep her busy."

"She does. It's music therapy today. She likes that. And I hired one of the extra girls to keep her company."

"Oh, that's good. She won't be alone then." The PSWs weren't girls but she wasn't about to correct him.

"Exactly. She's fine, really." Her father cleared his throat. "So, what's up? You've enticed me here for a reason, haven't you?"

Martha touched her index finger to her temple. "Oh, you're much too clever for me." She laughed softly. "But can't a girl just ask her favourite guy out for lunch?"

He chuckled. "Yes, but what I'm really wondering is why that same girl sent a town car for him, or rather, me, when she knows that I am capable of driving myself." His grin didn't hide his irritation.

"I wanted to treat you, that's all. You didn't cancel the car, did you?"

"No, no I didn't."

"I was trying to be nice. I didn't think you'd be mad."

"Okay. But don't do that again." Her father opened the menu, then glanced up at her. "You got the restaurant right. There's nothing quite like one of Syd's steaks. Nothing."

Martha smiled, allowing herself to relax a little. "You do realize that there isn't really a Syd, don't you? And if there was, he gave up grilling a long time ago." She looked around at the dark wood paneling, dimly lit wall sconces and heavy draperies. "I sure hope the beef hasn't been aging as long as this decor."

Martha loved teasing her dad about Syd's. It was, by far, his favourite place to eat and it hadn't changed in years—or ever. Heavy crystal glasses, white linen tablecloths and worn leather captain's chairs contributed to the old-world atmosphere.

Martha had been here many times, sometimes after she'd started working with her father, but more often with Mom and Jonathan too. It had been a family tradition; a couple of times a year, and always just before Christmas, they'd get all dressed up, drive to downtown Toronto and park under Dad's building on Bay Street. She and Jonathan had loved that they had to take two different elevators—a short ride from the garage to the main level. And then up forty-two floors at breakneck speed to their father's office, which always made their ears pop. They'd run the halls, fill paper cups at the water cooler and spin each other in Dad's leather chair. Excited and hungry, they'd walk the few blocks to Syd's where they were served by austere waiters dressed in black pants and starched white shirts. When they were very young, they were given an extra cushion to boost their chins above the edge of the table. Jonathan always tried to order pizza or chicken tenders and a milkshake but the best Syd's could do was cheesy garlic bread and a bowl of vanilla ice cream with neon maraschino cherries.

"Martha?"

"Ah, yes? Oh sorry. I was just remembering all our dinners. Mom used to dress us to the nines to come here."

Dad smiled. "She did, but I think that was so she could show you off at the office."

The waiter hovered next to Dad and took their drink order—red wine and a Scotch. Her dad was still a handsome man, he wore his age well. His eyes were bright, and his hair, still full and all white now, complemented the crinkles and wrinkles that Martha preferred to think of as smile lines.

"So why are we really here, Martha?"

"It's not a big deal. I just wanted to talk to you, that's all." She was hoping he'd be full of steak and a little Scotch before she had to really get into things.

"What about?" He seemed genuinely puzzled. "Are you okay?"

Martha laughed under her breath. "Yes, I'm fine. Let's order our lunch, then I'll explain."

"Just tell me." He rattled the ice against the side of his glass.

The waiter interrupted. Martha glanced over the menu and ordered a green salad and grilled chicken.

Dad huffed his disapproval and asked for the house special, with all the extras, steak sauce, cheese, sour cream, chives and butter. "Yes, the works," he said. "But separate, in little pots on the side. Can you do that?" The waiter nodded. "Wonderful."

Martha started to object but quickly backed off. "So, Dad, how are you doing these days?"

"Just fine. Why?"

"Well, I got a call the other day, from The Hooomme." She tried to add a dose of levity by mimicking Ruby's spooky inflection, but Dad didn't react.

"You did?"

"Yes—they're worried about Mom. A woman named Helen—"

"Jesus Christ! She had no business involving you."

Martha sat back, bolt upright, surprised by her father's outburst. "Involving me? I'm already involved. You're my parents."

"I'm handling it." He sounded like a child.

"You are? You didn't mention that Mom had a fall."

"It was an accident."

"And she's lashing out. She hit you?"

"Not on purpose! Jesus Christ, your mother wouldn't intentionally hurt…a… She's not dangerous." His face hardened into a scowl, his voice low and rough. "I'm taking care of things. I know what's best for her." He pointed a finger at Martha. "Are they alleging that I haven't—"

"Stop. No one is accusing you of anything, especially me. You've done so much for Mom, but Helen, she's an RN, says Mom is getting worse."

"Chr-i-st." He swore softly under his breath.

Martha waited while the server filled their water glasses. "Helen says Mom has fallen into a pattern of sleeping all day and then she's restless and disoriented at night."

"Helen says. Helen says. Are you cross-examining me? I'm telling you. We're doing fine. Fine." He punctuated his last statement with a large gulp of Scotch, setting the glass onto the table with an imposing thud.

Martha reached for his hand but he pulled back. "Calm down. Talk to me." She looked around at the nearly empty dining room—the other early customers were scattered around the large room and were taking no notice of them. "I'm listening, Dad, but all I hear is an angry, defensive man."

"Stubborn old man. That's what you mean, right?" He glared at her, defiant. "There's nothing wrong. Yes, your mother is becoming more difficult. It's to be expected. But we have help. You know this, Martha."

"I do. But I also know how bullheaded you can be. Don't forget, we're a lot alike." She detected a small but wary smile. "I want to help. But how can I when you won't even concede that you might, possibly need help?"

"I don't."

Martha exhaled loudly. "Look, I know you aren't about to give up on Mom. But—"

"Stop!" Dad nearly shouted, then reined in his voice. "Did Helen tell you what they're planning?"

"It's not a plan, Dad. It's a proposal for care, suggestions, to improve Mom's living situation. It can be tweaked as her care needs change, so she'll be comfortable, live with dignity."

"Nice sales pitch. You came well prepared."

"Dad!" Now Martha was irritated. "Don't be petulant." He was getting the better of her. It annoyed her that, at seventy-nine he still could. But she was pleased too. Nothing wrong with his mind. She checked her phone, stalling to collect her thoughts. "Helen only suggested that Mom would be safer and more comfortable on the sixth floor. You're the one arguing like—like a goddamn trial lawyer."

His face twisted into a dogged, sardonic smile. "I'm simply fighting for what I believe is right."

"I know, but what if you're wrong?" He stared at her. Stubborn old man was right. But she couldn't back down. "Helen also suggested that maybe, because you're not getting a lot of sleep—maybe you shouldn't be driving right now."

"Holy Mother of God. Well, that explains the town car."

"Dad. Please." Martha didn't want to fight.

"Look, we spent a lot of time finding Whispering Pines so your mother and I could be together for as long as possible. I know you like facts so here they are. Yes, your mother is getting worse. She walloped me once, caught me on the lip with the back of her hand. She wasn't angry or upset, just couldn't control her arm. Yes, she fell. She was bruised and scared, but I calmed her."

"Oh, Dad."

"Let me finish, please. She does get angry. But then why shouldn't she? She barely speaks, but when she does, if she knows me, it's brief but she's there. She doesn't sleep much at night so I nap when I can. I have the gym now, a couple of friends and lots of help. I'm handling things and I am perfectly fine to drive."

"Oh dear. I didn't realize things had gotten so bad. I'm sorry."

"You're not hearing me. Things aren't that bad."

"But, wouldn't moving her upstairs make things better for you? You could visit, spend as much time as you wanted with Mom."

"Not an option. Not yet." He looked around. "What do you think happened to my steak?"

"Don't change the subject." She wagged her finger at him. "So why? Why rule out the sixth floor completely? And I need a better reason than just because you're stubborn. You must be able to see some of the benefits."

He hesitated, fiddled with his fork. "Yes, but then she'd be all alone." Martha watched as he struggled with his emotions. "And I promised. I promised her—"

"What?"

"I promised that…that…that…I'd never lock her away." He exhaled.

Martha wanted to reach over and take his hand. She wanted to get out of her chair and go to him, wrap him in a hug. And she wanted to jump in and argue, but she bit her lip as she saw him hesitate.

"But, now, that I'm faced with the possibility, the need—" He cleared his throat, lifted his shoulders and sat straight in his chair. "No. I'll figure it out."

"I know this is hard. Dad, I need you to be honest, so I can help. Just tell me. Are you really okay?"

He inhaled deeply and then let the air escape one beat at a time. "Okay, in a nutshell. I'm tired. And frustrated, often angry. I sit on the patio and I just want to holler or down a whole lot of whiskey. But I don't dare. Your mother needs me. Sometimes I can't stand to be near her. And then there's the guilt. It's—"

"Guilt? You have nothing to feel guilty about. You're Mom's advocate, her protector, her guardian angel!"

"Not always."

"What?"

"I didn't always treat her well. I broke promises. I hurt her—" He stopped and gulped some water. He looked away.

Martha could feel his pain, his guilt. Would it help if he knew that she knew at least some of the past?

"No," he continued. "I just can't move her. Not yet."

"Look at me," she said.

He raised his head slowly. She could feel his broken heart. Damn she was angry at the world, the gods or just at the random cruelty of life. "I'm sorry, so sorry. I haven't been paying close enough attention. I thought you were okay."

"No! This isn't on you. It's not."

"Yes, it is! I can't fix Mom, but I should be looking out for both of you. I'm so sorry."

"Don't apologize. It makes me feel worse."

"I'm sorry," repeated Martha. Dad cocked an eyebrow at her and added a wry half grin. "Right," she chuckled softly. "How about, I'm here and I'm listening?"

He nodded. "Thanks. Just talking about it, admitting it, out loud, helps a little."

"I'm glad." She hesitated. "And, for the record, I *am* sorry." She waved away his objections. "No, please let me do my *mea culpas.*" He nodded. "I think I just felt so relieved that you and Mom were in a safe place, with extra help, that I…I felt…kind of released. And when Jon was here, well he and Ruby were a huge distraction—for all of us. And then, I just dropped the ball."

"No, you've helped us so much. And I'm well aware that we've been a little resistant at times."

Martha laughed. "That's true. Did you guys ever eat all the healthy food I forced on you?"

"Most of it. Well, some, not all. Your mom just wouldn't eat tofu. Some of the casseroles were really good. You know, she still loves her ice cream. Some days it's all she eats."

"Smart woman," chuckled Martha. She leaned in closer to him. "Look, this isn't just your problem, it's ours. You should have talked to me sooner." She motioned to the waiter for another Scotch. "We'll come up with a plan together, okay?" He nodded but looked doubtful. "Chin up now. We'll work this out." He'd said it to her a thousand times.

He leaned back and tried a smile, but it was meek, unsure. "You know, I thought I was handling things. But, honestly, I'm a mess!"

Martha squeezed his hand. "No, you're just someone who's too proud to ask for help."

The waiter set down their meals. "Anything else?" he asked.

"Thank you, no. We're good," replied Martha. He nodded and then backed away.

"That's a lot of food." She pointed at her dad's plate. "You'd better dig in. My defences are down at the moment and it may be a long time before you see such a feast again."

He grinned, inhaled deeply and carved off a slice of his perfectly grilled strip loin. They ate in silence for several minutes. Martha was mesmerized as Dad tried each bite of potato with a unique combination of toppings. He looked happy.

"So, all you expected?"

Dad chuckled, "And more. It's excellent and I plan to eat it all."

"I figured as much." Martha pushed away her half-eaten salad. She waited, debating with herself and finally cleared her throat. "Um, Dad? Look, about the guilt thing. He looked up, stopped chewing. "I know some of which you speak."

Her father set his fork and steak knife beside his plate, deliberately aligning them on the white linen. "Go on," he said.

"It's not healthy to hold onto things like hate and guilt. I don't know the details, I don't need to know, but I have witnessed what you and Mom have now. I don't care if you made mistakes or if she did." She wasn't about to admit that she knew her mom and Mateo and suspected his transgressions. "But it's clear to me that you both forgave or were forgiven." She stopped for a breath. "I've tried to let go of my guilt, find forgiveness. I have the therapy bills to prove it. But I've learned the most from you and Mom—your marriage, your love, the kindness. You are my example of how to forgive. So, whatever it is that's got you stuck, let it go, Dad."

Her dad's eyes were watery. "She didn't do anything like—"

"It's none of my business, and it doesn't matter, at least it doesn't matter anymore. What matters now is you, and Mom, and doing the best we can."

"Thank you, Martha."

"For what?"

"Just being you. Taking some of the load and for not judging." He reached across for her hand.

"I love you, Dad. Nothing ever changes that."

Her father blinked back tears. "On that note—" He pushed back his chair. "I'm going to check the plumbing."

Martha chuckled. He'd used that line for years. Jon had taught it to Ruby, explaining that Grandad was really going to use the bathroom. Martha toyed with her salad, finishing most of the greens and the last bites of chicken. Just as she was starting to wonder if her dad had escaped in the waiting car, she saw him. He'd stopped to chat with one of the older servers. He returned to his place at the table, picked up his knife and dolloped butter and sour cream onto his potato.

"Are you okay?"

"All good. But I am going to finish this."

"I know. And while you were gone, I was thinking—"

"I would've been disappointed if you hadn't been." He winked.

"Well, I think I have a plan. But first, for the record, no one needs both sour cream and butter. One or the other, Dad. One or the other." She grinned.

"I'm indulging. Don't judge me."

"Fair enough." She felt more at ease now. The wine helped. Or maybe they'd cleared the air a little. "We're still going to need a meeting with Helen." She could feel his rising objections. "No hear me out. You and me, Helen and maybe Mom's doctor. We need all the facts before we do anything. As sad as this is, we have to do what's best, not just for Mom but for you too."

"Oh, I'm fine."

"Yeah, I know, for now you're fine." Martha waited while he prepared another bite of his steak. "Just chew and listen, okay? Once we have all the info, we'll decide on the next steps, but we'll do that together."

He was silent.

"Is that okay, Dad? I know it sounds a bit bossy."

He wiped his face on his napkin. "Yes, it's a solid plan, but—" He hesitated. "Well, I haven't been completely honest. In fact, I may have understated the situation a little."

"What do you mean?"

"Well. I didn't disclose all the facts, to you or that Helen woman."

Martha's heart started racing. What now? She forced herself to stay calm. "Let's hear it."

"Well, besides the falls—"

"Falls?"

"Yes. Just two. Well, your mother has started wandering, not often, but one night, a while ago—"

"Dad."

"She…she got out onto the patio. She didn't go far. Well, further than the other times."

"Dad!"

"I handled it. I walked her back in, no problem. But I'm worried the nurses are going to catch on. Or that she'll get out into the hall."

"Yes! Exactly why you should tell them."

Her father screwed up his face but otherwise ignored her. "I think she thinks she's still at the house, looking for her garden, or maybe her glasses." He closed his eyes and slowly shook his head. "You know, maybe we should've stayed there. We dismissed that whole *aging at home* idea pretty fast."

"Dad, stop, this isn't just aging. Mom's sick."

"Yeah, I know."

"Whispering Pines is a good place. That's why we chose it."

"Yeah. Still—the sixth floor—it's locked, Martha."

"For safety. It's not a jail." He stared at her with heavy sad eyes. She wanted to tell him he couldn't have things his way. She had to be strong, honest. "Dad, we have to move Mom to the sixth floor."

"I know." His voice was weakened by a dry sob. "I know, just not yet."

"But soon?"

Her dad nodded and Martha sighed. The concession wasn't solid but she didn't have the heart to press for anything more definite.

They sat together, quietly mourning. Martha shared the tissues from her bag. The waiter approached and quietly set another Scotch in front of Dad. The Scotch alone justified the car!

"Okay then." Martha finished her wine and stood up. "I'm going to the lady's room and then we're having dessert. Do you think they still serve that amazing crème brûlée? I used to love cracking it with my spoon and I think we both could use a little something sweet. Cheesecake?"

"No." He patted his belly. "That's a little heavy, but maybe the apple crisp, with ice cream."

"Good choice. Order it all and something to take home too, for Mom."

"Are you charging this lunch to the firm?"

"Nope, those good old days are long gone, Dad."

CHAPTER THIRTY-SIX

Martha left for the office very early the next morning. The grey dawn, before sunrise, suited her today. Her temples throbbed from the wine at lunch and the additional two glasses she'd had last night. She hadn't made much progress with her father yesterday. She'd at least gotten him to open up, admit how hard it was for him. And he'd sort of agreed to the sixth floor.

She'd spent the whole night worrying. Maybe moving her mother wasn't the right decision. It would be hard on her dad. He'd literally just started smiling again. Just before bed she'd checked out the Whispering Pines website, hoping to get some insight into the care provided on the sixth floor. Not much there, but a further search into lock-down nursing care was harrowing and resulted in the extra glasses of wine.

Martha tried to call Jonathan, but he and Lennon were out for the evening, at an opera. She texted a scowling face emoji and added, *You? At an opera? Call me tomorrow!* She was sure he'd be no help at all, but maybe he could worry a little too.

As a last resort, she just had to do something, she'd left a message for Helen, asking for a meeting to discuss the situation. She'd gone to bed restless, hyped on wine and worry and she was going to pay for it for the rest of the day.

Martha used her key card to enter the office building. The security guard mumbled a sleepy good morning. He looked tired too. Her first task was coffee. She'd made a to-go mug at home but only remembered about it on the highway, half-way to the office. She planned her morning as the coffee streamed into the cup and then spent the next two hours without interruptions or distractions. Sylvie appeared through the frosted glass around nine but felt no need to announce her arrival. Martha had worked her way through countless briefs and contracts when her cell phone began vibrating under a stack of papers. Whispering Pines, Helen, returning her call. Last time, the only time they'd talked, Martha had found her unexpectedly steely, undeniably passive-aggressive. "So you are unaware of your mother's fall?" Martha had dealt with her well enough, but this time she was ready.

"Hello, this is Martha."

"Ms. Walker, Helen Frost here."

She'd never met her, but Martha had no trouble picturing her; a thin, angular woman, dressed in icy blue, whose surname defined her disposition. "Hello. Thank you for returning my call. I was hoping—"

"Yes, Ms. Walker. Are you on board then? Willing to facilitate Mrs. Walker's move?" Her words were imperious, sparse and adversarial.

Martha slowly closed her laptop, deciding to deflect the questions. "You've upset my father." Martha could hear Helen's tongue click. She almost heard her face tightening.

"That was not my intention. But I am concerned about Mrs. Walker's safety."

"As am I," replied Martha, adding just a touch of superiority. "But surely we should be considering the well-being of both of my parents, my mother *and* my father."

"Yes, yes, of course, my dear."

Martha bristled at the condescension but chose to ignore it.

"Look, your father is doing an exceptional job with your mother but it has become abundantly clear, and this is my professional opinion, that some decisions, albeit difficult ones, have been ignored far too long."

Martha wanted to pounce, remind this battle-axe that her job was to help, and no matter how she hedged it, this was not helpful. Martha drew in her claws. "I was wondering if we should have my mother reassessed to see how much things have changed, before we upend them again."

Helen clucked her reluctance. "If you insist. I can arrange for testing, at your expense, of course; there are cognitive and neurological tests, a brain scan, a psychiatric evaluation, blood tests. Whatever you like."

"Yes, all of—"

"However, the staff here feels that such procedures would be quite disruptive to your mother, confusing, frightening and completely unnecessary. There is little to be gained."

"In your opinion."

Helen continued, seemingly without taking in air. "We have accommodations for your mother, a private room, comfortable and safe on our secure floor. This is where she belongs—with or without further evaluation."

Martha waited for more. "Okay, then. Well, Helen, I appreciate your candour, but your plan, as it were, discounts my father. I think he at least deserves the chance to be heard. Don't you?" Martha coated this with all the sweetness she could muster.

"Yes. Yes, of course. I did speak to him, you know."

"Yes, I heard. You scared him and he felt you—" She wanted to say *you were a pushy bitch* but she bit her tongue. "He felt discounted, unheard."

Helen was unapologetic. "Well, then let's set up a meeting." The clacking of computer keys felt like tiny little slaps. "Monday at ten," she declared.

"Nine," said Martha. "In the suite, with both of my parents."

"That is not how we usually conduct our meetings."

"But I insist."

"Fine."

Martha hung up and silenced the scream rising in her throat. Wow, now she understood her dad's aversion to Helen. She closed her eyes and exhaled her exasperation.

"Oh, that sounds like big problems."

Martha jerked to attention and saw Mark standing in the doorway, looking like he'd just stepped off the pages of GQ. "Oh God, please don't tell me I forgot another meeting."

Mark chuckled. "No. At least not with me. Are you okay?"

Today he was wearing a midnight blue suit, tailored just right and a French cuffed shirt, open at the neck—no tie. Professionally casual? Casually professional? Either way it was perfect. How did he do it? Yoga, meditation, Botox? Whatever it was, it was working. He looked so damn good. "Yeah, I'm just a little tangled up with everything. Kinda stressed to the limit. Normal things. My parents need more of my time. Apparently, I've been neglecting them." She sighed. "And the Grayling hearing has been pushed up almost two weeks. Also, my junior is pretty much useless."

Mark slid into one of her client chairs. "Take a breath. Who's helping you on this?"

"Stewart."

His eyebrows shot up. "Oh, yeah. I'm doing his review. It won't be good."

"We can't keep him, and if we do, I'm not sure I can work with him again. He can't seem to get anything done on his own. Questions I can handle but he's so unsure of himself. He's been here awhile now, hasn't he?"

"Almost two years," said Mark.

"Well then, he should be able to work on his own more, right? It's a matter of self-confidence and I can't teach that."

Mark smiled again.

"What?" He was probably a lot more patient with his juniors.

"I came in to invite you for coffee."

"Oh."

"But I think you might need something more than a coffee break. How about dinner?"

"Dinner? Why?" That came out wrong.

"Why?" He shrugged his perfect shoulders. "Because we work together and you're my favourite partner—of all the ones under eighty."

"Thanks, I think."

"And," Mark continued, now itemizing on his fingers. "I quite enjoyed our breakfast last week. You seem like you need a night out." He grinned and lifted his right foot onto his left knee. He wore brown leather dress sneakers, no socks. "And I like you."

Martha could feel herself blushing. She swiveled her chair just slightly into the light from the window. "Just dinner or will we be able to bill this?" She grinned.

"Nope, no shop talk. Just dinner. How about tonight?"

"Tonight?"

"Yup. Where would you like to go?"

"Anywhere but Syd's." She scowled. "It's really old and stodgy now."

"Still your dad's place then?"

"It is. We just went there, yesterday in fact, and it was, well, let's just say it wasn't a relaxing lunch."

"I'm sorry."

"No, it's okay, but I'm really swamped here. I don't think I can get away tonight. Tomorrow, maybe? If that works for you."

He exhaled—an exaggerated sigh accompanied by a generous grin. He pulled his phone from his inside breast pocket. "Well, I guess I can move around a few things." He used his thumb to click and scroll, squinting just a little at the tiny images. He looked up, blue eyes and dimples. "It's a date. I'll book something a little more twenty-first century, okay?"

Martha nodded. Mark waited, as if needing a verbal response. "Perfect." Her voice cracked. She'd known Mark for years, but this felt different.

"Right after work then? I'll meet you here,"

"Great," she replied, trying to match his easy confidence. "I'll be ready."

"Yeah," he chuckled. "If I can drag you away from your desk."

She laughed. "Don't worry, I'm looking forward to it."

He stood and moved toward the door. "Me too." He stopped. "Your parents, are they okay?"

"Yes. No. I'll fill you in later, Okay?"

He gave her a thumbs up, more dimples, and was gone.

A date?! *It's a date.* He'd said it. But was it a date like an event in the calendar or a *date,* with wine and romantic potential? She had the rest of the day to decide.

**

The next morning Martha dressed for the office in an off-white linen sheath and classic flats. She looked professional, polished and boring. The dress was lovely, but—what clickbait had caught her eye the other day? *7 Day-to-Night Looks that Actually Work.* She grabbed her leather tote and tossed it on the bed. Her closet was full of possibilities. The first selection was easy—her favourite Hermes silk scarf with soft geometric patterns in burnt orange and gold. She moved through her large closet slowly, hoping for some further inspiration. Her black worsted wool jacket would work, but it was more day than night. She also dismissed a beaded shawl whose time had come and gone. Maybe a shoe upgrade—a nice leather pump would give her a little height. Or snakeskin stilettos! They hadn't been out for dinner in a quite a while. She picked them up and blew the dust off the toes. Sexy. From her jewelry box, she chose a pair of diamond chandelier earrings, held one up to her ear in front of the mirror and then slipped them into a tiny velvet bag. She laid everything on the bed before going back for her favourite perfume. Nerves and self-doubt threatened to reverse her decisions, but she forced herself to stuff everything into the tote. She had just packed a date bag! She slung it over her shoulder, surprised by her excitement. She was ready.

**

Martha stretched out her toes and fished around under the table in a half-hearted attempt to find her shoe. She'd remembered too late why the beautiful heels were covered in dust. Her feet were burning after the short walk from the office so she'd alternately dangled one shoe then the other off the end of her foot. The right one had escaped.

They'd had a delicious dinner, shared a bottle of wine, maybe two, and now, at the suggestion of the affable maître d', they were sampling cheeses paired with very fine brandy. Martha watched, enthralled, as Mark carefully curated a single bite for her. His gorgeous hand maneuvered it off the cheese knife and onto her plate. She popped it into her mouth— creamy French brie, fig compote followed by a mysterious but tasty kick that made her eyes water. She nodded in appreciation then sipped a little brandy. The shoe, the wine guy, Mark's hand—she was clearly tipsy. She pushed her glass away. "I think I'm done."

"Really? I believe there's more on the way."

"Brandy or cheese?"

"Both."

She hadn't realized it would be so substantial when Mark agreed to the liqueurs and cheese to finish. "Oh no."

Mark laughed. "I think our friend at the bar is trying to impress you."

Martha giggled. "I doubt that. I think you're more his type." She was teasing him, but she sounded silly.

"Maybe." Mark laughed. "Either way, I think we should humour him."

Martha smiled. "I agree." She reached for her brandy snifter. "I wouldn't want to offend anyone," she said as seriously as she could. But it came out playful, flirty.

Mark rewarded her with a winsome grin and placed his hand over hers—amorously or friendly, it was hard to tell.

"Well." He squeezed her hand gently. "Dinner was definitely the right call."

"Because?"

"Because, lately I've been worried about you. You are juggling so much and I'm pretty sure you're not taking any time for yourself. Am I right?"

"I run."

"That's good for stress."

"It is. But honestly, I haven't run in a while. I've been sleeping late most mornings and by the time I get back from the Home or work, I'm usually too tired." She chuckled ruefully. "But you're right about tonight. I haven't felt this foot-loose in a very long time." She cringed at her choice of words. She still hadn't found her shoe.

Mark smiled. "That's great. Mission accomplished."

"Sadly, this feeling will be fleeting. There are many calamities on the horizon."

"I know and I'm sorry. Do you want to talk about your mom and dad?"

"Nope, tonight I am the proverbial ostrich. You know that's not true, right? They don't bury their heads. Why would they do that? How would they breathe?"

Mark laughed. "Very good questions!"

Martha blushed. "I might be a little too relaxed."

Mark clinked his glass against hers. "Here's to burying all of our troubles in the sand."

"Oh yes! Let's run away to a desert island, somewhere far far away."

"With no clients or cell phones."

"Or WIFI or parents." Martha paused. "Hmm, that's a little mean."

"Not really. It's hypothetical freedom." Mark pushed back his chair, stretched his legs.

Martha sighed. "I'll miss them when they're gone."

"I know."

Mark finished his brandy and Martha picked at the cheese. She made one last ditch sweep for her errant shoe and located it under her chair. They sat in comfortable silence for several minutes.

"Ready?" asked Mark.

"Yes," she said, sad that the night was ending. She reached for her bag. "I'll order a car."

"Already done." Mark motioned toward the door. "It's waiting. Neither of us are driving tonight."

"Right," agreed Martha as she rose slowly, checking her balance. She casually hooked her arm through Mark's as they headed outside. Unsure how to end such a wonderful evening, she scurried into the waiting car. She'd barely begun with a *thank you,* when Mark slid in beside her. "Oh!"

He held up his hand. "I'm just going to make sure you get home safely," he said.

"I wouldn't expect anything less," she teased him, but wondered if there would be more.

Mark checked his messages on the drive home and Martha frantically pondered the state of her house, Thursday, yes! The cleaners had come— fresh sheets, no dirty dishes in the sink, and she had eggs and toast for breakfast.

Mark extended a hand to help her from the car, held on as they walked up the driveway and climbed the steps to the porch. The car idled at the curb.

"You can let him go," said Martha, with more confidence than she felt. Mark shook his head and pulled her close. The hug swelled to a kiss, a long, luxurious, inviting kiss. They stood so close.

"Come in," whispered Martha. She raised her hand to dismiss the driver, but Mark caught it, stopped her.

"I can't, Martha."

"Oh! I—I'm so—"

"No, I want to," Mark continued "But—"

Martha shrugged and turned to the door, hoping to find her keys and abandon him on the porch.

"Wait. Wait. Let me explain. Please?"

"My fault. I misunderstood." She turned to him. "I'm gonna blame the brandy."

"No, stop. Look, I'm surprised too. I invited you out as a friend, mostly. You see, I've always thought we might have something—but you had Peter and I had—"

"A plethora of ladies."

He chuckled and inhaled deeply. "The timing was always off. And now—"

"And now?" Martha was confused.

Mark scrubbed a hand over his face. "Well, that's *still* the problem." He motioned to the wicker chair on Martha's porch. "Sit. Let me explain properly."

She unlocked the front door and tossed her bag inside. "Do you want to come in and talk?" He shook his head. She sat, as instructed and slipped off her shoes. "The meter's still running."

"Fuck it. I don't care."

He held her gaze, his eyes the bluest blue. She shook her head banishing all such thoughts "Okay. Let's hear it."

"I'm leaving. Going away."

"What?"

"I'm taking a break from work, for a while."

What was he talking about?

"Next week. Friday's my last day."

"But you're a partner." Her mind was trying to process but it seemed to have turned to jelly.

"Sorry, I'm not explaining this well. I'm not quitting. I'm taking a sabbatical, six months, maybe a year." He paused, inhaled and then raced on. "We're trying to keep it quiet, so everyone doesn't decide to bugger off for a year. I wanted you to know, hence the coffee invite. But then coffee turned into dinner and dinner became…this…and—"

"But why?" Was he going to write? Teach? Neither of which would preclude him from spending the night. "Are you sick? Joining a monastery?" she asked, her brain still slowed by alcohol.

Mark laughed. "No." He moved closer, leaning against the railing now. "I'm going sailing."

"Sailing? For a year?"

"Yup, with my son."

She foraged for the name of the tiny child she'd met a couple of times. "Sam? But he's so—"

"Saul. He's twelve now, soon to be a card-carrying teenager and I hardly know him."

"I thought you see him all the time."

"Not enough. We're buddies, but I don't feel like his father. I've never lived with him; he's barely ever spent the night with me. He's a quiet kid—outnumbered and overruled by his mother and the stepsisters. Their house is chaotic at the best of times and Saul has started acting out. More importantly, he wants to do this. Sail with me." He looked pleased, incredulous and anxious all at once.

"Wow, that sounds—" Stupid? Risky? Hair-raising? Martha settled on, "amazing. Just the two of you then?"

"Yup, we'll either kill each other or grow very close. We're leaving at the end of the month, flying to the Virgin Islands, St John, to pick up the boat. I bought it a few years ago and haven't used it much. I just need to finalize a few things with Saul's school but then we're off."

"Off into the wild blue yonder." She felt sober-ish now but still couldn't stop blabbering.

"Not quite. We've made a plan, but, yeah, sometimes we'll just go where the wind blows us." He squatted in front of her, his back ramrod straight, his face close to hers. "So, I can't start anything right now."

She stared, dumbfounded.

"And I don't want this to be a one-night stand. I really don't. I think, maybe, it could be more."

He stood, held out his hands, pulled her to her feet. She was decidedly shorter than him now without the heels.

"Couldn't you have told me this earlier, like before you kissed me?"

"Yes. I could have, probably should have, but then you might not have let me. And I really wanted to."

She smiled and leaned into him, her head resting on his perfect white shirt. She inhaled deeply. He smelled like a man, an intoxicating medley of sweet, sweaty and sexy. "Shit, shit shit," Martha whispered into his chest. He slid his hand up and down her back.

"It's not over. It just can't begin yet."

She raised her eyes to meet his. They kissed again.

"Fuck bad timing," she said.

He laughed. "I'll be back," he said without a hint of the famous accent. "It's only a few months."

"Or a year. That's a really long time. You might forget."

"I won't."

"Then—" She pushed open the door. "Let's make sure you don't."

He smiled, started to shake his head no, but she cupped his cheeks in her hands and kissed him. There was no way she was letting him get away tonight.

"You sure?"

"Very."

"I won't be around to, you know, follow up."

He slowly slid his hand lower, pressed the small of her back.

Martha inhaled sharply. "That's okay," she breathed. "You're here now." She leaned into him. "And I think that driver would really like to go home, you know, to his wife and kids."

Mark laughed. The dimples, the eyes, and probably so much more!

CHAPTER THIRTY-SEVEN

Martha sighed as she looked up from her computer. What the hell was going on here? She'd thought they'd settled the asset negotiations of this divorce last week, but this email had the opposing lawyer demanding more, more, more. And the husband, who had been so aggressive about having custody of the family dog that he'd pounded his fist on the boardroom table, was now returning it. Martha's client didn't want the scruffy little terrier either. Poor unwanted little guy.

Sylvie knocked softly and opened the door. Martha looked up, half expecting Mark, but that ship had literally sailed a month ago.

"Sorry," said Sylvie. Her face was flushed.

Martha removed her earbuds, disconnecting the music meant to relax and block out distractions, but doing neither. "No, it's fine. What is it?"

Sylvie hesitated and bit her lip. "There are two policemen here to see you."

"For me?"

Sylvie nodded.

Martha had driven in that morning singing along to the *Fleetwood Mac Essentials* playlist, probably going a little too fast, but they wouldn't come to her office to give her a speeding ticket, would they? This must be a mistake.

"Are you sure they want me?"

"Yes, yes. I checked. They're waiting in reception." Sylvie paused then added. "They were very stern, official like." She smiled nervously.

"Okay then." Martha closed her computer and swept her fingers through her hair. "Better not to keep them waiting." She smiled to reassure Sylvie and calm her own nerves.

The two uniformed officers were standing in reception, appearing, for a moment, to be guarding the door. They were almost identical in size and shape, tall and muscular, both officially posed and Sylvie was right, very serious.

"Hello officers, I'm Martha Walker. How can I help you?"

Neither smiled but the older one nodded. "Ms. Walker." He didn't offer to shake her hand. "I'm afraid I have some bad news for you. Would you like to sit?"

Martha shook her head, impatient and suddenly terrified. She looked around, trying to establish the reality of the moment. The room was as it always was, chairs, artwork, a silver tray of bottled water, all in place. "What? What is it?"

"Ma'am, I first need to confirm that Nicholas Walker is related to you."

"Yes, he's my father. Why? Is he alright? What's happened?" She wanted to scream, but her voice was small, barely a whisper. The officer glanced at the receptionist and took a couple of steps back. Martha followed.

"I'm very sorry ma'am." The officer leaned forward, his shoulders drooped, his voice softened. "There's been an accident. Your father was alone in the car when he drove off the road."

"Is he okay?"

"No, I'm sorry, ma'am. He passed at the hospital."

She felt his hand on her arm even before she felt her legs give way. She swayed precariously on her high heels. Flashes of light blurred her vision. An ocean of waves flooded her ears. He steadied her, gently leading her to a nearby armchair.

Martha tried to speak, form thoughts, questions, ask for details but she couldn't. Her mind was ablaze, her body cold. She kneaded her hands together. "Are you...sure? I...he's—when?" The elevator chimed and before the door was fully open, Peter rushed out.

"Peter?" Martha blinked, willing him away, rewinding...*car accident, passed...dead. DEAD!* She tried to grasp the moment, understand any of it, but her mind lurched and spun, processing only flecks of time, distant words and heavy, incomprehensible moments.

Why was Peter here, beside her, bending so close? She heard his knees crack, inhaled his cologne—that was new. He placed his hand over both of hers. It was marked by veins and spots, a thin pale line on the fourth finger. She didn't want to want him so close. She stared at their hands. "My father is...dead."

"Yes, I know. I know Martha. The police called me."

"Why?" Peter wasn't family anymore.

"Because your father still had me down as his emergency contact—on a card, in his wallet."

"Oh." Martha vaguely recalled the long-ago argument, something about male equanimity. She raised her head, met his eyes. "Well, you're here then, but I don't need you. No, you don't need to be." She stood, wobbly, a little lightheaded. "I'm okay." She stepped out of her shoes and felt small but steady and stronger.

"Officer—" She tried to read his name tag.

"Collins."

"Thanks. Officer Collins. I've never done this before. I guess that's a good thing, right? That I'm inexperienced in accidental death?" He nodded politely. She choked back her despair and tried to find some pieces of her professional self. "So, what happens next?" She could feel her body regaining its equilibrium.

"The hospital, ma'am. We can take you or—"

"I have my car. I'll take you." Peter stepped forward.

No. She could drive herself. She needed time to think. Still, she was relieved when Peter followed her back to her office and waited while she talked to Sylvie, slipped into flats and collected everything she'd need for the rest of the day.

**

Martha hated Peter's new red car; it seemed indecent for a trip to the hospital to see her father—her dead father. She pressed her right foot into the spotless floormat, willing him to accelerate, ignore the speed limit. *Faster Peter. Faster. My Dad*—But then there was no need for speed, was there? She should call Jonathan. It was still very early there, so she'd wait until she knew more. "Ruby."

"Pardon?"

Peter wouldn't understand. *Poor Ruby—her Grandad.*

Peter helped her from the car and held her arm as they went through the automatic doors under a huge red sign—*Emergency*

Officer Collins met them at the desk, his partner a few steps behind him, still silent, but available. A young nurse, assured them that Mr. Walker's body had not yet been taken to the morgue and that a doctor would be out to speak to them shortly.

Peter selected seats in the crowded waiting room. Martha looked around at the sick and damaged—all waiting—but all alive. Martha sat on the edge of her chair and tried to shift it back just a little. "These chairs are awful." Peter looked confused. "They're plastic," she said, "and bolted to the floor."

"Practical, I suppose. Safe, easy to clean, always in place."

Martha nodded. "Safe." A car accident. Only horrendous ones resulted in death.

"Walker. WALKER?"

She jumped up. *Who—where?* Peter took her arm.

"This way," He whispered.

"Are you with Nicholas Walker?"

"Yes, he is my father. No—" Martha stammered. "Was my father."

"I'm Doctor—"

Yes, she looked like a doctor, just like the ones on TV—white lab coat, stethoscope, slightly rumpled, tired overworked.

She read from a tablet. "Nicholas Walker. DOB 01-02-1938, right?"

But something was off, like the wardrobe department had messed up. Yes. She had two stethoscopes around her neck—how strange. "What? Sorry. What did you say?"

"Maybe a little slower, please," said Peter. "This isn't easy for us and yes, that is his birth date."

The doctor sighed, nodded and continued, slightly slower. "Okay. Mr. Walker experienced a myocardial infarction while driving."

Martha still wasn't following. "What?"

"A massive heart attack. Heart failure. He was pronounced dead at the hospital, after the cardiac team was unable to revive him. He died quickly without regaining consciousness."

"So, it wasn't...bad driving?"

"No, the heart attack likely caused his accident. I'm sorry for your loss. The staff will help you with any other questions."

She turned and walked away quickly.

"Great bedside manner, that one," said Peter. He gently directed Martha back to the plastic chairs. "Are you okay? Did you get what the doctor said?"

Martha inhaled slowly. "I did." Officer Collins sat down across from her. "My father had a heart attack."

"Yes, so I understand."

"It wasn't the crash then?"

"No, we believe that your father's heart failed, causing him to lose control of the vehicle, um, his car. The accident was rather minor, a decelerating roll into a cement light standard."

"Oh, thank goodness." Her dad would be pleased to hear—or would be if—Martha sighed and stared ahead, still trying to focus. Finally, she nodded and turned back to the officer. "I wonder where he was going. He didn't drive…he…he didn't go out on his own much anymore."

Officer Collins nodded. His long face was kind and sincere. "It appears he'd been to a bakery. Baked goods, mostly donuts were found at the scene. Er, sorry, were on the floor, passenger side."

"Probably Boston Creams, He loves those. Or honey crullers for my—mother!" Martha gasped for air. "Oh no! Peter. I forgot about Mom." She turned to the officer. "My mother isn't well. She's in a home. I need to call…someone. Dad spends all day with her."

Peter placed a hand on her shoulder. "Not today. He went out so I'm sure she's fine."

"Maybe—"

"Don't worry. I'll call." Peter held out his hand. "You finish up here and I'll let them know, okay?"

Martha handed him her phone. "It's under *Whispering Pines*. Don't call the suite. Use the general number." Peter nodded.

"Good." said Officer Collins. "We did call there earlier, but of course we didn't know about your mother." He dismissed Peter with a nod. "Okay, just a couple more things and I'll be on my way." He explained about the paperwork, the accident report, and said he'd send her some information about the car, for the insurance. Next, he suggested that it might be less upsetting to identify Mr. Walker's body here, rather than at the morgue. He suggested Peter, but Martha said no, she needed to be sure.

Martha followed the nurse into the emergency ward. Half open curtains revealed patients, resting, breathing, some even smiling. Her dad would not be—

The nurse stopped in front of a closed door.

"Your father's in here. I know this is hard, but thankfully he went quickly." She pushed a loose strand of bleached hair off her forehead and added, "Take your time."

As she walked away her shoes squeaked, repeating *quickly quickly.* He died quickly. So what? He was still gone, quick or slow, she'd lost her father, forever. She leaned her shoulder into the door and pushed.

Dad looked pale, but peaceful and unscathed. He just had to open his eyes and—"Dad?" She choked back a sob. All the critical monitors were blank and silent. Red and yellow wires protruded from small plastic electrodes that were stuck to the hairs on his chest. She lifted his hand, wove her fingers through his. She'd had this hand, this man and his love, all her life. He'd led her so many places, taught her, challenged her, kept her safe. She pulled the sheet up to hide his naked chest and the wires, then gently laid his hand on the thin white sheet. His hand, lifeless now; the nails still meticulously clean and filed to a square tip, the right thumb nail damaged, knobby from a hammer strike many years ago.

Where was his ring? She glanced around and noticed an opaque plastic zipper bag on the stainless-steel cart, labelled with a red marker. *Nicholas James Walker.* Martha ran her finger along his name. *Dearly departed. Deceased. Gone forever.* She could feel his wallet, his watch, sunglasses, maybe his readers, but no ring. She was reluctant to open the bag, actually face the contents. She tried again, his comb, a few coins and then, deep in the corner, the wedding ring.

"Found it," she muttered, blinking to hold back the tide. She bent and kissed his forehead then combed his thick silver hair through her fingers. "I wish you would've said goodbye. I know you would have—but I never thought we'd runout—I'm sorry the few last years weren't— we should've talked more, Dad, about everything. Like, how I'm going to live without you." He seemed about to answer, reassure her as he'd done so many times. He'd given her so much. Everything. "Thank you," she whispered. She picked up the plastic bag and clutched it to her chest. "I love you Dad, always."

She pulled open the heavy hospital door and hurried back to reception. She nodded to the waiting police officers.

"Yes, that's my father, Nick Walker."

Officer Collins pointed to a single sheet of paper and handed her a pen. "Just a signature please."

Martha scrawled her name and watched the ink fan out to meet the edges of her tears.

Peter was waiting for her. She sat beside him and leaned into his shoulder, taking comfort from his calm strong presence.

"Mom?"

"She's fine," said Peter. "I spoke to Enid."

"Yeah, she runs things."

"She sends her condolences. Your mother is fine. She has a friend with her, but they haven't told her about Nick—your dad."

Martha choked back a sob.

"I told her you'd be there as soon as you finished here. Is that okay?'

"Yes. Thank you."

Peter nodded.

"I should call Jon, before I do anything else. What do you think?"

"Yeah. He needs to know." Peter reached into his pocket and handed her the keys. "Go to the car. Call him from there. Shoot me a text when you're done."

"Thanks."

"I'll find us some coffee. Caffeine can't hurt, right?"

Peter's car seemed cozy now, safe and private. Martha settled herself with yoga breathing before she placed the call. Jon's phone buzzed so many times she almost hung up.

"Martha?"

"Hi Jon. I'm…I'm sorry." She was trying not to cry.

"Martha? What is it?"

"I'm sorry I have to tell you this—Dad…Dad…is—" Dead, died, deceased—all horrible words. "Dad's gone, Jon. He—" She exhaled a deep, painful sob.

"Oh Martha. No." Silence, then. "Martha? Are you alone? Oh shit. Martha."

"Sorry, sorry. Yes, I'm fine." She snuffled and wiped her tears. "I'm not alone. Peter's here."

"Peter?"

"Yes, a long story but it's okay. He's helping and I'm glad he's here—to not be alone. I'll explain later, okay?"

"Dad is…dead? How? I have so many questions"

Martha nodded. She watched a young man walk past the car carrying an empty baby car seat, likely a new father.

"Martha?"

"Sorry. Dad had a car accident—this morning."

"Damn! He shouldn't have been driving."

"I know. I know. But he's…was…stubborn. And truthfully, I think it was good for him—like mentally. Just not today."

"Jesus." Jon sighed. "So, what happened?"

"He went to a bakery!" She choked back another sob. "And—on the way back he…he…he drove into a cement pole but—" The sobs escaped. She swallowed. "But that didn't kill him. He had a heart attack. Thankfully he was alone in the car."

"Jesus, poor guy. I'm sorry Martha."

"I know, look, I just wanted to tell you but I don't have a lot else right now. I'm still at the hospital."

"What about Mom?"

"She doesn't know yet. I'm heading there next."

"That's going to be—"

"Horrible? I know."

"How will you tell her?"

"I don't really know. I guess I'll figure it out when I get there."

"Okay. Okay." His voice cracked.

"Jon?" She waited, feeling his tears. "Look, let's talk again tonight. After I see Mom and maybe—I don't know how this works. But could you find a funeral home?"

"Sure, okay. I'll call around. Text me the hospital info." He sounded steadier. "Look, take Peter with you."

"What?"

"Peter, when you tell Mom. She always liked him."

Martha allowed herself half a smile. "Good idea, but I'm not sure Peter will think so."

"Bye. I love you. Call tonight, or before if you need me."

"Okay. Bye." Martha watched the screen go dark as the connection ended. Jonathan. Had she really been holding a grudge against him, pretending she could block him out of her heart? She had—almost. What a fool! Any smidge of resentment she'd been feeling for him was washed away. He'd be here soon. And she was glad.

Ready to go. She texted Peter and he almost immediately appeared at her window with two Starbuck's coffees.

Martha opened the door and he handed her a small paper bag. "They didn't have any muffins, so I got you cake pops. I think you need some sugar."

"Thank you, Peter. Ruby loves these."

He closed the door, walked around to his side of the car and settled in. "We're going to *Whispering Pines*, right? You'll have to navigate."

"You don't have to go with me." Martha took a big bite of the treat. "Just take me back to the office and I'll get my car."

"No. I don't mind. And you shouldn't be alone right now."

"I'm fine. Really."

"I know."

Martha smiled. "But Jon suggested I take you along. Mom always liked you better than me."

Peter laughed. "Okay then. That settles it."

"Take the highway," Martha instructed Peter as they pulled out of the hospital parking lot. "It's faster."

"Okay," agreed Peter.

"The highway, east, and then exit at Ninth Line."

Peter nodded. They drove in silence for several minutes. Martha closed her eyes, exhausted and anxious. She tried to calm her mind, to block out the image of her father's body, remember him before her mother's dementia. They were happy then, weren't they? Martha started to the sound of the turn signal, the car slowing down.

"You drifted off," saif Peter.

"And you found your way without me."

"Google maps."

As the car turned into the familiar drive, Martha felt her anxiety return. "Are you sure Mom's okay?"

"She's fine, really. Enid said the police called there asking about him. That's the address on your dad's driver's licence, right?"

"Oh course." She'd helped Dad find all the change of address forms online, driver's licence, insurance, taxes.

"Enid said she'd keep an eye on your mother. Violet is staying with her until we get there."

"Violet? That was your grandmother's name."

"Yes. That's how I remembered it, but I have no idea who she is."

Martha smiled. "Dad had enlisted some of the ladies who live here to sit with Mom when he worked out or went out for lunch. He thanked them with bonbons."

"Bonbons?"

"Yup."

"Smart guy."

Martha couldn't find another smile. "She's not alone, then." Except she was alone, lost and now without her husband. Martha dabbed at the new flood of tears. "I've...I...I just can't process all of this."

Peter pulled into a parking spot. "You're doing great. Really. It would be a lot for anyone."

"Thank you," she whispered.

They were greeted by a couple of the staff, all saddened and respectful. Martha mumbled her thanks, unable to add much more. They walked to her mother's suite, thankfully meeting no one along the way.

"Peter, what do I say? How do I tell her—tell her that he's—gone?"

"Slowly," said Peter. "Let her set the pace. Don't push her. Just wait and see what she's picking up."

Martha glanced sideways at him. "I wouldn't push her."

"Look, I haven't seen your mom in quite a while now, so I don't really know, but that's what worked with my grandmother."

Martha stopped and faced the door to her parent's suite. She inhaled deeply. "Right, I guess I'll take my cues from Dad. He was always kind and gentle, slow and steady, not always my strong suit."

Peter smiled and opened the door for her.

"Hello," she said, affecting a cheerfulness she didn't feel.

Peter followed close at her heels. He touched her elbow and whispered, "Shh, quiet now, bring it down a notch."

She bristled but realized he was right. She was wound up tighter than a—what would Dad have said? She choked back her tears.

Her mother was sitting at the small dining table with another woman. "Hi Mom," she said, gently. "What did you have for dinner?"

Martha waited for several seconds then turned to her mother's companion. She was round and rosy, a picture-book-grandma. Her face was framed with gold wire rimmed glasses, her white hair pulled into a loose knot, a few wiry curls escaped at her temples.

"Hello, I'm Martha and this is Peter. You must be Violet."

"Fri...end," said her mom.

"Yes, we're good friends, aren't we, June?"

Mom nodded, but she was staring at Peter. "P...Pee?"

Peter smiled. "Hello, June. It's nice to see you." She extended a shaky hand but it dropped into her lap before Peter could take hold.

"Well," said Violet, pushing herself back from the table. "We've had a lovely day together, but I'll get out of your way now."

She was at least Mom's age, maybe older, but she was robust and lively.

Violet quickly gathered up her things—an Agatha Christie paperback, her cardigan and something wrapped in a napkin. "A cherry tart," she explained. "My bedtime snack. Your mom didn't eat hers and it'd be a shame if it ended up in the bin." She moved closer to Martha and spoke almost into her ear. "I am so very sorry about your father, dear. He was a real sweetie."

Martha allowed herself a smile. "Thank you, that's nice to hear. And thanks so much for today. Is there some way I could repay you?"

"Don't be silly. It was my pleasure. I'm just glad I could help out." She reached out with her free hand and pulled Martha in for a hug.

"Oh!" She started to resist but found herself embracing the doughy warmth of this kind woman.

"Good night, then," said Violet as she walked to the door.

"Can I walk you home?" asked Peter.

Violet giggled. "Goodness no, I live only one floor up, next to the elevator. And you all have a lot to talk about, I'm sure." She smiled sadly, turned and was gone.

Martha sat across the table from her mom. She looked calm and comfortable, despite the unrelenting trembling. She was pale, her skin seemed paper thin and the lines on her face had grown deeper. Martha fought back tears, her nerves were on edge, her stomach seethed. How could she possibly tell her?

As if reading her thoughts, Peter squeezed her shoulder. Martha looked at him and was comforted. Slowly, he'd said in the hall. Just be kind and gentle. She realized he was cleaning up. He'd stacked the dishes on a tray in the kitchen and wiped the crumbs from the table. Then he offered her mother his arm and walked her to her chair.

"Tha...nks." Mom smiled at him a little coquettishly. "Tall Petey."

Any other day it would have been funny. Peter disliked nicknames and had never even gone by Pete. But Martha was impressed when he just patted her mom's hand and smiled sweetly.

Mom held his gaze. "Who...are you?"

"Just a friend of Martha's," he replied.

Martha's mind raced. How could she tell her? How would she react? She had no idea what to say, so instead, stalling, she pointed out the birds on the feeder outside the window. "Look Mom, the cardinals are back."

"Nick?"

"Mom."

"Nick." She was addressing Peter. "Home...soon."

Martha moved to her mother's side and crouched next to her. "Mom, I'm sorry, really sorry, but Dad…Nick, well he can't come home."

Mom's eyebrows shot up; her head jerked to attention. "Home…soon." She flung her arms in the air and bellowed. "Nick!"

Martha inhaled shakily and shifted back on her heels. "Dad had an accident, Mom, in the car. He's gone Mom. Dad died today."

Her mother's eyes grew wide. She shook her head from side to side. "No." One crystal clear word.

Peter started to speak but Martha waved him off. "Do you understand, Mom?"

"Home soon."

Martha exhaled her irritation. Mom needed to know, to understand, but pushing her might make things worse. "Okay, you're right," said Martha. "Soon. Soon."

Mom nodded and sat back, suddenly calm, quiet. They sat in silence as the sun dropped lower in the sky. Martha had lost track of time. Her body ached. She wanted to cry or scream, any kind of release, but keeping calm and quiet seemed the wiser choice.

Peter had pulled out his phone and was typing. *Sorry*, he mouthed silently. It's work. She nodded. He was unaware that he'd chosen Dad's favourite chair.

Mom was lost in thought or just lost. Was it her bedtime soon? She had settled now, but Martha had no idea how long this would last or if she'd absorbed any of what she'd told her. Martha breathed a sigh of relief when the evening helper arrived.

She greeted Mom warmly and escorted her into the bedroom. Martha could hear all the steps involved in the lengthy nighttime routine: clothes off, toilet, pull-ups and pajamas, teeth cleaned, face washed. Peter left quietly about halfway through, encouraging her to call on him if she needed anything. She squeezed his forearm, surprised and flustered by her emotions. "Thank you, for today—you didn't have to—"

"You'll get through this Martha. You're strong. Just don't forget we all need a little help sometimes." He leaned in and lightly kissed her cheek.

He closed the door just as the attendant came out of the bedroom.

"Your mother should be asleep soon, Ms. Walker." Her name tag said Rose. "Have you arranged for someone for the night?"

"I'm staying." Martha hadn't even thought of it before now but it just seemed right.

"That's good. Have you had dinner?"

"Not yet." Just breakfast, when everything was normal, and then cake pops. "No, but I'll be fine."

"I could send something up for you."

"There's food here. But thank you, Rose. You're very kind."

"Good night, then. And Ms. Walker, I am very sorry for your loss. We all really liked your father. He was always so kind."

"Thank you."

When she'd gone Martha locked the door and turned off all the lights, hoping the darkness would quell the persistent thudding in her head. Moonlight coated the room. She opened the fridge and was surprised to find half a bottle of Pinot Noir and a fine selection of cheeses. *Oh Dad, really?* She poured a generous glass of the wine and poked around for some crackers, laughing, and crying when she found a bag of Oreos with a florescent pink sticky note, in Ruby's unpredictable printing, *Ruby and Grandad only.*

She sat in Dad's chair and watched the lacy shadows from the trees flit across the room. There were no memories here. She wished Dad had died at home—his home, not here, or in the car, but in the house he'd bought for his family so many years ago. If she'd known how little time he'd had left—maybe. Martha emptied her glass and then walked quietly into the bedroom. It was dark and still.

"Mom? Are you awake?" Silence. She sat on the side of the bed, close to her mother's frail body. "Mom? Mom, I'm so sad. I'm sorry but we've lost Dad. He died, Mom." She almost gave in to her desire, her need for love, but she couldn't risk frightening her with a hug. "He was a good man, wasn't he? He had a big heart." She sighed, gulped back the heavy sobs that had been gathering all day. "But his heart, well, it just stopped. He had a long life, right? But I wasn't ready to give him up yet. Can you even understand this? Mom?"

Her mother's eyes fluttered open, once, twice, then drifted shut. Her face calm, so beautiful in the glow from the nightlights.

"Mom, Dad isn't coming back. He's gone now." Martha watched the chenille bedspread rise and fall slowly, steadily. She tried to force back her tears, blotting the defiant ones with the back of her hand. "What will we do without him, Mom?"

But her mother was sleeping or faraway, unaware, unmoved by the day's events.

Martha slipped her feet out of her dad's slippers and carefully stretched out on his side of the bed. She faced her mother. It had been years, decades since they'd shared a bed. She reached out to whisk a stray hair from Mom's cheek but stopped when she flinched. Martha let her hand slide slowly onto her mother's pillow and was surprised to find it soaked in tears.

CHAPTER THIRTY-EIGHT

Still no word from Jon. Martha checked her phone just in case. Nothing. She'd strangle him! Though not really. When she'd met him at the airport, they'd just folded into each other's arms. She'd thought she'd feel some ill will and resentment but no. Her grief left no room for such petty nonsense, and really it was just her and Jon now.

Still, she'd strangle him. Martha scrolled through her messages from the last few days, stopping at Mark's. Her pulse slowed as she focused on his kind words, so warm and sympathetic. She knew it was magical thinking but maybe if he hadn't left—? She missed him but wasn't sure she had the right to.

Damn it! Where were they? Jon had gone to The Home hours ago. They'd had a plan—Jon offered to take on Mom while Martha supervised things at the church and the reception. Jon had the itinerary. It was all perfectly timed and now they were behind schedule.

Martha had arranged for Frannie, Mom's current favourite *Gloria,* to help her get ready and then stay with them for the rest of the day. The funeral home had sent a car. So, why weren't they here? Dad was such a stickler for punctuality. At least he wouldn't know if things started a little late today. Martha texted Jon again. *Where are you!* noticing the punctuation error just as the message left with a decisive swoosh. No immediate answer.

Impatient and now fighting anger, she stood and ran her hands down the front of her pencil skirt, coaxing out the wrinkles. She retrieved her compact from her handbag, determined to disguise her red and puffy eyes. A mirror hung next to the door, no doubt for just these cosmetic purposes. She stepped closer, recalling the small spiderweb cracks that stretched randomly out from the gilded frame. Still here, the same after so many years. The last time she'd waited in this stuffy anteroom she'd been nervous, but happy, dressed in a white lace gown. She couldn't sit still that day either. But Dad had calmed her, held her hand, joked a little, as they waited to walk down the aisle together. She usually wasn't one for pacing but today seemed to warrant it. The funeral was set to begin in less than fifteen minutes.

She stepped into the narthex and peered outside through the open church doors. No sign of them. Mr. Lawson, the funeral director, was welcoming people into the church. He caught her eye and mimed his concerns. *Where are they?* Martha shrugged. So many people, dressed in black or grey, the occasional flash of colour, all whispering and earnestly trying not to smile too much. Quiet chatter, some stilted laughs. She inhaled perfume and spicy aftershave, winter air and the funeral smell of lilies. Sylvie was walking towards her. She clutched a handful of tissues.

"Oh Martha, I'm so sorry. How are you doing?" asked Sylvie as she pulled Martha into a generous hug.

"I'm okay…good, I think, for the most part," stammered Martha.

"I just can't believe he's gone. You know, he was just, you know, such a force." Sylvie wiped fresh tears from her cheeks. "I just can't stop crying. You and your family—take care of each other. Okay? I'll keep you in my prayers."

Martha nodded. "Thank…Thanks." She still hadn't worked out what to say to the words of comfort that seemed to make her so uncomfortable. She squeezed Sylvie's hand. "I'm glad you're here. Dad was really pleased when you and I started working together."

Sylvie smiled. "I'm glad. Can I help with anything? Today or later. Anytime?"

"No, no we're good. Unless you know where Jon and my mother are."

"What? Really?"

"No, don't worry. They're just running a little late. You should go in, find a seat. I'm worried there may not be enough."

"Okay, I'll see you later." Sylvie rejoined her partner Thérèse, who'd been hanging up their coats. Martha watched as they entered the nave. The pews were almost full and the funeral attendants were unfolding chairs in the side aisles.

"Geez Dad, turns out you were quite a popular guy." She was talking to him again. It had happened a lot in the last few days and it freaked her out a little. It probably wasn't wise to get into the habit of talking to the dead. Jon had overheard her in the kitchen yesterday. He'd started to tease her, but then, seeing her tears, came in with a bear hug.

Her mind vaulted to the catering order she'd placed at the country club. Would there be enough? She attempted a quick head count. Not a chance. She'd tried to calculate the numbers—friends, colleagues, associates, buddies, neighbours, and ordered food and drinks for about a hundred but there were easily twice that many people here. She checked the spreadsheet on her phone again, running up and down the columns confirming that, yes, they should have probably doubled the order. An event with no guest list, no invitations was impossible! She was about to call the club when she heard Jon's voice.

"Martha?"

She looked up to see Jon, without a coat, but sweaty and a bit rumpled. He was hovering over Mom as both shuffled slowly across the stone floor. Frannie followed close behind.

"This way. Over here," she called out and stepped aside so they could shepherd Mom into the anteroom. "Where's the wheelchair?" Martha nearly barked at Jon.

"Don't, Martha, just don't. It was all we could do to get her to use the walker. It'll be fine. I'll stay right beside her."

Martha exhaled loudly. The plan had been to have Mom seated before everyone arrived. But that wasn't going to happen now. She felt hot and faint. Rivulets of sweat slid down her spine. "Let's walk her up together then, okay? Can we do that?" She looked at Frannie. "Can *she* do that?"

"Yes, I think so. If she's willing." Frannie stood next to Mom now, steadying both her and the walker.

"Okay, but maybe she should sit for a minute?"

"No," said Jon, placing a hand on Mom's shoulder. "Let's just keep moving. If she sits down, we'll have a problem."

"Oh."

Jon bent down on one knee. "How're you doing Mom?" He didn't wait for an answer. "We're going to walk a little more now. I'll be right beside you, with Martha. Okay?"

Mom didn't answer. She didn't protest when Frannie helped her out of her coat. Martha unbuttoned her mother's cardigan and smoothed out the pleats in her dress. To Martha's surprise and relief, her mom allowed Frannie to comb through her hair.

"Ready," said Frannie. "Just don't go too fast." She helped June turn around and move out of the room. "I'll sneak up the side aisle and meet you at the pew."

Martha and Jon each put a hand over their mother's on the walker and an arm around her back. Mr. Lawson, who'd been waiting just outside the door, followed close behind them. They walked slowly, up the aisle, a reluctant procession. Sadness and grief hung in the air but there was also a low discernible buzz. Martha bristled. Tongues were wagging. About her mother's decline? Or Jonathan's presence? Maybe both.

Martha straightened her shoulders and lifted her head. She saw a few recognizable faces as she passed; Jack and John Harris, brothers and the firm's oldest active partners, Norah, some of their old neighbours, the Maxwells, the real Gloria, Tony, Arthur and Enid, and then Peter, sitting next to his parents. He leaned forward in the pew, shifting his body as if to stand, offering to help. *Oh Peter*. She fought back tears and mouthed a silent *no*.

They carefully maneuvered Mom to the front of the church, stopping at the first pew. Frannie was waiting, ready to help. Jon stepped in first, sliding next to her. Martha guided Mom in and settled her beside Jon. Mr. Lawson slipped away with the walker as Martha took her seat on the aisle. She exhaled. They'd done it. They held Mom safely between them, like bookends.

The church felt cool, comforting in a way Martha hadn't expected. "I'm sorry," she whispered, reaching behind her mother to rub Jon's shoulder. "I shouldn't have snapped at you." His smile absolved her. "Mom looks really nice, her dress and her hair, even the slippers."

"That was all Frannie," whispered Jon. "She's a miracle worker."

Martha nodded. The ambience in the church shifted. The quiet purr of many voices replaced by the rising notes of the organ. Altar boys appeared and lit the candles. Dad's coffin rested just in front of her, almost exactly where she'd been baptized, confirmed and married. It was the wrong place to admit it, but she'd lost her faith in the church a long time ago. Still, she couldn't completely rule out God or all things spiritual, especially not today.

She studied the casket, a very fine wooden box. She and Jon had chosen it together. The last resting place of her father. She pictured him inside, then willed herself to stop. Instead, she focused on the highly polished exterior. Dad would have liked it—if you could like your own coffin. He certainly would have appreciated the rich mahogany, the finely carved details and the solid brass hardware.

The flowers were so much better than expected. She'd placed the order late, focusing instead on so many other details. The florist had warned against her choices, out of season and expensive, but Martha had insisted, ordering a large cascading spray of white peonies and gardenias from Mom. Next to it was a small perfect heart of pink carnations, the tiny gold letters on the white satin ribbon read *Grandad*. Jon had requested two matching arrangements of yellow roses and peace lilies. "Twins," he'd said as if it wasn't obvious. Flower arrangements of every size and colour filled the altar and the steps. The obituary had asked for charitable donations instead of flowers, but now Martha was silently grateful that so many people had chosen to ignore the request. Sunlight, tinted by the rich hues of the stained-glass windows, caressed the blooms. It was simply beautiful.

The minister stepped forward and stood silent and erect in front of the altar. The low mournful chords from the organ faded away. Martha felt her mother's body slump into her. She leaned forward just enough to confirm that she was still awake. The pastor raised his hands only slightly and the conversational buzz ceased.

This pastor was new. Dad had pointed out that he looked more like an altar boy than a spiritual leader. "He's too young to know much," Dad had told her after he'd made a couple of visits to The Home. Dad had complained that he was nice enough, but a little too chatty, too eager and still wet behind the ears. "Father Axel," Dad had huffed. "What kind of a name is that?" Martha had sighed, pointing out that his real complaint was that he wasn't Father Mike, who as a young Anglican priest, and in this very church, had assisted at the wedding of Martha's parents. Her dad and Father Mike had become friends. They'd been golf buddies and partners on the tennis court until the years had robbed them both of their games. When Father Mike had passed away, he'd left behind a shrinking congregation of loyal but aging worshipers.

Martha had spoken to Father Axel only once, by phone, earlier in the week. He was pleasant, sympathetic and seemed capable enough. They'd settled on the time and the date and then resolved all further funeral related questions by text. But now, seeing him, realizing how just young he was, she hoped he'd be able to integrate some of the personal notes she'd suggested into the service. Having rewritten far too many legal briefs lately, her faith in the competency of these millennials was almost non-existent.

"Good afternoon, friends. I'm Father Axel Larson. We are here today to celebrate the life of our beloved Nicholas Walker, a devoted husband, loving father and friend. And I've been told, a pretty formidable lawyer." The murmur from the pews confirmed this.

The sound calmed Martha. She inhaled and released the breath slowly. Father Axel was talking, his voice authentic and strong. Martha sensed rather than felt a change in her mother, her hands folded in her lap, her head resting against the sleeve of Jon's suit jacket. Mom had stiffened, only slightly, as if touched by a feather. Martha patted mother's thigh and purposely rested her hand there— comforting, protecting, monitoring.

Father Axel had, following the agreed-on order of service, asked the congregation to rise for the first hymn. The sound of so many shifting bodies startled Mom. She cowered, now curling into Jon. He put his arm around her and pulled her close. As Martha rose to sing, the first chords of the hymn triggered her tears. It was one of Dad's favourites. Well, it used to be.

She couldn't find her voice. The words—*Lord of all hopefulness, Lord of all joy*—Dad loved to sing in church—*Be there in our sleeping, and give us, we pray*—belting out the words, in his powerful tenor. No longer trusting her legs, Martha sat down and rifled through her purse to find a fresh tissue.

The last fading notes of the hymn were drowned out by the rustling of hymnals closing and people settling. Mom flinched. Was that a whimper? Jonathan leaned forward and attempted a smile. His face was taut, nervous. The hum and soft rhythmic click from the overhead fans filled the silence.

Martha watched the service unfold, just as they'd planned; the readings, a message from Father Axel, too brief to be called a sermon and then the eulogy. Martha and Jon had spent most of last night trying to get it right.

Jon waited for Frannie to shift closer before he stood and transferred his mother's weight to her. Mom had slumped a little more now, and again Martha wondered if she'd fallen asleep. But as Jon stood and took a step toward the aisle Mom grabbed his pant leg. He bent and kissed her cheek, gently placing her hand back in her lap. He waited for Martha to stand and as she slipped out of the pew, she heard the first of her mother's moans, low and guttural. She glanced back. Mom was slouched against Frannie.

Martha stepped forward with Jonathan at her side. They walked past the coffin and up the steps that had suddenly grown steeper. When they reached the lectern, Jon produced the single sheet of paper that held their notes. They would take turns, as they had always done as children, but this time Jon would go first. He turned, squared his shoulders to the congregation, inhaled deeply and started to speak.

"My father was a good man. Many of you knew this long before I did." Nervous laughter rippled toward them.

Martha had cautioned Jon against being too frank. But he'd insisted and now continued, seemingly unfazed.

"Dad and I never had an easy time of it, but in the last while, thanks to his ability to love and forgive, we managed to find a way to move forward. It seems a bit of a miracle but, Dad and I became friends. No, even better, we found the love of a father and a son. It took us a while, but it turns out he was a really great guy, tough sometimes, but I get that now that I'm a parent." Jon smiled at the nodding heads. "Really, it's not as easy as it looks." He took a sip of water and waited for the quiet laughter to subside. "Dad was an extraordinary grandfather to my daughter Ruby. They had an incredible bond which was forged over *Oreo* cookies. He welcomed my husband and our daughter into the family with generosity and respect. He loved us all and I will miss him every day."

Jon slid the paper across to Martha. How had he done that, laid bare his heart in front of all these people? She wanted to vanish—poof—or hide, maybe just be alone, mourn alone. She felt Jon's hand on her back, gathered her wits and focused on the handwritten words. "Nick Walker, Dad, was …everything to me. I have so many memories, so many—"

A long, low wail came from the front pew. "NICK! Wh…where…s…s Nick…" The words were slurred and the pitiful sound was almost obscured by the collective gasp that filled the air. Frannie was trying to hold her back, but Mom flailed at her, knocking her back with a force that shocked Martha. What was happening? No Mom! There was more to say, the service wasn't over yet. Father Axel, his view blocked by the altar, stood up and abandoning all decorum muttered, "Oh Hell."

As Jon bolted from the lectern, Martha watched their notes, her words for Dad, float slowly to the carpet. She hurried after Jon, feeling the heel of her shoe pierce the thin paper. She came to a standstill when she reached the casket, confused by fear and the sweet scent wafting from the gardenias. *Dad, we need you.* She felt faint again and clutched the cool brass rail on the side of the casket. Through a hazy uncertainty that she hoped was a dream, even a nightmare, she watched her mother grasp the wooden rail in front of her and using both hands, pull herself up off the pew.

"Nick! Nick? Nick!"

Her mom was screeching. Panic contorted her face. Frannie tried to intervene but again Mom shook her off, her weakened body somehow gaining strength, her slippered feet adding pace to her purpose as she moved toward the aisle.

"Nick!"

People, including Father Axel had moved in to help, but not wanting to get too close, they formed an unintentional barricade, blocking Jon's path.

"Move!" Jon shouted. "Stand back!"

They disbursed, but not fast enough. No one was there to catch Mom as she let go of the rail and lurched forward. She managed just a few shuffling steps into the aisle before falling, careening forward, nearly striking an urn of mauve and white gladiolas.

Mom! Martha gasped—the wail frozen with her breath.

Her mother, crumpled on the floor, her cries now filled with pain. She sobbed, loud and unrestrained but still managed a sorrowful fading chorus of "Nick, Nick, Nick…"

Jon bent over her, whispered and stroked her silver hair. Martha heard Frannie's "No, don't move her" as Jon gently lifted their tiny, shattered mother into his arms, his back shielding her from the congregation.

Martha tried to blink it away, a series of stills, jerky freeze frames she couldn't escape. She was numb, weakened, drifting, suddenly relieved to be anchored to the coffin. She heard a noise, a cough, maybe a sob. The people were still here. Mom was safe with Jon. She saw Peter, his face ashen, freshly shaved. He looked so sad. She was crying. Peter stood and came to her. He held her briefly, barely a hug, then gently tugged her hand from the brass rail. They followed Jon and Mom, Frannie and Father Axel through a curtained doorway. The velvet brocade grazed her face. It smelled old and heavy with dust. She could hear sirens, far away, coming closer. Frannie was crying. Jon, still holding their mother, murmured a familiar lullaby.

CHAPTER THIRTY-NINE

Martha stepped off the elevator and held her key card under the scanner. *The Sixth Floor*. It had been inevitable after her father passed; no discussion, no debate, but still a lot of guilt. Her mother's health had deteriorated. Her heart was causing problems, congestive heart failure according to the doctor. But Martha believed it had been damaged, broken when she'd lost her Nick. Either way, her mother couldn't live on her own anymore. A notably *unfrosty* Helen Frost was overly pleased with herself for having had the forethought to save the room for them, *the very room that your father turned down*, she'd reminded them, although Martha suspected it had been vacant for a while. Martha had packed up the suite into the boxes they'd labeled *MOVING* almost two years ago. One of the movers remembered them and asked about Ruby. They'd taken everything to her house and stored it in her garage, along with Peter's canoe.

The small red light flickered, turned green and the door opened with a quick, almost silent swish. Martha hurried for a few steps, outpacing the door before it slid back, then slowed her pace. No need to rush. She switched her leather tote to her right hand, shaking the left one back to life. She seemed to bring more stuff every day, laptop, food, her book, an extra sweater.

Martha paused to read the white board which rested on an ornate artist's easel. Each day's message was meant to comfort or inspire. Today's did neither. *You are doing your best and it is enough.* "Ugh," Martha groaned. "I doubt that." She felt like she was failing miserably, at everything. *Stop it!* Her therapist had told her to breathe deeply and focus on the positive. Well, it's good that Mom was still here, at Whispering Pines instead of in the hospital or a long-term care facility. She wanted to believe her father would be pleased. He'd fought hard to keep her off the dreaded sixth floor, but he'd chosen Whispering Pines for her comfort and care. He'd made the right choice.

As she passed the nurses' room, she smiled at the woman at the desk who, in the middle of a swallow of water, waved her pen, signaling for Martha to wait.

"Ms. Walker."

"Hi, Candy. Martha. Please." Her mother had been on the locked floor for two months, no, it was ten weeks already, so Martha knew most of the staff. Candy was her favourite, kind, patient and appropriately sweet. "How are you?"

"I'm good, Martha. Thanks." Candy set her water bottle on the desk. "I was with your mom this morning, woke her up and all."

Martha stiffened. Please not another outburst. "And—?"

"She was in quite a mood when she woke up. Not happy at all. I have no idea why, no bright lights or weird noises, but she was very animated." Candy clicked her tongue. "Something was really bothering her. I had the feeling she was trying to tell me something. But I couldn't figure it out. She seemed scared of me—or something, maybe a bad dream. I couldn't tell. I sat with her for a while and that seemed to calm her down. No extra meds. She's been fine ever since."

That was all? Martha allowed herself to breathe again. "Thank you, for…for not…for working your magic."

"All good," said Candy. "I'm here until eight today, if you need anything."

"Wonderful," said Martha, digesting the good news, no screaming, no hitting, no sedatives, no restraints.

It had happened only once. Martha had arrived later than usual that day and was shocked and devastated to find her mother's wrists bound in padded straps and secured to the bed. She'd try to explain that her mother wasn't dangerous, only angry and confused. Martha shouldn't have left her alone. The nurse had apologized, and then explained that they had simply followed protocol, for her mother's safety as well as their own. The restraints were removed at dinnertime. Martha had fed her mother and stayed most of the night. And then she'd promised her dad, she only talked to him in her head now, and herself that it wouldn't happen again. So, she came more often, stayed longer and developed a rapport with the nurses, especially Candy.

Martha thanked Candy again and continued to her mother's room. She paused before going in and took a deep breath. Her mother was confined to her bed now, by choice rather than capability. Physically, she'd recovered quickly from the fall at the funeral, but since then she'd refused to get out of bed, even when Martha or the nurses tried to help her into a chair, she fought back, hollered and landed blows of surprising force. Martha put it down to grief. June might not know her Nick was gone—Martha hoped dementia had at least given her that mercy—but she was sure her mother felt his loss. Felt it as deeply as Martha herself did.

Martha dug deep for a smile. "Hi, Mom. How're you doing today?"

No answer but her mother was awake. Her eyes shifted toward Martha without a hint of recognition. "It's a beautiful day. Still a little chilly, but the sun's warm." Martha dumped her bag and coat on the straight-back metal chair and dragged the armchair closer to the bed, just like she'd done yesterday and the day before and the day before that. "So, I'm good. Nothing new to report. I spoke to Jonny last night. He and Ruby send their love." Her mother stared at the ceiling light.

Martha drew back the covers as she talked and straightened out her mom's hospital gown, pulled up her socks and furtively checked her diaper. All good. Martha had purchased soft bamboo pajamas, a beautiful floral print for her mother but they were too impractical and inconvenient. Now she wore only open-back smocks, upgraded hospital gowns available in a variety of pastel colours. Martha pulled up the crisp cotton sheet and then gently covered her with the blanket—her blanket. Her mom's fingers clutched the woolly fringe, frayed and matted, worn out after so many years of unconditional comfort.

Martha settled into her chair and opened her book, an eight-hundred-page biography of Ruth Bader Ginsburg, that Jon had sent with a note that said *A worthy distraction. Love you.* He'd included a *Notorious RBG* tee shirt and had purchased one for Ruby too. When her mother woke up, Martha read several pages aloud and then realized she was hungry.

Martha opened her insulated lunch bag and took out a container which she'd filled with leftovers from last night's dinner—chicken, rice and spinach. She'd save the bags of snacks for later, celery, carrots and nuts. "Look, Mom, I have a new lunch bag, not quite as fancy as the one you gave me in grade two."

The last lunchbox she'd owned was *My Little Pony* and it had come with a matching thermos. She'd hadn't brown-bagged it since law school. At work, her lunches were healthy but delivered from local restaurants. Her life had changed a lot in the last few months. Martha no longer set her alarm and seldom went into the office. Her phone and her laptop allowed her to stay in touch with her clients, be with her mom and, as Jon pointed out, look after herself. It was true. The stress of the last few months, hell years, had caught up with her—a rash on her back that had resisted treatment, sleepless nights and even some chest pains, but she hadn't told Jon about those.

Martha watched her mother's chest rise and fall. They were having a good day. She was breathing easily. Mom smiled. Yes, it was sadly crooked, and probably an involuntary reflex, but Martha claimed it as a good omen.

Her phone vibrated in her pocket. A text from Mark. She hadn't heard from him in over a week. He and Saul were in the Caribbean, anchored off some small island with a good marina and a surf side bar that served great rum punches along with the free WIFI.

Wanna join us?

Martha smiled. It was hard to tell from texts but she felt they were growing closer. Her pulse quickened every time he messaged. She tried to convince herself it was nothing, that he was an escape from her daily routine of home, her mom, log-onto-work and bedtime. They'd made no promises. She hadn't seen him since the morning after *that* night. He'd sent a photo of the sunrise when he and Saul had set sail. She'd texted a happy face and a hug but then deleted the hug and replaced it with *Happy sailing. Be safe.*

But then he'd called a couple of weeks ago. They'd talked for over an hour, Martha sparing him all but the barest details of her mother's health. He'd filled in the conversation with tales of their adventures, sailing stormy seas, fish stories and exotic locales. Martha's phone shook in her hand. More photos. Mark looked good, fit and tanned—his hair bleached by the sun. Saul, a younger version of his father.

I wish I was with you. Her thumb paused, suspended above the message. She closed her eyes and pressed send.

Well, come. ASAP. With emojis—a heart and a hug! If only she could.

Her mom groaned and stirred, her feet barely disturbing the covers. Martha rose and softly touched her mother's forearm, then slowly lifted her hand. She gently massaged her palm. Mom opened her eyes.

"Hi Mom. It's just me. Martha." She held her breath, but instead of fear, she saw a hint of recognition in her mom's eyes. "Hi Mom," she repeated softly, delicately brushing her fingers across her mother's cheek. Mom winked, another reflex but it felt warm and intimate. Martha gently squeezed her hand, then kissed her on the forehead. She felt her mother's breath on her cheek and stepped away, her eyes warm with tears.

A young man, dressed in cleaning-staff scrubs, came in and emptied the trash can. He nodded a stiff hello and left quickly. Martha settled back into her chair and unwrapped the piece of milk chocolate she'd packed with her lunch. Chocolate. Another new addition to her life. She let it melt on her tongue, just like Ruby had instructed. *It tastes better that way, Aunt Martha.* And it did.

Martha checked her email and sent a quick reply to Sylvie, then as she did every day, she talked to her mom. She could tell her anything now, even her deepest darkest fears. But she tried to keep things light. Mom didn't need to know how sad she was, how much she missed Dad or that the house had been sold and now Martha had to deal with the final clear out.

"Norah called this morning. She sends her love." True, but she also reported that Mercury has an egg-size lump on his back, hopefully just a fat deposit. They were doing tests and Norah would report back. Martha asked that the bills be sent to her, and please God, let him be fine. Mom didn't need to know. "Mercury is doing fine, still chasing squirrels." Martha never expected a reply or even a reaction. She just talked. "That new lawyer we hired, Anita, I think I told you about her. She's working out well. She's smart, Mom and I really like her."

Her mom was staring at the light. Martha stood up and switched off the overhead fixture.

"Is that better? Easier on your eyes? Sylvie likes Anita too, so that's something, isn't it? I've even given her some of my clients so I can spend more time here, with you." Martha chuckled to herself. "It's true. I don't have to go into the office very often. Crazy, right? Can't you just picture the look on Dad's face?"

Mom's eyes were closed, but—was that a grin? "Dad... Dad...Nick...Nickolas Walker, Dad," Martha tried to find the magic words, but there was no response. She stood, walked to the window and pulled back the curtains. The darkening sky echoed her mood.

"Hello."

Martha jumped. "Oh!" Dr Amos, a geriatric specialist, came to check on her mom a couple of times a week. He literally wore rose coloured glasses, stylish wire frames with tinted pink lenses and these, along with a round baby-face and a perpetual cowlick made him look too young to have graduated medical school, let alone have a specialty. Martha liked him.

"Sorry." He smiled. "I didn't mean to scare you. It's these shoes. They're practically soundless."

Martha looked at his electric blue crocs and tried to suppress a snicker.

"Ridiculous, right? My wife hates them. I'm not allowed to bring them home, but they're so darn comfortable."

"So I'm told," said Martha. She wouldn't be caught dead in them. "How's my mother doing?"

"Oh, about the same." He warmed his stethoscope between his palms then bent to listen to her mom's heart. She didn't move or even open her eyes. "You know, given her cognitive issues, and her immobility, your mother is doing, well, let's say better than expected." He pulled back the cover and pressed his fingertips into her mother's ankles. "We seem to be getting the edema under control, so that's good." He noted her swollen belly. "Still too much fluid here though, which isn't good for her heart or her lungs. I'll increase her meds, see if that makes a difference."

Martha nodded. "She's failing, isn't she?"

"Yes, I'm sorry. Her heart just isn't working as well as it should. She has some time, but it's impossible to tell how much."

Martha winced and took a few steps back. "Do you think…can she hear? Understand?"

The doctor lowered his voice. "I really don't know. Each patient is different, but I'd like to think that your mother is still here, somehow present."

Martha nodded. "Me too."

"You know, I can treat the body, but the dementia is beyond reach." His smile was tempered with sadness. "I'm sorry." He pulled the sheet over her mother's feet and left without a sound.

The room seemed empty without him. "I'm so lonely," Martha whispered to herself. She felt lonely and alone, sitting here with only the ghost of her mother. She wished Jon lived closer. She could really use a dose of Ruby. She blinked through her tears as she tapped his name on her phone. Her call went to message. She cancelled it and texted. *Hi. Doctor just left. Mom is about the same. Miss you.*

His reply was quick. *Hey, sorry. Busy day. Ruby's very late for school. She's trying out stubborn and unreasonable this week. Lennon down with the flu. Talk tonight? Tomorrow?*

OK, love you. Martha sighed, trying not to envy Jon his family. Strange how things had changed. She'd always thought she was the lucky one.

"That was Jon, Mom. Texting." Martha chuckled to herself, remembering her mother's reluctance to embrace a cell phone, let alone text messaging. "Just call me at home or better still, drop by for a visit," she'd often told Martha.

"Mom?" Martha set her phone on the bedside table. "Remember when we talked about Jonathan? Well, you talked and I didn't listen." Martha shifted closer to the bed. "You told me that sooner or later I'd have to forgive Jon, because—well, that he wasn't as strong as me. It took a while, Mom, but you were right." Martha waited for any kind of a reaction. "I just wanted you to know, before you—that things are fine now, just fine, you know, between Jonny and me. Oh, don't get me wrong, he still knows how to get me going. His diet is atrocious and he's always late for everything. But you know what?" Martha leaned close and whispered in her mother's ear. "He's pretty strong now, too."

Her mom's breathing was deep, peaceful for once. Had she heard? Was she there?

Martha relaxed and closed her eyes, drifted off for a minute or two.

Her mother growled, low and mournful. Was that fear? Pain? She clutched at her blanket, croaked as if her lips and tongue were attempting words.

"What is it, Mom?"

Where am I? Why am I here? Help me. Martha imagined these words, conjured them from the low, cheerless sounds that struggled out of her mother.

"It's okay, Mom. The doctor, you know, he told me you're doing great." Martha choked on the false enthusiasm. She straightened her mother's pillow, lifting her shoulders, pulling her close against her own chest. Mom shuddered, involuntary twitches that Martha knew to ignore. "Quiet now. It's okay." Mom drew in her breath as Martha settled her against the pillows. She exhaled a sharp cackle, an eerie singular sound that Martha used to believe was reserved just for her, but had since figured out that it was generic, impersonal and senseless.

Martha used the buttons at the foot of the bed to raise her mother to nearly sitting. Despite the soft purr of the bed's motor, the gentle lift, her mom startled. "Oh, I'm sorry. Are you okay?"

More gibberish, angrier now, her frustrations bawled.

"It's okay, Mom." How many times a day did she say that? Martha sat and took her mother's hand in hers. She stroked the boney fingers and hummed. It had worked before. She added words, *twinkle twinkle little star*. Mom's breathing slowed; her limbs relaxed. Martha waited, barely moving for several minutes, then tucked her mother's hand under the covers. She leaned back in the chair and closed her eyes, surrendering to her tears.

"Oh, Mom," she whispered. "What are we going to do? I wish I knew. Or maybe I wish that you could tell me. Are you in there anymore? Do you know me? Can you hear me? I wish—" Where was her mother? Not this mother, but her old mom, the one who could listen, solve problems and hug the biggest hugs.

"Yesterday, my therapist, asked me to describe how I felt about—" she waved her hand around the room, "—all of this. Well, to be honest, she asked me to write it down and I flat out refused. I'm too old for homework. I told her it felt like you were already gone, kidnapped in all but body. That's a bit weird, isn't it? If only I could pay the ransom, I would—even a king's ransom—just to get you back. Pipe dreams, right Mom?"

Martha could hear the meal cart in the hallway. "Are you hungry?" Although it was barely four o'clock, a kind and gentle PSW had arrived with the dinner tray, a misnomer for what was really just sustenance. Today Mom started with a little water from a spoon and then something akin to baby food, a mush of pears or apples or bananas and powdered protein. Imara was patient, encouraging each minute bite. Martha busied herself on her computer, trying not to watch the slow, tedious process. The head nurse had already told Martha that they could speed up the meals with a feeding tube. She had declined the offer.

"Well, if your mother refuses to swallow, stops eating altogether, it's the next logical step." Logical, maybe practical, but no. Martha wasn't about to prolong the suffering. She'd told Candy about her decision: "Starvation can be a painfully slow death," Candy had warned her. "So is this," declared Martha. She'd used her power of attorney and left written instructions with the nurses and Enid. No feeding tube and a *Do Not Resuscitate* order. No way did she want her mother to be resuscitated. And she'd make sure there were drugs for the pain. Her mom had suffered enough.

After dinner Imara gave her mother a quick sponge bath and changed her. She was awake now, bolstered by the food. This was often her best time. Sometimes Martha would read to her but today they looked at photos. Martha had gone through the albums and had the best ones blown up—eight by tens she used like flash cards. Sometimes Mom smiled, sometimes squawked, which Martha hoped was, *Who is that? Where is that?* She'd tell her again, as if for the first time, day after day: *Jonny and Martha, your garden, Italy, Ruby, Mercury and Dad.* She always lied about Dad—*he'll be here soon.* What did it matter? If Mom believed her even for one moment, it was enough.

The photos didn't hold her mom's attention today so Martha switched to music. She carefully placed a lightweight headset over her mom's ears. Martha inserted her own earbuds, which she'd linked to her mother's headset, checked the volume and pressed play on her phone. She'd made a playlist of popular tunes from the eighties, the songs she and Jon and Mom had bounced around to when they'd played dance party. She'd introduced them to *Billy Joel, Fleetwood Mac* and *Wham.* These songs seemed to pique her mom's interest more than the classical pieces suggested by the therapist. The thrilling notes of *I Will Always Love You* filled Martha's ears. Whitney Houston was Mom's favourite. She smiled, a real smile and slowly rocked from side to side, wiggled her toes, approximated a few hand claps. It was magical but it never lasted long. Mom tugged at the headset.

Imara returned with some meds. She lowered the bed and turned down the lights. Martha always stayed until her mother was asleep, until her breath, with the help of a spoonful of crushed sleeping pills and applesauce, became calm and steady. She collected her things, careful to leave nothing behind, then pushed the heavy chair back into place. She kissed her mother's cheek and whispered, "You can stop now, Mom. Just let go. Give in. Give up. It's time." She willed her mother's broken heart to miss all its beats. "Dear God, please just let her die. Set her free. Please God."

CHAPTER FORTY

The call came just after midnight, when Friday night becomes Saturday. Martha had fallen asleep listening to a podcast, her phone next to her pillow. The call display read *Whispering Pines*. She sat up, fully awake now, gulping back the acrid taste of panic.

"This is Martha."

"Hello, Martha."

"Candy?"

"Yes, I'm sorry. I know it is very late but—"

"Yes?"

"I'm very sorry, Martha, but your mother has passed."

"Sorry. What?" She'd left her mother, sleeping, breathing, only a few hours ago.

"She went quietly, in her sleep."

Martha hoped this was true. "I'm on my way."

She dressed quickly and drove too fast. She took the highway, remembering her father's complaints about the travelling distance to Whispering Pines. Tonight, it seemed to take forever. What did it matter? Her mother was dead. Martha had asked for this, prayed for this but now didn't want it. She shivered, feeling the chill of the night, and took several deep breaths to clear her head, calm her body.

Her key card didn't work. Her hand was shaking. She tapped on the glass and waited until the door swung open.

Candy met her in the hall. "I'm so sorry, Martha."

"Thanks. I—I'm—did she—was she—what? Oh, I don't know."

Candy slipped her arm through Martha's. "Hush now. Plenty of time to figure things out later." She walked Martha to her mother's door. "She's ready for you."

Martha nodded to hide her confusion.

Candy opened the door and stepped back. "Take as long as you need to say your goodbyes."

"Thank you." But, no, thought Martha. No goodbyes. Her mother had been gone for a very long time. Martha walked to the bed and inhaled sharply, surprised, awed by mother's face; tranquil, serene. She looked so calm, younger, finally at peace. Martha smiled. Candy had brushed her hair and dressed her in the flowered pajamas. "You look beautiful, Mom." Martha held her hand. It was surprisingly soft, still. "Mom?" She didn't expect a reply, but her mother's appearance, her demeanor, confused Martha. She seemed less absent, less broken, now that she was dead. Martha straightened the collar on her mother's pajama shirt and stroked her cheek.

"Don't worry about us, Mom. Jonny and I will be fine. We'll take care of Ruby." She had no tears. This death was a gift. Martha reached into the pocket of her sweater and took out a small porcelain figurine. "Mom, I brought Goldie. She's a little faded, weathered, but then I would be too if I'd spent nearly forty years in the garden."

Martha had remembered the fairy houses just last week. She'd been at her parents' house, waiting for the movers. The house had been sold. She still had several weeks to achieve what the realtor had called vacant possession, but that day she'd arranged to take the patio set and a few special pieces to her house. She'd open the gate for the movers and then wandered around. Her mom's gardens were a little wild, but still beautiful. Sadly, the putting green had all but grown over. Martha and Jon had spent many happy hours out here when they were young. The long-gone wooden play set had, at various times, been a castle, a pirate ship and their not-so-secret hide-out. Mom had even let them sleep in it once, until Jon heard a coyote.

What ever happened to the fairy houses? The ones in the trees would be long gone but what about the one in the back corner, behind the hedge? Martha had squeezed behind the tangled boughs choking on the cool, prickly bouquet of cedar. She could almost see Mom hammering the nail into the corner post. Martha ignored the sap and the scratches, and reached through the branches, amazed when she found the little plastic house still hanging from the chain. It was dilapidated, dingy and blackened with mold, but it still housed Goldie, the busiest and best fairy of them all. She and Mom had imagined her chasing stars, riding on unicorns, and granting wishes.

Now, Martha carefully placed Goldie in her mother's palm and folded her delicate fingers around the tiny fairy. "Safe journey, you two. Say hi to Dad for me."

**

Martha splashed water on her face and was startled by her reflection, dark circles, wrinkles and some new wiry grey hairs. She barely remembered driving home from Whispering Pines and had slept off and on for only a few hours. Maybe she'd dreamt her mother's death, but no, Goldie was missing from her nightstand.

Martha checked her phone before turning on the shower. She'd texted Jon last night—no details, just a request to call her. It was still so early there. Let him sleep. He'd know soon enough. She undressed and stepped under the warm spray allowing the tropical smell of her coconut body wash to relax her until the wail of her phone interrupted.

She reached out with a dripping hand. "Jon! Hang on. I need a towel."

"Hey. What's up? Did you miss me?" He chuckled but stopped when she inhaled a ragged sob. "Martha? What's wrong?"

Martha slipped into her terry cloth robe and sat on the bench at the foot of her bed, ignoring the clothes she'd dumped there last night. "I...I...oh, Jon."

"Are you alright?"

"Yea, yes, I'm fine. Jon, it's Mom. She's gone. She died late last night."

"Oh no."

"We knew it was coming, right? But it's still a shock. And...I wasn't with her." The connection between them was silent, invisible. She glanced at the screen. "Jon? Are you still—"

"Sorry, yeah. Oh shit. I'm sorry. Jesus." His voice caught. "Poor Mom, but it's better—"

"Yeah, she's better off. I know, but...She looked so calm, and younger, more like herself." Martha reached across the bed for her box of tissues, remembering just in time that it was empty, stuffed full of her morning tears.

"Yeah, it sure wasn't easy for her. Or for you, Martha."

"I didn't mind. I only hope she knew—" Martha sniffled and collected herself. "Now we need to figure out what to do next. I saw her, last night, after she died. I don't think I have to go back there until it's time to collect her things. I do have to go to the funeral home. We'll use Langston's again. Okay?"

"Oh course. Jesus, you're like an expert at this."

"God no, more like reluctantly capable."

Jon chuckled sadly. "I'm sorry I'm not there to help, but I'm coming to help you. I'll book a flight and be there—"

"Okay, check out the flights, but don't book anything. Not yet."

"Really? Why?"

"Let's talk it through, later today. I don't think we should have a big funeral—something else, maybe?"

"Okay. Whatever you want. Are you sure you're okay?"

"Yes, I think I am."

"Okay, call me later. Don't forget!"

She laughed a little then caught herself. "I won't forget. Bye."

"Bye. Martha. Love you."

The call ended, leaving her alone again. Martha dialed the office and filled them in, not even bothering to leave instructions for Anita. She'd be fine. She called Langston Funeral Home and arranged to meet with them in a couple of hours. She made coffee and a light breakfast, and sent a quick text to Jon. *Maybe you could put together an obit? Langston will post it on their site.* She dressed in black trousers and a silk blouse, forgoing makeup. No amount of concealer would hide the bags under her eyes so she opted for her largest sunglasses.

On the way out the door she caught a glimpse of herself in the hall mirror. Oh god, was this blouse too cheery? No, Mom had liked it, the deep coral colour, the softness. Martha remembered her mother's compliments, "Lovely shirt dear. Is it new?" She'd run her fingers along the sleeve, touched the mother-of-pearl buttons, her smile tightening into lines of confusion. "What is this colour?" she'd whispered under her breath. That was early on—before Martha knew that dementia had already begun to lay waste to her mother.

Oh Mom! She wished they'd talked more. She wished she'd listened, been more patient, spent more time. Asked more questions about her past, her dreams, her regrets. She didn't know then that too late would come so soon.

**

Martha stepped out of her shoes and headed to her kitchen. It had been a hard day and she'd missed lunch and now she needed dinner. She checked the fridge and then the cupboards but found nothing to tempt her. She spotted the large cardboard box she'd meant to drop off at the food bank. She'd filled it with food from her parents' suite, unopened boxes of crackers, bags of chips, several packages of Oreos and a single box of cereal. Martha studied the ingredients and shrugged. What could it hurt? She filled a large bowl with sugary multi-coloured flakes, added a handful of almonds, some dried cranberries and drenched it in oat milk. She glanced at her watch. It was almost four o'clock out west, a decent time to call Jon. She clicked on the FaceTime app and waited, then tapped her fingernail on the screen, trying to expedite the connection between her iPad and Jon's.

Jon's face suddenly filled the screen. "Hi," she mumbled through the cereal and nuts.

"Hello! I've been waiting for you." Jon leaned into the screen. "What're you eating?"

Martha swallowed. "Mom's cereal. It's not nearly as disgusting as I thought."

Jon grinned. "Yeah, Mom and Ruby seem to really like that stuff." He looked tired, sad. "How did everything go today?"

Martha wiped her mouth on a napkin. "It was okay, fine. The Langston people were really helpful again. I decided to go back to the Home—to be there when they came to collect her." She inhaled quickly. "And, just so you know, I took her rings."

"What?"

"Mom's rings. I have them." She'd felt sheepish sliding them off her finger, but she'd made a promise. She'd keep them safe.

"That's fine, Martha." He smiled his approval. "Really. They're special, and valuable. And again, I'm sorry you have to do all this."

"It wasn't horrible. Just sad. She was so little, Jon. It was like she'd just melted away." Martha inhaled deeply. "Wait, where's Ruby?"

"In her room. She's having a bit of a time-out."

"Oh?"

"Yeah, she's been a bit of a terror lately. Pushing boundaries, talking back. She yelled at me, Martha!" He grinned sheepishly. "Yeah, I know."

"Surely it just growing pains."

"Yeah, except yesterday she pushed a boy at school. He was teasing her so she shoved him and he fell on his ass."

"Yay, Ruby!"

"I made her apologize and now she hates me."

"She doesn't hate you, Jon."

"You should've seen the death-stare. If looks could kill. And the side-eyes! Seriously, she's a six-year-old teenager!"

"Ah yes, the cruelties of daughterhood."

"What?"

"Do you have any idea how mean I was to Mom?"

"No, not really."

"Oh Jon, I had all the weapons. I used to freeze her out, roll my eyes at every suggestion. I wouldn't go shopping with her and then hated the clothes she brought home for me. I stole her clothes and used her perfume. I borrowed her gold earrings and then lost them and denied it. I was impatient, petulant, always annoyed with her. Trust me, no matter what Mom did for me, she couldn't win."

"Really, and why?"

"Yes, really." Martha grinned. "Because I knew she loved me, Jonathan."

"Still confused—"

Martha laughed. "Look, maybe I couldn't have articulated it then. It was visceral, but I knew in my soul, that no matter what I said or did my mother's love was a given, safe, secure and constant."

"Oh."

"A part of me will always be that little girl curled up in her mother's arms."

"Ruby doesn't have a mom—at least not an everyday mother."

"She has you and Lennon. Don't worry about Ruby. Just keep loving her."

"Easy for you to say, Auntie Martha."

"I know." Her little pep talk had left her sad, realizing it was now too late to apologize to her mother.

"Are you alright?" Jon's face was somber, lined with concern. His hair was shorter now which made him look more like—Dad; he had the hairline, the eyes, the jaw. How had she never noticed it before?

"Yes. I'm fine," she said "Really. I would like a drink though."

"Go ahead. You've had a hell of a day. You can have one for me too, but I'm not supposed to think like that." He picked up a glass and tipped it to the screen. "Pink Grapefruit Perrier."

"Nice," she said. "A fine vintage and sparkling too!" Jon nodded. "So, are *you* okay, Jon?"

"Yeah, pretty good. Lennon's a rock and I went to a meeting at lunch today. That helped. "Not sure how I'll tell Ruby, though."

"Yeah, she'll be sad, but she's got you and Lennon."

"Just too bad she didn't have Mom and Dad longer. That's on me."

"Don't go there. You made it right. You did good, Jon." Martha could see his tears.

"Martha?" Jon dabbed his eyes with a tissue and took a long drink from his water glass. He smiled and looked even more like their dad. "Did things really go so smoothly today?"

"Yeah, pretty much. I had a little trouble deciding on an urn. I was going to go with one that matched Dad's but it just didn't feel like Mom, you know? I chose this—" She held up the photo on her phone. "I can change it if—"

"No, it's perfect. Mom will…" Jon stopped. "…would love it."

"There's this one too." Martha held up her phone again.

"No, the first one. I'm having trouble thinking of her in there."

Martha nodded. "They'll cremate her tomorrow."

"Geez."

"I know. It seems a little irreverent, doesn't it?"

Jon nodded.

"So, I have an idea." Martha held her breath.

"About?"

"The funeral. What if we did something less traditional, more private for Mom? Nothing like Dad's. Just me and the few of her friends who are still alive and able."

"And us, right?"

"No, see that's the thing. What if I just had a little ceremony here, and then brought her to you?"

"To *me*?"

"Yes, well, think about it, we could scatter her ashes, you know, together." Martha squirmed at his silence but she let him think it through. It really was such a good idea.

"But what about Dad? Didn't we decide to bury them together?"

Martha hesitated. "Yes—we did."

"We met with that *delightful* woman at the cemetery, remember?" Jon leaned in. His face filled the screen. "And chose those very expensive plots because you insisted they be side by side under a tree and with a view."

"Yes, we did and I was supposed to find a date and make the arrangements and you were supposed to come home for the internment and remind me when I failed to complete my mission."

"Right. So, where's Dad?"

"Still at the funeral home, hopefully at rest."

"Okay then."

"I've been busy, Jon. And I'm sorry." She hadn't forgotten, just procrastinated. The funeral home had called a few months ago and offered to do the whole thing for her, with decorum and respect, but she certainly wasn't going to let that happen.

Martha poured herself a Scotch. Her dad's bottles hadn't made it past her kitchen table. "Well, I—"

"It's okay. I get it," said Jon. "Now, we can bury them together, right?"

"We could, but I thought that maybe, unless you don't agree—that I bring both of them, Mom *and* Dad, out west and find a beautiful spot for them to be together, always. Perfect right?"

"Why here?"

"It's so beautiful, the mountains or the ocean or just somewhere peaceful."

"Martha you can't just dump ashes wherever you want, you know."

"I'm pretty sure you can, if no one catches you."

Jon laughed. "How much of Dad's special Scotch have you had?"

"This is my first one and there's still lots." She seldom drank Scotch anymore. It just didn't taste the same.

"Yeah, Dad was never short of booze." Jon chuckled ruefully.

"So," said Martha, unwilling to give up on her plan. "What do you think? Our parents together forever in some gurgling mountain stream?"

Jon sighed. "Look, I don't hate this idea, but—"

"Ahhhh. There's always a *but*." Her enthusiasm was waning.

"Look, I'm okay with your *scattering* idea." He added air quotes and a smile but it did little to hide his misgivings. "But I don't think this is the right place. I mean, Mom liked it out here but Dad, not so much. It wasn't that special for either of them, except that I'm here." He twisted his face into a wry grin. "And then there's the whole Mateo thing."

"Oh shit!" Martha exhaled her frustrations. "It just made so much sense in my head."

"I think it still makes sense. But, what if we, um, *disperse* them somewhere else? Somewhere special to both?"

"Where, like the house?"

"Maybe, but the new owners may not be very happy about that."

"How would they know?"

"We'd know, so no."

"The club?" This whole idea was falling apart on her.

"How about Italy?"

Martha watched his face to see if he was kidding. He didn't move. She tapped the screen. "I think you're frozen."

"I'm not. I'm waiting for you to—"

"Venice! They both loved Italy so much. Mom used to talk about it. They stayed in some quaint bed and breakfast. Was it near a winery?"

"That's a pretty good bet."

"True." Martha grinned. "Is that where they went for their honeymoon? Not in the touristy Venice, but somewhere on the ocean?" Jonathan was nodding, wiggling his fingers as if trying to coax out the memories. "And Dad, he had that photo in his office of them riding horses on the beach. Was that Italy too?" Martha took a deep breath. Her heart was racing. "Jon, could we do that, like really?"

"Yes, at least I think so. It wasn't in Venice. They stopped there for a few days and then went on to Caorle, it's a coastal town. Mom told me. She wanted to go back, you know. We joked about going together. But I think she knew, even then, that it was too late."

"Oh, that's sad. I had no idea." Martha sat back, sobered by an unexpected prick of jealousy. Why hadn't her mother told her about Italy? They could have gone together. *Just stop it*, she scolded herself. That was clearly Jon's domain, just as the law was hers. She knew her mother had loved them both, given them each what they'd needed. She'd been kind, wise, funny, seldom strict and always a dreamer. Most of all, her mother had been a real family woman. *Family woman*—why was that not a thing, like *family man*? Why did men get extra credit just for hanging out with their kids?

"Martha?"

"Yeah, sorry. Italy, eh?"

"Yup. I've never been to Venice."

"Me either. Do you think there are laws against travelling with human remains, like ashes?"

"We might have to look into that," said Jon. "So, let's make that our working plan. See if it's even possible."

"We might have to FedEx them." She imagined wrapping her parents in bubble wrap.

"Maybe. But hopefully not," Jon chuckled, then turned serious. "Also, I'm coming home. I'm booking the flights today. No matter how small the celebration, I'm coming. I've missed too damn many family events. We'll all be there. Ruby and Len too. For Mom."

"Okay," agreed Martha. "Thank you." She checked her phone. "I'm thinking Saturday."

"Sounds good," said Jon. "Get lots of flowers—not the funeral-y kind—happy ones." Jon's eyes welled with tears. His lips trembled. "It's hard to believe that Mom is gone too. Both of them in the same year. It's almost like they just had to be together." He slouched back into his chair. "They had quite the life, didn't they?"

"They did, a long and mostly happy marriage, right?"

"I think so," said Jon. "But I'm betting those wedding vows were stretched pretty thin at times."

"But they held on, didn't they?"

"Yeah," agreed Jon. "They stuck together to the end. Maybe that's marriage."

"I hope it's more than that." Although she'd probably never know for sure. "They were quite a pair."

"Indeed. You did well by them, Martha. Thank you. I mean it. You're a hell of a good person. Mom... Mom was always so proud of you. You have to believe that. She just knew that I needed her more."

"Don't make me cry." Martha blinked back her tears.

"I'll call you tomorrow, from the airport. We'll be on the early flight."

"Thanks, Jon." She blew him a kiss and closed her tablet.

Venice. Italy—maybe. They could take them back to the same place in Caorle, scatter them in the ocean or maybe they'd decide on the cemetery. Did it really matter? As long as—she pictured them together, hoping their spirits would be young again or at least at peace, all mistakes forgiven or forgotten. Starting out on their new journey.

Martha lifted her glass and let the last drops of the warm amber liquid fall onto her tongue. Her mother was gone. She should feel sad, alone, lonely, but no. She was relieved. She wanted to rejoice, give thanks to the heavens, that her mother had finally been set free. Mom had suffered so much—slowly, painfully consumed by a relentless disease. Now, hopefully, by the will of her god, she was at peace. Mom had finally reached the finish line. But it wasn't the end. She'd left behind some of herself, her spirit in her children, her family. Martha and Jonathan. Ruby. Lennon. Even Peter.

Martha tore a sheet from her *To-Do-Today* notepad and wrote *Celebrating Mom* at the top. She'd keep the guest list short, close friends only. Norah could bring Mercury. She made a note to reach out to Gloria who'd emailed Martha a couple of weeks ago, thanking her again for the trip home. She'd stayed with her family for several months and was back now, working for an older couple in Rosedale.

Martha added champagne to the list and sparkling water for toasts. And lots of fancy little cakes—petit pours and flowers. They'd have it in the garden, Mom's garden. She'd ask Father Axel to do a blessing or something. She yawned, her body willing her to bed.

A message popped up on her phone. *Hey gorgeous.* Mark. She smiled, felt her face flush. The next week would be busy. And later there'd be Italy or she'd go out west for a visit. But between the two, maybe a few days in the Caribbean?

Martha poured a scant inch of Scotch into her glass and placed the cut crystal stopper back into the neck of her father's decanter. June Walker. Her final years had been hijacked, but she'd left her mark— stronger, brighter and deeper than Martha had ever imagined. She raised her glass.

"Thanks, Mom."

THE END

ABOUT THE AUTHOR

Wendy Simpson is a writer from Oakville, Ontario. Recently retired from a career in real estate, she now divides her time between Toronto, Victoria and Grand Cayman Island to spend time with her three grown children and spoil her ten young grandchildren. Originally from Kitchener, Wendy moved to Toronto to study English Literature. She holds a BA and an MA from York University. Although her university days are long behind her she has never lost her love of reading and prefers literary fiction and the occasional mystery. She is a long-time book club member and enjoys crosswords and Wordle, trivia nights with her friends and family time at the beach, the cottage or a Blue Jays game. For many years, she has attended writing classes and workshops with Brian Henry and has had short stories published in *Quick Brown Fox*. This is her first novel and she is currently writing the second under the warm Caribbean sun.

ALSO FROM MIDDLEROAD PUBLISHERS

MiddleRoad | Publishers

www.middleroadpublishers.ca

Making Literature See The Light Of Day

**All books available at amazon worldwide
ebook versions available from all ebook channels**

A TIME TO LOVE AND A TIME TO DIE
[a novel]
By Michael Joll

ATTITUDE
[a novel]
By Dave Moores

CIRCE'S DANCE
[Short Stories]
By Heather Laltoo Ferguson

DANCING MY WAY TO 80
Biography published privately not available for sale.
By Doris Naraine

DEATH IN THE SUBURBS
[a novel]
By Donna Kirk

DOWN INDEPENDENCE BOULEVARD AND OTHER STORIES
[1st Prize Guyana Prize for Literature (Fiction) 2022]
by Ken Puddicombe

FROM MY WINDOW
Memoir and fiction
By Rena Flannigan

GABRIELLE
[a novel]
By Michael Joll

GENERATIONS
[Biography published privately and not available for sale]

HACKER
[a novel]
by Michael Joll

I WENT TO THE END OF THE RAINBOW
[Children's story]
by Pramita Chakraborty

JUNTA
[a novel]
By Ken Puddicombe

LIFE'S AWE AND MYSTERY
[poems]
By George Secko

LOVE HAS TWO MOONS
[Short Stories]
By Franklin Mohan

MEET ME AT THE FOUR CORNERS
Anthology of Brampton Writers' Guild Authors

OUTSIDE THE WIRE
[Short Stories]
By Michael Joll

PAGES FROM A NOTEBOOK
[Non-Fiction]
By Ken Puddicombe

PEOPLE OF GUYANA
[Poems]
By Ian McDonald and Peter

Jailall

PERFECT EXECUTION AND
OTHER STORIES
by Michael Joll

PERSONS OF INTEREST
[Short Stories]
By Michael Joll

POEMS FOR MARY
By Ian McDonald

RACING WITH THE RAIN
[a Novel]
By Ken Puddicombe

RAMLALL'S STRANGE
COURTSHIP AND WEDDING
[Short Stories]
By Kennard Ramphal

RUTHLESS RHYTHMS
[Poems]
By Judith Gelberger

SCALING NEW HEIGHTS
Anthology of Pakaraima Authors

THOUGHTS TO MEDITATE ON
[Health and Lifestyle]
By Kennard Ramphal

SLIPPERY OCHRO
[a Novel: 3rd Prize Guyana Prize
For Literature (Fiction) 2023
By Kennard Ramphal

SNAPSHOTS OF OUR LIVES
[Anthology]
By Ram Jagessar, Roop Misir
and Kennard Ramphal

SPARKLES AND KARIM
[a Novel]
By Dave Moores

TASTE MY WORDS
[Poems]
By Lisa Freemantle

THE DARKEST HOURS
[a Novel]
By Michael Joll

THE GARDEN
[Poems]
By Ian McDonald

THE PRICE OF FREEDOM Bk1
[a novel]
By Judith Gelberger

THE RIVER CROSSING
[Poems and non-Fiction]
By Harry Persaud

TROPICAL SCENES
[Poems]
By Ken Puddicombe

**UNFATHOMABLE AND OTHER
POEMS**
by Ken Puddicombe

**WEALTH THROUGH REAL
ESTATE INVESTING**
[Self-Help]
By Jay Brijpaul

WINDWARD LEGS
[a Novel]
By Dave Moores

www.ingramcontent.com/pod-product-compliance
Lightning Source LLC
Chambersburg PA
CBHW062025170626

46813CB00001B/288